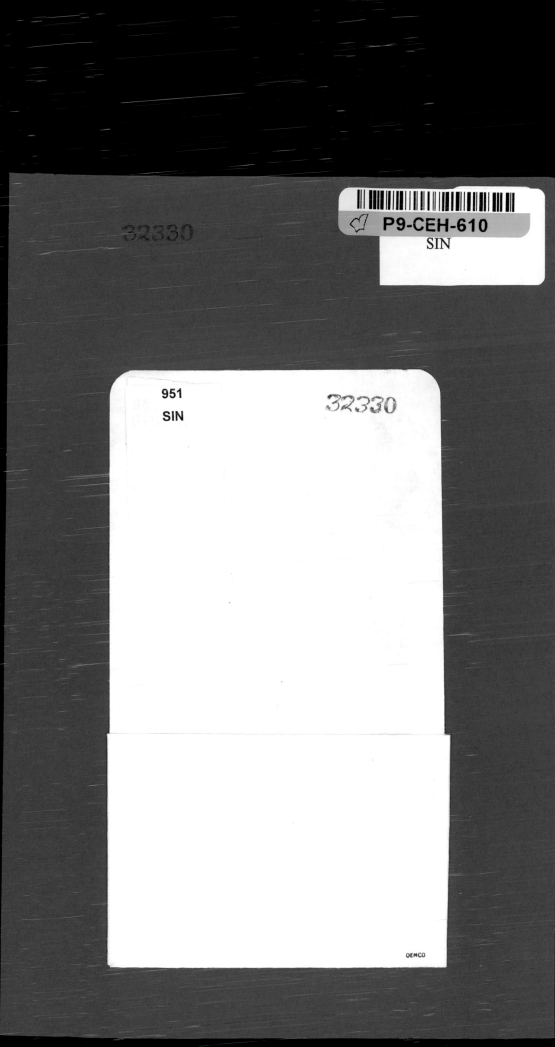

SINGLE SPARKS

CHINA'S RURAL REVOLUTIONS

Studies of the East Asian Institute, Columbia University

THE EAST ASIAN INSTITUTE OF COLUMBIA UNIVERSITY

The East Asian Institute is Columbia University's center for research, publication, and teaching on modern East Asia. The Studies of the East Asian Institute were inaugurated in 1962 to bring to a wider public the results of significant new research on Japan, China, and Korea.

SINGLE SPARKS

CHINA'S RURAL REVOLUTIONS

KATHLEEN HARTFORD
STEVEN M. GOLDSTEIN

Editors

AN EAST GATE BOOK

M. E. SHARPE, INC.
ARMONK, NEW YORK/LONDON, ENGLAND

An East Gate Book

Copyright © 1989 by M. E. Sharpe, Inc.

Available in the United Kingdom and Europe from M. E. Sharpe, Publishers, 3 Henrietta Street, London WC2E 8LU.

Interior design by Angela Foote.

Library of Congress Cataloging-in-Publication Data

Single sparks.

    Includes index.
    1. China—History—1928-1937. 2. China—History—
1937-1945. 3. China—History—Civil War, 1945-1949.
4. Communism—China—History. I. Hartford, Kathleen
II. Goldstein, Steven M.
DS777.47.S493 1989 951   87-4823
ISBN 0-87332-427-7

Printed in the United States of America

CONTENTS

LIST OF ILLUSTRATIONS

Maps

Tables

Figures

ACKNOWLEDGMENTS

Several of the essays in this volume are based on papers presented at a workshop on Chinese Communist base areas held at Harvard University's Fairbank Center for East Asian Research and sponsored by The Joint Committee on Chinese Studies of the American Council of Learned Societies and the Social Science Research Council with funds provided by the Andrew W. Mellon Foundation. Preparation of this volume was assisted by a grant from the Ida and Louis Katz Foundation.

The editors wish to thank Thomas P. Bernstein, Michel C. Oksenberg, and Elizabeth J. Perry for their critical comments on earlier versions of the volume. Our thanks also to Jason Parker of the American Council of Learned Societies as well as to those who have helped in various stages of the volume's preparation: Mary Ellen Alonso, Ann Blum, Barat Ellman, Jean Jackson, Craig Malone, and Hugh Shapiro. Doug Merwin and Anita O'Brien at M. E. Sharpe have most ably seen us through the numerous details attending publication, with the eleventh-hour addition of Kathleen Silloway. Finally, our heartfelt thanks to the authors in this volume, who cooperated with our editorial suggestions in exemplary fashion, and have patiently awaited the published evidence of their efforts.

ABOUT THE CONTRIBUTORS

Gregor Benton teaches in the Anthropology-Sociology Center of the University of Amsterdam. He is currently completing the first volume in a two-volume study of the origins and growth of the New Fourth Army up to the New Fourth Army Incident of January 1941.

Steven M. Goldstein teaches in the Department of Government at Smith College. He has written on issues of Chinese domestic and foreign policy.

Kathleen Hartford teaches in the Political Science Department of the University of Massachusetts at Boston and is an Associate in Research at the Fairbank Center for East Asian Research at Harvard University. She is presently working on a study of the Communist movement in rural Hebei from 1921 to 1949.

Steven I. Levine is presently visiting professor of Political Science at Duke University. He is the author of *The Anvil of Victory: The Communist Revolution in Manchuria, 1945–1948* and is presently working on a comparative study of Mao and Stalin.

David Paulson received his doctorate in Chinese history from Stanford University. He spent a post-doctoral research year at Harvard's Fairbank Center for East Asian Research, where he completed a study of the Shandong base area.

William Wei teaches in the Department of History at the University of Colorado in Boulder. He is the author of *Countrerrevolution in China: The Nationalists in Jiangxi during the Soviet Period.*

SINGLE SPARKS

CHINA'S RURAL REVOLUTIONS

1

Introduction: Perspectives on the Chinese Communist Revolution

KATHLEEN HARTFORD and
STEVEN M. GOLDSTEIN

We are at a new juncture in the study of the Chinese revolution. A new generation of scholarship is emerging which promises to resolve old debates, bridge old dichotomies, and join formerly separate strands of analysis. We are accumulating a rich body of empirical data making possible a fruitful exchange between those studying the Chinese revolution and those attempting comparative generalizations. We are gaining a clearer sense of the interrelations of domestic and international factors, of the Communist movement and its opponents, of spontaneous peasant impulses and revolutionary organization and leadership. These strands are being joined by intensive studies of the Chinese Communist revolution in local contexts, of which the essays in this book are a highly instructive sample. Although these local studies deal with milieus far more limited in geographical and, at times, chronological scope than much of the earlier work on the revolution, such limitations have allowed more comprehensive examination of relevant actors and causal factors than has heretofore been possible. The result is a seemingly paradoxical development. The exceptions to previous generalizations on China, the catalogue of "local idiosyncrasies," are pointing to a pattern that promises a new set of tentative general hypotheses on the revolution. In this pattern one finds a greater consonance between the Chinese revolutionary process and the generalizations of compara-

The research assistance of Barat Ellman, Julia Erickson, Donna Milrod, and Christine Torre is gratefully acknowledged as is the financial assistance of the Ida and Louis Katz Foundation. This chapter has also benefited from helpful readings by Lloyd Eastman, Craig Malone, Michel Oksenberg, Elizabeth Perry, and Stanley Rothman.

tivists than was evident in earlier, more general works on the revolution.

Clearly these are large claims to make for a body of work that is still maturing. In support and elucidation of them, we provide in this introduction an overview of the intellectual background to the work presented here, as represented by studies on the Chinese revolution and by those on comparative revolutions.

The Study of the Chinese Revolution:
Early Images, 1932–1949

Not until the CCP's forced removal to China's rural hinterlands did it emerge as a significant object of study by Westerners. Before 1927, most observers regarded the Guomindang (GMD) under Chiang Kai-shek as the (pejorative) extreme in Chinese radicalism. But once the GMD achieved control of the national political apparatus, Westerners reporting on China's military, political, and social upheaval turned their attention to the growing Communist movement. They tended to find the sources of its dynamism in three factors: popular (especially peasant) support for the CCP, partisan warfare, and organization.

In 1944, the Shanxi warlord Yan Xishan accounted for CCP strength in an apparent tautology: "The reason why the Communists today have such powerful forces is that so many people are following them."[1] The Western reporter who recorded this comment accepted popular support as central to an explanation of the CCP's strength, a view that figured in almost all discussions of the Communist movement in the pre–1949 period. For most authors, one question was paramount: Why do the peasants so enthusiastically support the CCP?

The reasons for this preoccupation lie, in part, in the prior experience of analysts assessing the Communist areas: most knew Guomindang China well. Whatever their political leanings,[2] these Western observers were overwhelmed by the country's massive social dislocations and disgusted by the GMD's continuing inability to respond to these problems. Popular dissatisfaction in the Nationalist areas highlighted the perceived enthusiastic peasant support in the base areas.[3] Even by the mid–1930s most accounts (primarily of the Jiangxi Soviet) located the sources of Communist success in the party's ability to address rural economic hardship.[4] This approach figures in perhaps the earliest systematic discussion of the Communist movement, written in 1932 by O. Edmund Clubb, then a young American vice-consul. Clubb saw the Guomindang's 1927 break with the CCP as an important watershed. The GMD had lost its "roots in the great body of the people" and had turned to a policy of "grasping militarism." It was simply unresponsive to China's worsening socioeconomic problems. By contrast, the Communist program—land redistribution, fiscal reform, and labor legislation—had created "considerable popular support."[5]

A second factor focusing observers' attention on peasant support was the type of warfare conducted by the Communists. "Partisan warfare," later to be known as "people's war," was to many observers a new and exciting phenomenon. And those who wrote in the 1930s and 1940s agreed that the key to success in such warfare lay in popular support.[6]

Popular enthusiasm was needed if the CCP's armies were to get the recruits, supplies, and intelligence they needed to fight. But enthusiasm was of little use unless there was an organization in place to channel and deploy it.[7] Almost all visitors to the Communist areas commented upon the pervasiveness of organization. Organization was the vehicle for the education, discipline, and further indoctrination that helped elicit support. But organization did more than this: it transformed propaganda into popular policies. Relief from military threat or economic insecurity was impossible without the intercession of party-led or sponsored organizations. Peng Dehuai made this point to Edgar Snow in 1936 when he asserted that only by "constant political and organizational work" could the CCP "fulfill the promise of its propaganda." Foreign residents of the GMD areas had seen how government venality and brutality sapped popular support. In the CCP areas, they concluded that the reverse was true: organization was essential to building support.[8]

Few authors during these years would have denied that strong and constant organization was needed to avoid a return to peasant passivity and indifference. And even fewer would have quibbled with the United States War Department, which asserted that the CCP was "the most effectively organized group in China."[9] All these writings recognized that the Communists had created organizations that had generated the commitment of the masses, channeled it into apparently popular policy directions, and so created policies and institutions that a growing proportion of the population considered worth fighting for.

Some analysts saw power in Communist organizations flowing primarily from the top down. Traditionally passive peasants had to be organized, and the resultant bodies were intended to implement the will of the party leadership.[10] Others spoke of "democracy" in the base areas, suggesting that they saw more mass spontaneity and popular control in these organizations.[11] Some traced the sources of peasant support to the CCP's socioeconomic policies, while others, during the Anti-Japanese War era, tended to stress the mobilizing effects of the war. The major differences of emphasis are illustrated by three works: Edgar Snow's *Red Star over China*, George Taylor's *The Struggle for North China*, and Theodore White and Annalee Jacoby's *Thunder Out of China*.

For Taylor, writing in 1941, the emphasis is clearly on the importance of the Japanese invasion and Communist resistance organizations: "[Japanese] brutality was, of course, an excellent argument for the guerrillas, *but only* on condition that they were there to state it, that they had been in a district long enough to organize and infuse a new morale and political outlook into the peasantry."[12] In Taylor's view, socioeconomic reforms were a secondary but complementary factor stimulating peasant involvement. He sees the war not merely as a catalyst but as a crucial intervening variable which generated a peasant consciousness unprecedented in Chinese history. He suggests, however, that peasants might lapse into apathy again once the war had passed and, further, that classes brought together to fight the Japanese might divide again along economic lines. Maintaining the momentum, Taylor believed, took considerable political acumen. The Communist movement was not a passive beneficiary of GMD decay and Japanese invasion. Rather, the basis of Communist success lay in organizations able to channel mass dissatisfaction and implement ameliorative policies.

Snow's contrasting view of the Communist movement was decisively conditioned by his visit to the border areas before the Japanese invasion. The CCP leaders with whom he spoke were naturally tentative about the new policy of promoting anti-Japanese nationalism. Indeed, Snow's conversations with the Communist leaders suggest their belief that a conservative, parochial peasantry could only be incorporated in the movement for national liberation if their immediate economic needs were first addressed. The CCP leaders remained skeptical of the efficacy of anti-Japanese resistance policies as a mobilizational device. Zhou Enlai, for example, spoke of food and land as "the primary demands of the revolutionary peasantry."[13]

For Snow the Communist movement was part of an inexorable process fueled, for the most part, by China's serious, long-standing economic ills. The war was a catalyst, not a precondition of revolution. It would speed the growth in awareness of the Chinese people. The CCP, of course, would benefit from popular mobilization brought about by the war; Snow certainly recognized the importance of nationalist appeals in building Communist support. But in contrast to Taylor, he argued that a socioeconomic reform program had to draw the peasants into Communist organization *before* the issue of anti-Japanese nationalism could become salient.[14]

White and Jacoby viewed the Communist revolution from the very different vantage point of the immediate postwar era. Theirs is the perspective not only of economic misery and brutal Japanese occupation but also of a degenerating, and to them thoroughly corrupt and reprehensible, Guomindang. For them, the simple act of bringing an alienated people into the governing process created support crucial to party success. The reason for this success, they wrote,

> could be reduced to a single paragraph: If you take a peasant who has been swindled, beaten, and kicked about for all his waking days and whose father has transmitted to him an emotion of bitterness reaching back for generations—if you take such a peasant, treat him like a man, ask his opinion, let him vote for local government, let him organize his own police and gendarmes, decide on his own taxes, and vote himself a reduction in rent and interest—if you do all that, the peasant becomes a man who has something to fight for, and he will fight to preserve it against any enemy, Japanese or Chinese.[15]

Thus we see their strong emphasis on Communist political institutions as an integral part of the movement's appeal. The role of international forces is unclear in their analysis. They saw the Japanese invasion as an important event, as was the postwar rivalry between the Soviet Union and the United States and the growth of Asian nationalism. Still, the Chinese revolution remained essentially a domestic phenomenon.[16]

If one pauses at the 1949 juncture for a retrospective look at evaluations of the Communist movement, several qualities of the literature stand out. One is struck first by the diversity of those writing on the Communist movement. In contrast to later years, academics played a secondary role. Although George Taylor and Laurence Rossinger, for example, made important contributions, they were overshadowed by newspaper reporters and free-lance writers who introduced the Communist movement to the public outside China. This was quite natural. Most academics were historians, and the Communist movement was current events, to be described by participant observers on the spot.

Second, a clear evolution in sources of evidence took place. The movement was, until the mid–1930s, largely inaccessible to foreigners. During the period of the Jiangxi Soviet, commentators such as Clubb and Harold Isaacs had to rely on scarce written sources or hearsay. Snow changed all that. After 1936, and until the final Civil War, studies of the Communist movement relied heavily on firsthand observations which circulated among a small community of CCP-watchers in China. This factor not only provided a means by which the reporting of diplomatic personnel like John S. Service and John Payton Davies influenced public writings but also contributed somewhat to the uniformity of themes in writing about the CCP during these years. Indeed, some would argue that the dependence on such shared impressions and conversations with Communist leaders, to the neglect of examination of party publications, presented a somewhat misleading image of the CCP.[17]

Finally, the reliance on on-the-spot observation meant that conditions within China—primarily Guomindang corruption and lack of purpose—were the major determinants shaping Westerners' views of the CCP. Distaste for the GMD conditioned a tendency to see the Communists as an indigenous revolutionary movement responsive to the grave social problems being ignored by the GMD. As the only major force pressing for change in a steadily deteriorating China, the CCP was assumed to have deep indigenous roots. The Soviet tie was thus viewed as quite secondary when compared to the CCP's links to the Chinese revolution.[18]

Such was the mainstream view of the nature of the Chinese Communist movement, characterized by a common set of preoccupations but distinguished nonetheless by considerable internal pluralism. It by no means went unchallenged. Many within the American government, and outside of it, felt that the strength, popular following, democratic nature, and military effectiveness of the CCP had been overstated. The Communists, this school asserted, made only a slight contribution to the war while maintaining their hold over the population by means of propaganda backed up by organized coercion. They viewed the Guomindang as making the major contribution to the war against Japan. Charges of undemocratic practices and corruption were largely dismissed with reference to the exigencies of war. How, Walter Judd asked, could freedoms be extended to people during wartime?[19]

In the eyes of many who subscribed to this view, the prevailing drift of analysis was part of a deliberate plan to misrepresent the Chinese situation by discrediting the Guomindang. This argument presaged what was to be known during the cold war era as the "conspiracy theory."[20] But as Ross Koen has argued, until 1947 those defending the Guomindang from its critics made little headway. Paradoxically, they began to win out only as the tide of civil war turned against the increasingly corrupt and inept Nationalists. Perceptions of the Chinese Communist movement were coming under the pressures of the growing cold war mentality and the "who lost China" debate that it spawned.[21]

"The Organizational Weapon," 1949–1962

During the 1950s many who wrote on the Communist revolution ignored earlier insights regarding the relationship between Chinese Communism and China's ongoing revolution.[22] Many also discarded the analytical categories—party/mass relations, people's war, organizational ties with the populace, etc.—that had dominated earlier discussions. Treatments of the emergence of Chinese Communism were thus intellectually detached not only from China's earlier history but also from the scholarship of less than a decade earlier. They were now written against a preoccupation with three immediate issues: the prevailing scholarly view of Communist revolutions, the cold war, and the nature of the Communist system.

Scholarly studies of Communist revolution passed through two stages during the period from 1949 to 1962. In the first, which lasted until the mid-1950s, conceptualizations of Communist revolution were largely post facto extrapolations from the takeovers in Eastern Europe. In the second stage, starting with the mid-1950s, Communist revolution became associated with the emergence of the third world and the movement of Marxism eastward. Communism became a "disease of the transition" to economic takeoff, a "problem of development."[23] Despite this shift, the intellectual categories used to study Communist revolution remained remarkably consistent throughout the thirteen-year period.

The most striking consistency was the propensity for the study of Communist revolution to become the study of Soviet foreign policy. It was assumed that national Communist parties were best understood as instruments of Soviet foreign policy. Some writers spoke of Soviet "fifth columns" in various states, and Sigmund Neumann used the concept of "international civil war" where "a central revolutionary authority . . . can direct its orders by remote control.''[24]

Commentators throughout these years recognized, however, that the quality and strategy of national Communist organizations were also crucial to the revolutionary success. Most important was the creation and proper use of what Philip Selznick called "the organizational weapon." Those emphasizing this instrument referred to the Leninist prescriptions for a thoroughly disciplined, professional organization seizing power through ruthless manipulation.[25] Success, in the view of earlier analysts of the Chinese revolution, had to be *created*; in the view of these later commentators on Communist revolutions, it had to be *engineered* through such techniques as bogus coalition governments or the seizure of crucial ministries.[26]

The mid–1950s' shift toward a study of Communist revolution as a species of anti-imperialist, nationalist revolution only added a new variant to this tendency.[27] Most who looked at Communist movements in these areas argued that the crucial revolutionary factor in third world countries was the intellectuals who were attracted by the Soviet foreign policy stance and socialist developmental model. An understanding of their nature, aspirations, and ideology as well as their ties with the Soviet Union, it was believed, provided the most important insights into Communist revolution.[28]

Obviously the trend of scholarship was related to the political currents of the decade. As the cold war mood grew in the United States, so did the intellectual currency of the conspiracy thesis. The conspiracy thesis found its greatest acceptance in the Congress and in the mass and international affairs media. Two elements are present in all the variants of the conspiracy thesis. First is the argument that the outcome of the Chinese revolution was determined primarily by international factors rather than domestic ones. The Communist movement, the argument ran, prevailed only because Soviet aid to the CCP, combined with grievous deficiencies in American aid and damaging diplomatic concessions to Moscow, had crippled the Guomindang's ability to fight. With the Communist movement now depicted as the surrogate and beneficiary of Soviet policy, it was no longer important to study its domestic roots. The second common element is the assumption of conscious conspiracy. Different proponents of the thesis identified different villains, but all assigned some blame to short-sighted American policy makers misled by traitorous advisers seeking to bring the Communists to power.[29]

Both the organizational weapon argument and the conspiracy thesis imply that a model of elite politics is more appropriate for studying the Chinese revolution. Communist revolutions were by and large considered not to command the following or loyalty of the majority of the populace; they were illegitimate. Organization, Selznick argued, was a way "of eluding the need to win consent."[30] Success lay in the party's ability to manipulate legitimate mass needs and aspirations, particularly for agrarian reform and national independence so as to weaken the established authorities and promote seizure of power.[31] In the fifties, most commentators seemed indifferent to what attracted the masses to Communist movements; their thoughts or aspirations were considered to bear little relationship to the actual course of the revolution.[32]

The actions of the Chinese themselves helped foster this view. Not only did China, until the late 1950s, closely follow the Soviet lead in foreign affairs and contend that Soviet aid had been indispensable for victory; but also, beginning in the early 1950s, a series of mass movements culminating in agricultural collectivization suggested the sovietization and regimentation of China. The People's Republic of China bore little superficial resemblance to the old base areas. Many fell easily into viewing the past history of the party through the prism of its present, more nearly Soviet form.

The work of one group of scholars—David Rowe, Richard Walker, Franz Michael, George Taylor, and Karl Wittfogel—seems to reflect the conspiracy thesis. Like the thesis, their work often reads like an exoneration of the Guomindang. The CCP, we are told, was victorious in the first instance because a viable Nationalist government was grievously weakened by the Sino-Japanese War, and second, because its own strength was augmented by Soviet aid, both direct and indirect. These writers see the Communist Party using such devices as the united front to seize power by exploiting popular demands for anti-Japanese resistance and for social reforms, after which time the organization became "dictatorial," imposing leadership preferences on the masses.[33]

The emphasis on the Soviet connection so permeated the scholarship of the 1950s that it appeared in the very important and certainly nonconspiracy thesis studies of Benjamin Schwartz and Robert C. North. For both authors the focus of attention is on CCP policy and personnel shifts on the elite level. They agree that these shifts were the key to understanding the nature of the Chinese Communist movement, a key that could not be understood without reference to Soviet influence.

The emphasis on broad policy questions and elite struggle—views from the top—is quite consistent with the other emphasis in the work of these two men, the organizational question. In this respect, however, their views differed somewhat. North's study remains close to the typical 1950s' view of the organizational weapon. He is concerned with the use of united front tactics and front organizations as a means of building support within China and isolating the party's enemies. This "program for revolt," North makes clear, was a Russian product applied to Chinese conditions with only minimal changes.[34]

Schwartz, while recognizing Mao's debt to the Leninist conception of organization, found the principle given rather un-Leninist applications in China. He argued that Mao's willingness to develop his revolutionary formulae independently of Moscow and in response to national conditions was demonstrated by the movement to the countryside and by the CCP's reliance on a base of "peasant discontent." Although emphasizing the importance of organization, Schwartz thus also touched upon the "needs" of which the Communists made themselves "spokesmen." He wrote of the amelioration of peasant grievances and the CCP's ability to harness "national sentiment to its own cause."[35]

Schwartz's work thus called for scholars to focus more on the indigenous Chinese development of the Leninist organizational weapon and its application to peasant warfare and revolution. In his extraordinarily skillful hands the Soviet connection figures as not an alternative but an aid to understanding the indigenous roots of the CCP.

John King Fairbank, Schwartz's colleague at Harvard, also stressed the indigenous roots of the Chinese revolution. Fairbank's argument was atypical of the 1950s. Rejecting the premises that the Japanese invasion could exonerate the Guomindang from responsibility for its failure, he argued that "historical trends" were "no one's monopoly and may be ridden by alternative power groups."[36] In other words, the inability to meet the crisis of the war had highlighted the limitations of the Guomindang just as it had brought out the political prowess of the CCP. What, then, explained the Communist victory? Fairbank emphasized the CCP's "grip on the two essentials of power—agrarian revolution as the dynamic of the peasantry and national regeneration as the dynamic of the intellectuals."[37] He was returning to those interpretations—including that of George Taylor himself—that explored the popular appeal of the Communist movement in China.[38]

Perhaps the most striking characteristic of the 1950s' scholarship, with Fairbank the only exception, is the general emphasis on the impact of international events. Earlier authors had recognized the Japanese invasion's crucial impact on the fortunes of the CCP, but under the influence of the conspiracy thesis some placed this event and the diplomacy surrounding it at center stage. More strikingly, it was during these years that the nexus between Soviet foreign policy and the CCP was most exhaustively explored. Soviet intervention in CCP policy and leadership was thoroughly documented; on these points much of the scholarship of these years remains definitive.

The related emphasis on elite politics focused attention on high-level leadership conflicts over personalities and policies. Intraparty disputes over policies concerning relations with the GMD, approaches to the peasantry, and emphasis on rural or urban areas were the subject of extensive research and writing.[39] The effects of those policies in practice were largely ignored.

What of the masses? In keeping with the elite politics approach, the common view was that the party's leadership was indispensable to a mass of peasants clearly unable to organize themselves.[40] There were general discussions of the appeals made by the Communist Party for popular support. All seemed to agree that national resistance to Japan and moderate economic reforms were the principal rallying cries used by the CCP.[41] Yet the actual details of party/army organization and, most importantly, party relations with the people were rarely discussed. The masses and their attitudes played a decidedly secondary role in studies of the Chinese Communist movement.

The Debate on Appeals, 1960s and 1970s: Nationalism versus Social Revolution

The terms of debate began to change with the publication of the most important study of the Chinese revolution in the 1960s, Chalmers Johnson's *Peasant Nationalism and Communist Power*.[42] Johnson argued that the roots of Communist success in 1949 are to be found in the bond the party forged with the mass of Chinese peasants during the Anti-Japanese War of 1937 to 1945. The brutality of the Japanese occupation spurred the development of anti-Japanese nationalism among the peasants, championed by the Communist Party. The party's anti-Japanese stance, rather than the peasants' economic grievances and the party's platform of socioeconomic reform, gave the CCP the popular mandate that carried it to victory. Johnson's evidence of mass support for the party is found simply in the fact of successful guerrilla warfare, a strategic mode, he asserts, that could not possibly have succeeded without broad mass support. The CCP thus came to power

with legitimate (but conditional) authority based on popularly supported nationalist goals.

The influence of contemporaneous events on this analysis is obvious.
Johnson is exploring the nexus between nationalism and communism.
This, along with the comparison with Yugoslavia, clearly demonstrated
the impact of the Sino-Soviet conflict. In addition, as Johnson mentions
briefly in a contemporary article, his interest in guerrilla war was to
some extent a reflection of growing American concern with Asian
manifestations of what the French in Algeria had called *la guerre
révolutionnaire*.[43]

But if Johnson was responding to current events, he was also self-
consciously writing in reaction to the scholarship of the 1950s. He
argued strongly against the ''organizational weapon'' approach, rejected the conspiracy thesis, and criticized those who would focus on mass
discontent based on economic deprivation.[44] In doing so, he returned to
hypotheses suggested by works of the 1930s and 1940s. Johnson's
focus on guerrilla warfare led him, like Taylor and Evans Carlson,
immediately to the issue of popular support and, like many others, to
the mobilizational potential of Japanese brutality. As he himself would
later admit, he was merely using different sources (Japanese intelligence reports) to substantiate hypotheses generated earlier by others.[45]

Still, certain central elements in the analyses of the 1930s and 1940s
are absent from Johnson's study. Although he spends some time de-
scribing the broad outlines of the CCP's military organization, he
shows little of the appreciation of the centrality of organization that one
finds in the works of Snow or Taylor. There is no clear sense of the
concrete organizational nexus that linked the people and their leaders.
Instead, in this and later works Johnson depicts this linkage in the
ephemeral terms of an authority relationship.[46]

Johnson also omits any systematic treatment of an element typical in
the analyses of the 1930s and 1940s: the role of the party's socioeconomic program in generating support. To be sure, he does not deny that
agrarian reform might have played a secondary role in heightening the
party's appeal. Nor does he deny that, given time, festering economic
problems might have brought revolution. He simply asserts that since
the CCP failed when it advocated ''radical'' agrarian policies and
succeeded when it abandoned these and promoted nationalist policies,
the nationalist policies were essential to Communist success.[47] Earlier
authors rarely had been ready to treat the nationalism issue in such a
one-sided fashion.[48]

It was on this point that Johnson came under attack by Donald Gillin, whose review of the book took issue with what he saw as Johnson's major thesis: that the CCP was successful among the peasants only when it "virtually ceased advocating revolution." Gillin argued that appeals to nationalism found a responsive audience only among the elite. The peasantry was involved by policies aimed at alleviating their social and economic distress.[49]

The Gillin article, forcefully argued and widely read, was a natural starting point for a major debate over the sources of Communist success. However, there was no response by Johnson, or others, until the late 1960s.[50] The Cultural Revolution in China and the concurrent radicalization of the political mood in the United States changed this situation. Some were moved by the Cultural Revolution to seek the roots of the apparently bitter elite conflict in the policies of the revolutionary era.[51] Others saw the Cultural Revolution as a Maoist attempt to revive China's revolutionary thrust by reintroducing many of the policies of the base areas.[52] Some, proceeding from this point, were drawn to the pre-1949 period because it was then, they felt, that the bases of an attractive and humane form of society were laid, and it was from this perspective that the peasant nationalism thesis came under renewed criticism.

Those who attacked *Peasant Nationalism* initially proceeded from the assumption that the singular contribution made by Chinese Communism to socialist theory was "uninterrupted revolution" intended to secure an egalitarian, just society. And revolution was to be the work of the masses. In one respect they were sympathetic to Johnson's analysis: they too believed that the "organizational weapon" approach obscured the close spiritual bonds that linked the party to the people. However, they differed strongly with Johnson on the bases for the authority relationship. Socioeconomic deprivation, not nationalism, was the fuel of genuine mass revolution. To suggest that Communism had to "disguise" itself as nationalism in order to be successful was, in their minds, to deny the revolutionary quality of Communism or the legitimacy of the Chinese revolution. Johnson's book was attacked as a "political tract in social science guise."[53]

Similarly, the emphasis on the war was seen as a way of exonerating a reactionary GMD regime and denying the validity of the Chinese revolution. In short, the major issues of analysis for the 1960s and 1970s became the role of socioeconomic factors, the role of organization, and the impact of the war. We will consider each of these in turn.

With Johnson himself surprisingly sounding the charge (or perhaps blowing the retreat), the nearly monocausal analysis of *Peasant Nationalism* was revised. Five years after the book's publication, without so much as mentioning how great a change in his orientation it signified, Johnson stated simply that *both* "appeals to nationalism and mild reform of agriculture [rent and interest reduction]" constituted "the twin faces of Mao's mass line." Johnson seemed to be suggesting that economic appeals, insufficient by themselves to bring about revolution, required war-generated nationalism.[54] He thus quietly returned to the double appeal analysis of the 1930s and 1940s, minus any real discussion of organization. Other authors joined the discussion, arguing for both kinds of appeal rather than one.[55]

Some scholars remained dissatisfied, considering the double-appeals approach a compromise that waffled on the key issue. The most prominent expression of this view was Mark Selden's study of the central party base of Shaan-Gan-Ning, *The Yenan Way in Revolutionary China*.[56] Selden divides his analysis into three periods: pre–1936, 1936–1941, and 1942 and after. He argues, contra Johnson, that in the early period "agrarian revolution" was the very popular and necessary first step to engage peasant support and "[pave] the way for the increasingly effective military and political participation of the rural population" (p. 79). During the second period, the imperatives of the united front against Japan necessitated moderation of land policy, but land revolution was not the only way to solve peasant economic distress. Rather, Selden argues that peasants' support for the CCP stemmed from its meeting their basic needs and integrating them into responsive political organizations (pp. 119–120).

The final period was a response to leadership concerns over the loss of revolutionary fervor and the need to solve new economic problems facing the base area. It required directing the "creative energies of the people" toward "transforming the fabric of social and particularly economic life at the village level" (p. 209). Peasants' egalitarian, participatory efforts to meet the economic and political problems of daily life constituted the "Yenan way" to revolution (ch. 6). Emerging out of the Communist revolution in China was a "humane" alternative to the alienating systems spawned by "technocratic liberalism and Bolshevism."[57]

There is much that is extremely valuable in Selden's study. His was the first case study of a base area since George Taylor's work. Besides providing a wealth of data regarding broad shifts in CCP political and economic policies, Selden focused on the dynamics of party/peasant interaction at the local level. In contrast to Johnson, Selden was concerned with the kinds of exchanges between peasants and the CCP that gained involvement in and support for party programs. He seemed acutely sensitive to the importance of meeting immediate peasant needs as a prerequisite for the continuation of such involvement. Like Snow before him, Selden believed that the simple act of participation in the political process met an important peasant need and constituted an occurrence of revolutionary quality in rural China.

Here Selden's analysis, unlike Johnson's, moves into the area of organization. However, there are real limits to that movement. Because the point of his argument is to deny the necessity or efficacy of elite or administrative authority during the Resistance War period, he reacts even more strongly than Johnson against the organizational weapon view. However, like Johnson's, his alternative explanation—the mass line—is ephemeral. The emphasis throughout is on the participation, "creativity," and "dedication" of the masses.

After the early 1970s authors such as Kataoka and Thaxton, like Selden, emphasized the importance of socioeconomic restructuring in building support for the CCP. With this came a greater sensitivity to the enormous changes that seemingly "moderate" policies could effect in the countryside.[58] Yet work in this area of CCP policies slowed as most analysts settled for the path of least resistance and recognized the importance of both nationalist and socioeconomic appeals in generating support during the Resistance War period.

The question of organization proved less tractable; it became difficult even to define its contours. Scholars increasingly emphasized the contribution of organization to CCP growth in the pre–1949 period, but agreement on the nature of that organization was hard to come by.[59]

In his study of the Jiangxi Soviet, Ilpyong Kim argues that Mao's success stemmed from his appreciation of the importance of organization in mobilizing "passive and irresponsive" masses toward revolutionary ends—in other words, the mass line.[60] Participation roused peasants from their usual apathy, exposed them to party propaganda, and gave them the opportunity to vent their frustrations and to have the sense of shaping their sociopolitical environment (pp. 131–33). Peasant participation in organization, Kim suggests, was an appeal in itself. The feeling "that they were participating in bringing about revolutionary change and economic well-being" was "as important to revolutionary strategy as was peasant nationalism" (p. 89). However, in contrast to Selden, Kim suggests that mass organizations were more important in enhancing party awareness of mass feelings and eliciting popular participation in policy implementation than in allowing mass control over leadership selection or basic policy.

Tetsuya Kataoka's *Resistance and Revolution in China*, published in 1974, presents the strongest brief since the 1950s for the centrality of organized leadership in the Chinese Communist revolution.[61] His analysis portrays a highly traditional and parochial peasant. In contrast to Johnson, Kataoka sees the war provoking peasant reaction along quintessentially traditional lines. In response to outside threats, traditional defense organizations are formed and the peasantry prepares to defend the locality. There is no war-induced organizational void; the CCP must vie with traditional elites and other groups (bandits, secret societies, and so forth) for leadership in the countryside (pp. 279–302). Always ready to defend local or self-interest, the peasantry is not easily drawn to the party calls for self-sacrifice in the name of anything beyond the local community.

Thus the Communist Party's problem was to use economic incentives (land revolution, albeit by moderate means) to gain initial peasant involvement and then through military organization to create a structure to coordinate disparate local fighting groups. Such organizational control was essential; without it, the peasants deserted the Communist cause and slipped back into parochial attitudes. Moreover, local control could be lost to traditional leadership groups. In contrast to both Selden and Johnson, Kataoka sees no natural community of interests between the peasants and the CCP (p. 116).

Kataoka's picture of rural revolution, stressing difficult organizational work in the face of peasant apathy, is directly related to his view of the war's role in bringing party success (ch. 8).[62] In essence, he argues that the force of Communist-led rural revolution was insufficient before 1937 to bring victory. The urban areas, controlled by the Guomindang, had the strength to defeat rural revolution. Without the respite provided by the war, and without Wang Ming to call the party's attention to the cities, the rural Communist movement would have been crushed by the growing urban power centers. No war, no Communist victory.[63]

Given the research findings of Johnson and Kataoka, it was increasingly difficult to gainsay the impact of the war on the CCP's revolutionary success. But for the most part, the question of the precise role of war was resolved during the 1970s in a manner reminiscent of the settlement of the appeals question. Most scholars admitted that the war played a crucial, catalytic role in creating a vacuum in the countryside which the CCP could fill, weakening the GMD and laying the basis for Communist appeals to nationalism in the city and the countryside. But almost all tried to avoid categorical statements.[64]

The scholarship of the 1970s, then, provides something of a cyclical, perhaps even dialectical, quality to the past four decades' scholarship on the Chinese revolution. In the 1930s and 1940s the dual-appeal concept was advanced, only to be largely ignored in the 1950s and dichotomized in the 1960s. In the 1970s it was recombined. Few issues in the field of Chinese politics had generated as much heat and light as the nationalism versus socioeconomic appeals argument. Yet in the end the debate was never really resolved. On one level, it ended in a draw on terms somewhat reminiscent of the 1930s. On another level, the terms of resolution in the late 1970s seem disturbingly abstract and parochial.

In fact, the earlier conflict between Chalmers Johnson and his critics was often more apparent than real. Most of Johnson's critics shared with him a largely identical conception of the explanation for Communist success: widespread peasant support. Both sides very clearly assumed both a radical transformation in peasant mentality and pervasive, consistent support of the Communist movement. But their conclusions proved as abstract as those offered by the scholars focusing on elites: the translation of popularity into action, or support into power, and the relation of action or power to victory remained to be demonstrated precisely. To the level of abstraction was added the problem of parochialism in the body of research as a whole. Studies that did concentrate on limited geographic areas focused on the central base areas (Jiangxi and Shaan-Gan-Ning); those that chose a broad field were confined primarily to the Anti-Japanese War period. Thus hypotheses about the sources of the Communist movement's success were tested on atypical cases and limited periods of time. The combination of abstractness and parochialism may explain why, despite their fruitfulness for sparking more research, the generalizations simply do not square with a good deal of information on the relationship between the peasants and the Communist movement that was available at the time and has been plumbed since.

A second type of parochialism characterized the debate as well. Although scholars of comparative revolutions drew generously upon the empirical findings of specialists on the Chinese revolution, the flow of information and ideas remained essentially unidirectional. Whereas some scholars in the 1950s and 1960s had drawn on theories or models in comparative fields, that sincerest form of flattery was never exercised on the work on comparative revolutions. Even in the 1970s, Elizabeth Perry's was the only major work on the Chinese revolution to draw upon hypotheses and generalizations advanced by that body of comparative scholarship.[65] Most China specialists remained largely ignorant of or unconcerned with the different problematiques and conclusions being drawn by comparativists out of the empirical findings on China. China scholars' contributions to generalizations on comparative revolutions thus remained largely passive, and they drew no intellectual profit from the uses to which those contributions were put.

Comparative Theories of Revolution

One finds in the "third generation" of scholarship in comparative revolutions[66] a concern with the major issues so hotly debated by the China specialists: the appeals of revolution or revolutionaries to the peasantry, the role of revolutionary organization, and the impact of international factors. These factors, however, have been rather differently conceived by the comparativists, particularly in view of their attempts to derive some general statement valid for a variety of revolutionary histories.

Most attempts at studying revolutionary causation fall into two types: structural and volitional approaches. The structural approach draws upon such concepts as social structure, economic forces, and world systems in an endeavor to trace the sources and dynamics of revolutionary events. To the structuralist, although individuals and groups may act consciously for particular ends, motivations and attitudes must be traced to structural factors and therefore matter not one whit as independent explanations of either the occurrence or the outcome of revolutions. For those taking the volitional approach, on the other hand, the motivations of participants in revolutions are key, whether these are understood as primal urges propelling *levées en masse*, as the development of a group consciousness making collective action possible, as responses to revolutionary leadership or organization, or as the ideology and strategy of a revolutionary elite.

Few attempts at explanation of revolutions have avoided resort to both such approaches at some point in their analysis, and a number of explanations are self-consciously eclectic in resorting deliberately to both. Nonetheless, most can be said to rely predominantly on one or the other approach. A handful of recent studies seminal for debates in the comparative field offer sufficient examples of the current generalizations about revolutions. Two of these, Theda Skocpol's *States and Social Revolutions* and Jeffrey Paige's *Agrarian Revolution*, fall on the structuralist side of the spectrum. Two others works, James C. Scott's *The Moral Economy of the Peasant* and Samuel Popkin's *The Rational Peasant*, fall on the volitional side.[67]

Structural Approaches

Theda Skocpol takes an explicitly structuralist tack in her comparative study of the French, Russian, and Chinese revolutions. For Skocpol, the key process in the great revolutions was the collapse of state power, coupled with "widespread peasant revolts from below." Skocpol traces the crisis of the state to "international structures and world-historical developments"—wars and economic crises situated within the system of competing states and the developing world capitalist economy. The *ancien regime* state, seeking to respond to such challenges, encounters obstacles raised by the dominant classes within its own society, and it is this impasse that precipitates its collapse.

In the Great Revolutions examined by Skocpol, the collapse of state power was crucial in permitting "*widespread* and *irreversible* peasant revolts against landlords" to develop (p. 117). Peasant rebellions in this crisis environment may finish off the old regime or propel a new revolutionary elite into power. For Skocpol, the peasantry's capacity for revolutionary collective action depends upon its "internal leverage," which "is explained by structural and situational conditions that affect: (1) the degrees and kinds of solidarity of peasant communities; (2) the degrees of peasant autonomy from direct day-to-day supervision and control by landlords and their agents; and (3) the relaxation of state coercive sanctions against peasants [*sic*] revolts" (p. 115). Social revolution, then, becomes the "conjunctural result" of a crisis in the affairs of the dominant class and the potentially autonomous state structure on the one hand, and the rebellious activities of the peasantry, on the other.

Jeffery Paige's study of social movements in export agricultural settings concentrates on structural factors as well. Paige focuses on features of the social structure that, in his view, determine both the motivations of, and the capacity for effective action by, the masses of cultivators and the noncultivating elite. Paige distinguishes several types of agrarian social structures, each characterized by a particular combination of interests of the noncultivating elite and the cultivators, depending upon their sources of income (land or capital for the elite, land or wages for the cultivators). These sets of interests determine the type of agrarian class conflicts that may arise in each environment. Paige finds that it is primarily in a wet-rice sharecropping system that a coincidence of instability of tenure, cooperative reward structure, and independence from the noncultivating elite gives rise to a combination of radical ideology, collective action, and strong solidarity. Here one finds the growth of strong revolutionary communist movements. Other social structural settings are conducive only to nationalist revolutionary movements (the migratory labor estate), to reformist labor movements (the plantation), to agrarian revolts (the commercial hacienda), or to reform commodity movements (the smallholding system) (pp. 42–43, 45–48, 63–69).

Volitional Approaches

James Scott locates the rebellious potential of a peasantry in the perceived violation of a "moral economy" grounded in traditional values. Scott argues that not objective exploitation but peasants' indignation fuels rebellions. That indignation stems from trespasses against traditional principles of rights and obligations. These include a "norm of reciprocity" calling for exchanges of equal value in social relations, and a "subsistence ethic" dictating that all are entitled to a living out of village resources (in the form of a floor below which none should fall). Scott, exploring the 1930s' depression rebellions in South Burma and central Vietnam, contends that with colonialism and commercialization of agriculture, landlords and the state claimed resources at the expense of cultivators. Peasant reaction stemmed not from the magnitude of the exactions, but from the decline of social insurance as landlord or state demands eroded the subsistence floor. Peasants' adherence to a moral economy knit together rural communities in condemning and acting against these perceived illegitimate demands.

The implication of Scott's argument is that one may expect to find peasant collective action in those places where, first, the subsistence ethic and norm of reciprocity are being violated, and second, there is still a strong village community accustomed to acting according to such principles.[68] Scott is well aware, however, that even under such conditions, rebellion may be the exception rather than the rule. First, the societies in a better position to act collectively in rebellion may be less inclined to do so because they are less exposed to "economic shocks" than the "more differentiated and atomistic villages." Thus, in Scott's view, generalizations "relating peasant social structures to the potential for rebellion would be questionable" (pp. 201–203). Second, alternative survival opportunities may deflect rebellious potential, while also eroding the communal solidarity of peasants (pp. 223–25). Finally, effective repression by the state serves to drive peasants away from rebellious activity—just as the erosion of state power may attract them to the standard of rebellion (pp. 229–30). Despite these contingencies, Scott's approach offers a framework for comprehending peasant participation in rebellions, linked to revolutionary movements or not, as tied to peasant conceptions of justice and legitimacy rooted in the traditional village order.

Samuel Popkin, contrary to Scott, suggests that "peasant politics" is not so very different from any other kind of politics. He argues for a "political economy" interpretation of revolutionary causation, seeing participation in a revolutionary movement as an "investment decision" which a peasant weighs along with other options for balancing costs and benefits (p. 244). For Popkin, class grievances or norms of justice are beside the point. The central problem for a revolutionary movement is to provide the incentives and leadership that will induce peasants to participate in the movement, and not to participate against it. The key, he argues, lies in "organization, particularly communication and coordination"—or, if one will, the presence of a revolutionary, nationally based leadership (p. 251). Organization in such settings provides sufficient incentive to overcome individuals' resistance to collective action. In short, in Popkin's world, peasants do not automatically act to further group or common interests; social structures and cultural values do not preprogram their responses, and motivating them for collective action is much the same type of leadership problem as motivating any other group.

Here the free-rider problem enters the picture. Collective action aims at achieving certain "collective goods" in which all may—indeed, must—share regardless of contribution to the action. "Free-riders" are thus an endemic problem; if all make the free-rider's calculation of maximum benefit for minimum effort, of course, no one will act at all. Therefore collective action "requires conditions under which peasants will find it in their individual interests to allocate resources to the common interests—and not be free riders'' (p. 253). The ''political entrepreneur''—read, new leadership, or even old—is essential in solving this problem. The political entrepreneur demonstrates to peasants the efficacy of collective action; applies selective incentives to elicit participation or prevent defection; and selects the issues and offers goods most suitable for initial mobilization (pp. 253–64).

Common Emphases

Exploring the differences among these works in detail would no doubt teach us much about the orienting assumptions of each author, but for our purposes what is instructive is not so much the obvious differences as the less obvious similarities. For there are common threads of findings and interpretation running through all four of these works.

First, all these authors tend to assume the lack of natural consonance between the goals of revolutionary leadership and their potential peasant following. Only Paige appears to entertain the possibility of a close correspondence, and then only in one type of agrarian setting. Skocpol explicitly states that the outcomes of revolutions frequently bear little resemblance to the original goals of the revolutionaries, let alone to the ''peasant rebellions'' that help propel the revolutionaries into power. Scott implies in his book, and elsewhere makes into his central thesis, that rebellious peasants' intentions are far afield of those of any revolutionary organization that rides the tide of rebellion into a takeover of state power. And Popkin, whose line of argument certainly suggests that peasants and revolutionary leaders may find points of agreement, nevertheless makes it clear that finding those points and turning them to the benefit of a revolutionary organization is neither easy nor certain.[69]

Second, while all these authors are concerned with the question of ''what makes peasants revolutionary,''[70] they are concerned as well with the role of opportunities and countervailing factors. Skocpol indeed makes these the centerpiece of her argument, but it is remarkable to find that even in those works primarily seeking the sources of revolutionary/rebellious impulses among the peasantry, the presence or absence of countervailing forces, revolutionary opportunities, and non-revolutionary opportunities is eventually acknowledged as key in explaining peasant responses.[71]

The countervailing factors are of two types: the strength of the state apparatus, and the strength of the rural elite. In Skocpol's analysis, one may as well not bother talking about revolutions if these are omitted; the weakness of both is the only opening permitting peasant rebellions to blossom into full-scale revolutions. Only the inability of the state to suppress challenges to its own power, only the relative autonomy of peasant communities from elite control, will permit the forces of revolution to build up to a successful climactic confrontation. But although Skocpol treats these as structural factors, and therefore as givens in a revolutionary situation, the others introduce them in one form or another as the contingent factors that help determine a revolution's success. Paige recognizes that the "weakening of the repressive power of the landed aristocracy" can create the opening for revolution in a hacienda system; Scott acknowledges that the ease of repression may cancel the inherent potential for rebellion; and for Popkin, the calculation of likelihood of repression by state or elite is an integral part of the cost/benefit considerations weighed by peasants contemplating participation in a revolutionary movement.[72]

But the availability of opportunities is also crucial. Even Skocpol's structuralist approach must break away from a strictly structural explanation when she reaches the Chinese revolution, to find that a relative lack of autonomy of peasant communities was compensated for by the presence of able revolutionary organizers. For Skocpol, voluntarism thus creeps in by the back door. In a later article, she posits the presence of a revolutionary leadership as a key explanatory factor for most third world revolutions. Paige likewise must allow for chance or voluntarism in trying to account for revolutionary movements outside the lone social setting he considers conducive to a natural congruence between peasant and revolutionary purposes. He admits, for example, the possibility of revolution arising out of a situation ordinarily conducive only to agrarian revolt, if somehow the peasantry is linked to outside leadership by revolutionaries.[73]

The others note not only the strong incentive effect of revolutionary organizations, but also the potentially derevolutionizing effect of alternative opportunities for solution of peasants' dilemmas. For Popkin, of course, the cost/benefit calculation always weighs other opportunities against participation in a revolutionary movement. Popkin recognizes as well that there is a contest of action here, where the opposing side's ability to mobilize interests and resources changes the effectiveness of the incentives offered by the political entrepreneur. But both Scott and Paige offer examples of alternatives: Scott, in the possibilities for outmigration, technical modernization of agriculture, individual or state patronage, and local self-help; and Paige, in the "deal" that is offered by the agrarian elite (which, however, he sees as determined by their structurally defined interests).[74] Markets, migration, cooptation, and compromise thus all offer peasants solutions undercutting their propensity for integration into a revolutionary movement.

Third, and in large part due to the factors discussed above, all these authors offer basically the same roster of relevant actors in a revolutionary situation. The obvious central actors are there: peasants and revolutionary leaders, defined in varying degrees of clarity and precision. It is instructive that all recognize in one form or another the importance of the variety of peasants or peasant communities: Skocpol, in the relative autonomy of the peasant communities; Scott, in the difference between cohesive and atomized communities; Popkin, between corporate and open villages; and Paige, in a comprehensive inventory of peasant social structural types and corresponding interests.[75] But not one of the authors assumes that the proximate combination of peasantry and revolutionary leadership alone provides the powder keg that will blow away the old order and bring in the new. Rather, their appreciation of countervailing factors and alternative opportunities sensitizes them to three other key actors: the state, the rural elite, and international forces.

The state is crucial primarily as the repressor of rebellious or revolutionary activities. What constraints it faces on the uses or sources of its power, what alternatives it may offer to those contemplating rebellion, are therefore essential to a full consideration of revolutionary causation. If only Skocpol attends fully to this actor, it is because only she claims to be considering revolution as a unitary phenomenon. But clearly the state hovers in the wings as a critical player as Scott's peasants contemplate rising up in just rebellion, Popkin's peasants assess their risks, and Paige's square off in a contest against agrarian elites. The rural elite is another key actor whose responses to revolutionary or rebellious challenges must be anticipated by peasants and revolutionary leaders alike. And finally, the international forces of capitalist markets and military conflict play crucial roles: first in reshaping the peasantry in the modern era, second in defining the needs and interests of the state, third in shaping the rural elite, and finally in precipitating the collapse of the state or fatally undermining its capacity to weather domestic challenges to its power.

These common threads—the resort to opportunities and countervailing factors to complete historical explanations, the longer roster of relevant actors in a revolutionary situation—suggest that the scope of studies of the Chinese revolution should be widened. To be sure, we can find appreciation of each of these elements in some past work on the Chinese revolution. The difference for the comparative studies is that they find it necessary explicitly to define and acknowledge the role that each plays in determining the final outcome. And Skocpol's and Paige's studies go a step further also in suggesting that an understanding of the role of the state, the rural elite, and international forces is indispensable for understanding the options and actions of the peasantry and (for Skocpol) revolutionary organizations. Rarely in previous studies of the Chinese revolution do we find these conjoined, and never before the present generation of scholarship (though often in the writings of revolutionaries themselves!) do we find their interactions explored with any care.

The Essays

The essays in this book are examples of a new trend characteristic of much of the scholarship of the late 1970s and 1980s, which brings to life the interactions of elements stressed by comparativists. It is paradoxical that we find such correspondence, because, far from actively seeking grand generalizations, the new generation of China scholars would seem almost to have fled to the opposite extreme. Dissatisfied with debates in the China field, debates that ordinarily offered sweeping generalizations with little close testing in actual situations, they immersed themselves in detailed studies of local revolutionary milieus, tracing the birth, life, and sometimes death of the revolution in these locales. Their findings have tended to call into question not only the resolutions but the very terms of the earlier debates in the China field. Yet although we find considerable divergence between generations in the China field, there is a remarkable convergence between the answers (if not the questions) of these newer scholars and the approaches current in comparative revolutions.

Each of these essays is abstracted from a longer study on the area of focus, and therefore none is intended to serve as a general statement on the revolutionary process in the area in question. They are "fixes" taken on the revolution at different stages in its overall development and different points in the fortunes in the Communist movement— Wei's and Benton's in the early period at a time of defeat and failure, Hartford's and Paulson's in the middle period at a time of new opportunity (but with more difficulties than has until recently been assumed),

Levine's in the final period at a time of easy entry but uncertain success. William Wei argues that the Guomindang might not have succeeded in eliminating the CCP's southern soviets had it not compromised some of its own goals for controlling rural areas and shared power with the rural elite. Gregor Benton, tracing the survivors of the defunct southern soviets, argues that their survival owed to new adaptations to the society in which they found themselves, adjustments that fundamentally (and rather disastrously) shaped their adaptive capacities in the changed climate after the Japanese invasion, when they became the core of the New Fourth Army. Kathleen Hartford, focusing on Shanxi-Chahar-Hebei, the most successful Resistance War base behind Japanese lines, argues that combined repression by the Japanese army and the Chinese rural elite could have destroyed the base area, had the local CCP leadership not introduced strategic and tactical innovations that depart significantly from the prevailing image of the party's approach to the peasantry. David Paulson examines the Shandong base during the same era, arguing that the massive presence of Guomindang guerrilla forces impeded the growth of the Communist movement, that the eventual failure of the Guomindang owed to its national strategy and internal conflicts in Shandong, but that a few adjustments might have enabled it to attract a mass following and hold Shandong out of CCP control. Steven Levine, concentrating on Manchuria during the final civil war between CCP and GMD, contends that the CCP victory was not nearly so foregone a conclusion as previously assumed; rather, the victory depended on control of Manchuria, which in turn required a land revolution. That land revolution was permitted by the prior weakening of the rural elite under Japanese occupation and constituted the first step in an ''exchange'' relationship between party and peasants creating the army that would march to victory.

Clearly, then, we are offering a diverse group of studies. The essays nonetheless display a remarkable unanimity on the terms of debate. And it is here that we find their strong correspondences with the comparative work.

First, they tend to agree that it is very difficult to get peasants integrated into a revolution; or, having gotten them involved, to keep them that way. This departs significantly from the thrust of the preceding generation of work on the revolution. Current work on the Chinese revolution would seem, however, to have contradicted not only the ''peasant support'' argument in its pure form,[76] but also the comparativists who see in peasant-based revolutions some melding of rebellion and revolution. As Elizabeth Perry's magnificent study of the Huaibei area has conclusively demonstrated, traditions of peasant rebellion imbed in peasant society ongoing organizations that tend to resist any efforts to influence them for purposes beyond those of the locals or to turn them to new local purposes.[77] None of the essays in this book finds a tradition of rebellion of importance in explaining peasant participation in the Communist movement, though Hartford points to that tradition being turned directly *against* the movement at a crucial juncture. The peasant traditions most readily apparent in these essays are those of local self-defense. But, while this theme echoes Kataoka's on the rural militarization tradition, the authors here tend to view that tradition, again, as being perhaps more easily turned against the Communist movement than used for it. Wei shows the relative ease with which the GMD could harness the tradition once it decided to compromise with the rural elite; Paulson likewise considers the tradition a strong factor in the GMD's favor.

Failing the easy linkage of peasant traditions, rebellious or otherwise, with the revolution, one must seek explanations in the development of new patterns of thought or behavior among the peasantry. Comparative approaches have tended to offer one of two possibilities: the growth of a revolutionary consciousness among the peasantry, or the growth of contingent "exchanges" between peasants and revolutionary party as the building blocks of revolutionary mass organizations.[78]

We find both such possibilities forming part of the explanations in these essays, but given a different twist. Peasant revolutionary consciousness seems a handleless blade that can cut any who try to wield it. Benton, for example, discusses the peasants who have achieved the ultimate transformation of consciousness and made the leap into full-time revolutionary status. Presumably, without such a transformation among some individuals, the Communist movement would never have maintained a presence in the South after the Long March. Yet Benton points to the difficulties posed for strategic adjustments if this "revolutionary consciousness" was too intense (viz. those who wanted to execute Chen Yi when he arrived bearing tidings of the Second United Front). Hartford, in a similar vein, while suggesting that many peasant participants had little grasp of revolutionary goals, also indicates that too much revolutionary fervor among a minority could precipitate actions disastrous from a strategic point of view (and from the point of view of the less radical consciousness of most peasants). For both

Benton and Hartford, the success or very survival of the revolutionary movement depended at critical points more on linking the party to the environment than vice-versa; i.e., on compromising the ultimate revolutionary goals for short-term tactical and strategic purposes more in accordance with the ability or willingness of local peasants to act. This in itself posed problems of controlling those more committed to radical ends. Levine, on the other hand, favors an explicit exchange-theory formulation in his account of the growth of the movement in Manchuria, but he underlines the potential for group rather than individual exchanges and offers an explanation of conditions permitting the accelerated development of such exchanges in a crisis situation.

It should be noted that implicit in all three of these essays is some notion of the nature of the peasant environment in the areas under study, which defines the possibilities for peasant outlook and interests. Levine, for example, depicts an environment in which a radical land revolution can work because of the prevalence of tenancy in Manchuria; Hartford, on the other hand, asserts the inappropriateness of radical land policies in Hebei given the preponderance of freeholding middle peasants. The nature of the peasantry defines what *can* work in linking party and peasants, and thus defines the local revolution: two, three, many peasantries give us two, three, many different revolutions. Yet the nature of the peasantry alone cannot define what *will* work for the revolution's success. Rebellious or not, conscious or not, caught up in new exchanges or not, peasants are only one of the factors involved in the explanations advanced by any of these authors.

This brings us to the second point of correspondence between our essays and the comparative studies. For all five of these authors are painfully aware of the key importance of countervailing factors in defining the revolutionary (or counterrevolutionary) situation. This is perhaps inevitable in a group of studies all of which focus on areas or periods where the CCP was either on the defensive or just gaining a foothold. But some of these are the very areas or periods for which it has heretofore been thought that the CCP was on the offensive or that any opposition was easily turned to the party's benefit. However, more is at issue than whether the Communist movement was on the way up or down. If we may invoke a homely image for illustration, previous studies have tended to convey the sense of a conflict in which two sides lined up their forces and then slugged it out. These essays offer the flavor more of a dimly patterned general melee where the punches thrown at any particular point determined the way that the sides *would* line up. What the CCP's opponents did at each juncture determined both the way peasants could or would act and how the party could act in the next round.

In this vein, two essays argue explicitly that counterrevolutionary repression can indeed succeed against a mobilized peasantry. Wei, for example, suggests that the critical turning point in Jiangxi came not as a result of the massive military pressure of the encirclement campaigns, but rather as a consequence of the GMD's lining the rural elite up on its side. But the timing of this development may have been crucial, for the GMD's changed attitude to the rural elite coincided with the radicalization of CCP land policy and violent attacks on landlords and rich peasants. With the assistance (and accompanying material blandishments) offered by the GMD, the elite were then able to extend counterrevolutionary security organizations into the countryside and gradually to root out those who supported the revolutionary side. Hartford, on the other hand, while arguing that repression can succeed, also contends that it can be intelligently countered by the revolutionary side if it is willing to use methods that can lower the calculated risks to its potential mass supporters—even if that means lowering the calculated benefits as well. In both these situations, Jiangxi as well as Hebei, the implication is that the strength of repression by state or rural elite is key in determining the outcome; but the potential for repression can be altered at least marginally (and the marginal difference may be critical) by the revolutionary side.

But so can that potential be dissipated by the counterrevolutionary side, which is what Paulson suggests occurred in Shandong. In this case, the CCP's opponents on the GMD side diluted their own strength through internecine quarrels, ignored the very real opportunities for developing a mass base of support, and then vitiated their claims to legitimacy by joining the Japanese camp for instrumental purposes. Levine's analysis also affords some grounds for attributing the failure of repression to avoidable errors, in pointing out that the Japanese occupation undermined the capacity of the indigenous rural elite to mobilize effectively against the postwar communist land reform.

In this respect, therefore, while our studies confirm the comparativists' emphasis on the importance of countervailing factors for the revolutionary outcome, the local research indicates that those countervailing factors are no more static a given than is the revolutionary potential of the peasantry. We are, rather, viewing a dialectical process of contest among contenders for power, in which the *rules* may be written by the environment (local, domestic, and international), but the *moves* are subject to the intelligence, acumen, aims, and will of the contenders.

We come, finally, to the third point of correspondence with the comparative approaches, the central importance of alternatives open to those contemplating support of a revolutionary movement. Seldom in a revolutionary situation are most potential participants faced with such bald alternatives as land or starvation, liberty or death. Usually the opportunities are arrayed along a continuum, and most of the reasonable (or attractive) ones fall into the middle range of the spectrum. The winning side is usually the one that manages to stake out the middle range as its own territory; often, it does so because its opponents have left that area untended. This, for example, is the thrust of Paulson's argument that there was strong potential for GMD harnessing of local self-defense appeals, and that these could have offered enough to the peasantry to attract support away from the Communist movement. In Paulson's account, the GMD guerrilla forces' corruption, venality, and often brutal violation of local order in effect left the opportunity for self-defense, as that for effective social reforms, a clear field for the Communist movement. Others have of course noted similar effects, but heretofore scholars have tended to argue that the social base of the GMD dictated that it could not do otherwise. Paulson disagrees; he sees an alternative the GMD could have offered, and missed. Pointing to a case in which a local gentryman was able to organize such self-defense, build a popular base, and withstand CCP military pressures for an extraordinarily long time, Paulson finds a blueprint for methods that might have been employed by the GMD elsewhere in Shandong.

If the counterrevolutionary side may miss its opportunities, so may the revolutionaries. Here Benton's discussion of the roots of the New Fourth Army debacle is instructive. The fateful reluctance to relocate to a new and more hospitable environment, Benton argues, was an outgrowth of the southern guerrillas' approach to revolutionary action, fostered during their three years in the political wilderness from 1935 to 1937. Had they been more flexible, more receptive to new situations and opportunities, they might have proven far more effective.

The implication, of course, is that revolutionaries must offer realistic as well as attractive opportunities to a potential following. Here revolutionary leadership and strategy, ideology and propaganda, the very presence of a reasonably strong revolutionary organization, perform crucial functions. Revolutionaries must assess their environment correctly (and that means both the local and the larger environment), gauge their opponents' strength accurately, approach their potential constituents sensitively, respond to their opponents' moves creatively, and all the while keep their ultimate goals in mind. It is an assignment for master politicians, one which, as the essays here demonstrate, was as often missed as met.

What, then, do these essays offer in the way of generalizations? They suggest, first, that the China field must take seriously the interpretations advanced by comparativists, and the patterns detected in other revolutionary situations. But they suggest in fact that these are almost automatically taken into account by those who immerse themselves in a local situation and attempt to trace the development of the revolutionary process there. In making the necessary connections of cause and effect, one is led inexorably to trace the interactions among peasants, party, state, rural elite, and various manifestations of international forces, and to recognize the malleability of the fortunes of revolutionary war.

Second, they suggest that, in making these connections, the boundary lines between appeals and organization, domestic and international factors, structures and motivations, break down; that posing either-or questions for explanation points one either toward ambiguity or away from half the answer. The question, rather, is how all these factors are linked in the revolutionary process.

Third, with respect to this linkage, the essays suggest that revolution at the local level—without which no revolution would succeed; therefore, that The Revolution—is a political process, not the predetermined working out of structural factors or the inevitable Big Boom emanating from the mixture of revolutionary preconditions and revolutionary consciousness.[79]

Finally, they offer not so much a generalization as a proposition on the direction that future research should follow. That is to trace, with sensitivity to the different possibilities offered in different situations, just where are the boundaries of the givens, what is the leeway for political action, and what general patterns of interaction across diverse environments we can find. We may, in the process, discover that some locales of the Chinese revolution bear far more resemblance to local revolution in other countries than to other parts of China itself. We will be, at that point, much closer to an understanding of the Chinese revolution and of revolutions in general.

2

Law and Order: The Role of Guomindang Security Forces in the Suppression of the Communist Bases during the Soviet Period

WILLIAM WEI

Previous studies of the Chinese Communist revolution have explained the fall of the Central Soviet area of Jiangxi in 1934 mainly in terms of the weaknesses of the Chinese Communist Party. One of the most significant was the incessant power struggles and ideological disputes within the party.[1] In the eye of the maelstrom was Mao Zedong and his controversial strategy of rural revolution. In the name of Marxist orthodoxy, he was eclipsed by the International Faction led by the so-called Twenty-eight Bolsheviks, who were young Chinese Communists trained in the Soviet Union. They supplanted Mao's approach of mobilizing the peasant masses for a "people's war" with a harsh agrarian policy that undermined mass mobilization efforts, and a faulty military policy of positional warfare that played to the strength of the Nationalist Army. Since Mao and his strategy were vindicated by the belated success of the CCP during the Resistance War (1937–1945) and Civil War (1945–1949) periods, scholars have assumed that if Mao had remained in control of the base area, the CCP would have won earlier.

Because scholars believed that it was the outcome of the intraparty conflicts that determined the fate of the soviets during the 1930s, they have tended to give short shrift to the counterrevolutionary forces led by the Nationalist Party (Guomindang or GMD). By unduly discounting the effectiveness of these forces, they have inadvertently distorted our understanding of the revolutionary process in general and the

This essay has benefited from the comments and criticisms of Steven Goldstein, Chalmers Johnson, and Kathleen Hartford.

Chinese Communist revolution in particular. Explanations of the early failures and later successes of the CCP will always be skewed and incomplete unless they take into consideration the capacity or willingness of the Nationalist government to suppress its enemies. During the soviet period, it was eventually able to do so. I will argue that the decisive factor in the expulsion of the CCP from Jiangxi was the Nationalist leaders' decision to substitute, for the discredited strategy of military encirclement, an economic and communications blockade of Communist territory. Once that blockade was established, the tide turned irretrievably against the Communists.

Huge quantities of manpower and matériel were needed to construct and guard the network of roads and blockhouses that served as the blockade strategy's foundation. These would not have been available without at least some degree of popular support. But the Nanjing government initially received little popular cooperation with Communist-suppression efforts, even from the rural elite. Nationalist leaders therefore had to devise means for increasing that cooperation. Rejecting radical agrarian measures that might have preempted the soviet's popular base, they chose instead to extend and intensify the government's local administrative authority and to attract elite support in order to do so. The principal agencies used to accomplish this end were local security forces (police and militia). In this essay I will discuss the crucial role of the Jiangxi rural elite and the security forces in the Communist-suppression efforts.

My argument falls into two parts, applying to two periods in the evolution of the GMD's Communist-suppression strategy. First, in the period from 1930 to early 1933, the GMD attempted to construct security forces in a way that not only prevented Communist expansion but also either preempted or prevented the Jiangxi rural elite's influence over them. The rural elite generally saw this as a threat to their position, refused to cooperate with the Nationalists, and tried to subvert security forces for their own ends. The security forces therefore remained ineffective. Second, from 1933 on, the GMD devised a new strategy for suppression efforts, which they termed the *sanbao* strategy. This entailed Nationalist efforts to woo the rural elite by conceding them a greater share in local power, resulting in more effective local security forces. Those forces alone would not have been sufficient in the suppression efforts; the new strategy rested on the effective use of a three-pronged approach, of which the security forces constituted only a part.

The Initial Strategy, 1930–Early 1933

Even the early growth of the Communist movement in Jiangxi presented the Nationalists with ample opportunities for attracting elite support
against the soviet bases. GMD leaders, however, concentrated on extending their own control in opposition not only to the Communists but
also to the rural elite. Their military and other measures were designed
to meet the latter end even more than the former. As a consequence,
they alienated the elite and thus undercut the efforts to suppress the
social revolution.

The Rural Elite and Control of the Countryside

Before Nationalists (or Communists) could claim control of Jiangxi,
they had first to wrest the countryside away from the rural elite. This
group had adroitly moved into the vacuum created by the collapse of the
Qing dynasty to usurp political power in local areas. As a social class,
the rural elite could no longer be equated with the traditional gentry,
degree-holders who had dominated local affairs under the empire
through informal power. The gentry had become an endangered species
with the abolition of the imperial civil service examination system in
1905.[2] Their ranks were no longer replenished after that date, and
increasing numbers of them forsook their time-honored responsibility
for local leadership and headed for the relative security and better
amenities of the city.[3] Moreover, without a formal status designation to
distinguish them from the commoners, the remaining rural elite's class
cohesion began to disintegrate, and they became an increasingly amor-
phous social entity. By the 1930s, the rural elite were simply those who
held high official positions in a locality, or who dominated local social
and economic relationships, enabling them to survive the Hobbesian
environment of the early Republican period with their power and
wealth intact.

   A significant section of the rural elite were popularly known by the
epithet *tuhao lieshen* (local bullies and oppressive gentry), who Xiong
Shihui, chairman of Jiangxi from 1932 to 1942, described as comparatively wealthy and literate elements, village leaders who "bullied others as if the law were nonexistent."[4] Among them were landlords who
opposed the land registration program and encouraged others to do so
as well at public meetings.[5] Xiong considered them a type of bandit
who should be punished as such. Philip A. Kuhn delimited this group

even further, tentatively identifying them as the remnant of the lower rural elite of imperial days who were marooned by the closing of traditional mobility channels.[6] They were, as the term implies, a hybrid group that consisted of gangsters as well as lesser gentry. Those few higher degree-holders who had resided in the villages had fled to escape the pervasive rural insecurity and economic chaos. The lowest and most numerous degree-holders, the *shengyuan*, were those most apt to trade upon their residual social prestige to occupy a leading position in the villages. Alongside them were heavy-handed types who have sometimes been referred to as "new gentry," an elegant misnomer for a group of thugs with "no political ideology to teach the villagers except the silent message that there were times when the strongman won regardless of class background or moral conduct."[7] Their power derived primarily from their monopoly over the local means of violence, particularly the local militia, which they used as instruments for keeping recalcitrant or rebellious peasants in line.

Traditionally, the so-called upright gentry (gentry of unquestioned probity) had provided social leadership, for example, by maintaining public works programs and supervising educational activities. The *tuhao lieshen*, in contrast, were preoccupied solely with self-aggrandizement and evinced little concern for the welfare of the peasants they dominated. As imitators on a small scale of the militarists running rampant during the warlord interregnum, they used the militia units they controlled to carve out rural satrapies for themselves. They also speculated in grain, imposed unauthorized surtaxes, diverted considerable revenues out of regular channels on various pretexts (e.g., "militia expenses"), and engaged in numerous other unethical and illegal activities. The head of the Jiangxi Civil Affairs Department cited their exploitative behavior as one of the basic reasons for the growth of the Communist movement in the province.[8]

The CCP indeed tried to capitalize on peasants' disaffection by adopting a policy of "united front from below" against all in authority, particularly the rural elite as defined economically.[9] But it hit at many who did not fall into the *tuhao lieshen* category. By giving the peasants political rights and land, and by depriving landlords, rich peasants, and other "exploiting" groups of their political and economic power, the CCP believed it would win widespread peasant support. Cadres appealed to peasants' grievances against those who had oppressed and exploited them in the past, and to their desire for a just and equitable society in the future. Radical land laws were introduced, leading to mass meetings and trials that usually ended with the expropriation and redistribution of condemned landlords' and rich peasants' property. Peasants mobilized by land reform were recruited and trained to staff the mass organizations, including self-defense groups, that made up the soviets' infrastructure.

From the beginning of the Communist insurgency in Jiangxi, the local elite reacted to the establishment of soviet bases by organizing self-defense units. In Suichuan county, the seat of the Jinggangshan base, the anti-Communist initiative was taken by a Hakka named Xiao Jiabi, who donated money to purchase weapons and ammunition, organized the people into a self-defense corps (*ziwei tuan*), and rallied them around the slogan "Resist groups with groups, oppose organizations with organizations."[10] He often worked with Guo Mingda of neighboring Wanan county (see map 2.1). Guo himself, with the assistance of his clan, organized a pacification and defense corps (*jingwei tuan*) to resist the Red Army. An enterprising soul, he learned the military arts on the field of battle. Both Xiao and Guo earned the enmity of the Communists, who labeled them *eba* (local tyrants).

Even far away from the early centers of Communist activity, self-defense groups emerged as precautions against possible Red Army incursions. In Ningdu county in southeastern Jiangxi, the best-known resistance group was organized by Wei Xuexun, so-called master of the mountain and descendant of a Ming dynasty loyalist.[11] Wei helped to fortify Cuiweifeng, a nearly impregnable mountain redoubt dominated by sheer cliffs, where his forbears had fought against Manchu troops centuries earlier. The anticipated attack finally came after the Communists evacuated the Jinggangshan area and headed for southern Jiangxi in search of a new base. When the Communists occupied Ningdu in the winter of 1930, approximately five hundred people who wanted to resist them gathered at Cuiweifeng, many bringing along their movable worldly goods, including eight million dollars in cash. There they held out for twenty-one months, until hunger forced them to surrender.

The known leaders at Cuiweifeng, in addition to Wei, included six other men. Cai Jixiang had helped fortify the encampment and was in charge of food rationing during the siege. Yan Weizhen was the commander of the defense corps (*baowei tuan*) and Zhao Shouzha its secretary; these two were in charge of the defense. Cai Yi and Beng Ze were members of the county GMD executive committee and inspection committee, respectively. They were responsible for countering enemy propaganda among the defenders. Finally, Wen Zhaoyong, a known

Map 2.1. **Jiangxi Counties.**

carouser whose only claim to leadership was that his older brother was chairman of the county GMD executive committee, fought bravely during the siege.

There is also information on 107 other defenders at Cuiweifeng. Thirty-one had attended school. All but three of these had attended middle school or above, which was high by contemporary Chinese standards. Probably twenty-nine of the people listed had middle-class occupations.[12] Thus at least one-third of the defenders were almost certainly from the elite sector of society. Undoubtedly, the reason elite elements were disproportionately numerous among the Cuiweifeng defenders was that they felt they had the most to lose to the Communists.

As the foregoing evidence suggests, the Jiangxi rural elite were quite willing to resist actively the territorial encroachment of soviet bases, and if the Nationalist government had successfully enlisted their support, its own suppression measures would have been much more effective. Yet the Nanjing government from the outset focused on measures to extend centralized control over the countryside, to keep existing government security forces out of elite control or to wrest from them their control over indigenous security forces.

The government indeed tried to use socioeconomic reforms to make these measures more popularly acceptable, but without success. Its two major reform programs were the cooperative societies movement and the New Life movement. The former assisted rural economic development and the latter attempted to restore the conservative moral and social order in the countryside. These programs were intended in part to revive the GMD's local influence and to rally the people around the government's anti-Communist activities. They were primarily designed to appeal to (and the cooperatives movement, to benefit) the rural elite, and both were largely irrelevant to most peasants.[13]

The rural elite, however, resisted the blandishments of the GMD, viewing them as attempts to reduce their opposition to other measures that were undermining their local power. Consequently, efforts to persuade them that the government shared their interests and values failed. They remained adamantly opposed to any measures that increased the government's presence in the countryside, and they either boycotted or subverted all programs and organizations that facilitated its penetration of their local domain. This was particularly true of their reception of the various GMD local security forces and measures: the Western-style police, the *baowei tuan*, and the revival of the *baojia* system of household registration and mutual guarantee.

Western-style Police

The GMD leaders were aware that the absence of a strong central government since the late Qing dynasty had permitted a steady devolution of power into the hands of the rural elite. They planned to reverse this trend and reassert central government authority over rural areas. They were especially wary of the militarization of local communities, which augmented the rural elite's power. To weaken the indigenous elite, the GMD tried to preempt their local security functions by establishing the Public Security Bureau (Gongan Ju).[14]

The Public Security Bureau (PSB) was created in September 1928 as one of each county government's four regular bureaus.[15] Its responsibilities included fire prevention, public health and sanitation, and forestry as well as control of criminal behavior.[16] Elimination of Communist insurgents was tacitly subsumed under the PSB's general tasks of maintaining public safety; only as the Communist movement mushroomed did this become a major preoccupation for the bureau.

The Jiangxi county PSBs and their subordinate branch bureaus in towns in the districts were under the direct authority of the provincial Civil Affairs Department headed by Wang Yinxi.[17] His department appointed the heads of every bureau and kept close watch on the bureaus' operation through a team of inspectors.[18] Their candid inspection reports show that by 1930 the PSBs had clearly failed to live up to their mandate.[19]

The documentary evidence reveals a wide range of problems afflicting the PSBs. Principal among these were incompetent personnel, inadequate funding, and insufficient equipment.[20] The officials in charge of the bureaus mismanaged and misused them, often in direct violation of the very laws they were pledged to uphold. Hamstrung by these shortcomings, the PSBs were impotent organizations inadequate for Jiangxi's internal security, especially in the rural areas, where the Communists were most active. Policemen rarely ventured beyond the towns where they were stationed, save to extract resources from the countryside. If anything, they made rural security worse rather than better, by exacerbating the traditional tensions between urban and rural areas.

Some PSBs tried to alleviate their problems by combining with one of the ubiquitous militia groups to form a new, more militarized type of security agency called the Police Force (Jingcha Dui).[21] This organization was more effective against the Communists than was the PSB, but it had many deficiencies, some of which were inherited from its precursors, the PSB and the militia.

Provincial civil affairs commissioners, at a national conference in 1929, agreed that the provinces needed security forces expressly designed to suppress the Communist movement. They conceived of an explicitly paramilitary organization for this purpose, the county Police Force (PF). PF units were given both military and police functions. In their military capacity, they were to conduct operations against scattered Communist bands within the county; as police, they were to perform routine duties such as detecting and apprehending criminal and subversive elements.[22] The PFs were nominally under the authority of the county PSBs, but their command structure actually ran parallel to, and quite separate from, the PSBs. The county magistrate supervised them with the assistance of a PF commander.[23]

County PF policemen were recruited through the simple expedient of converting some pacification and defense corps, one of the many types of militia units existing at the time, into PF units.[24] Policemen in the PFs were similar to those in the PSBs except for their training. The goal was to train the PFs as regular soldiers so they could assist the Nationalist Army, engaging in search-and-destroy missions against the Red Army guerrilla groups. Their three-month training course therefore emphasized practical military techniques such as troop movements, infantry tactics, and use of weapons.[25] Only about one-third of their training time was taken up with instruction in police techniques.

The corps' incorporation into county PFs should have served the double purpose of solving manpower requirements and removing a thorn from the side of the local populace. The typical pacification and defense corps had largely been ineffective; the Civil Affairs Department had satirized them as "climbing a tree to look for fish."[26] They generally had neither adequate training nor sufficient weapons. Moreover, instead of defending people, the pacification and defense corps was more likely to outrage them with its lack of discipline. One Nationalist general, while serving as Military Police Inspection Office head, reported that both the corps and the military garrisons frequently used torture to extract information from suspects, a practice that hardly endeared them to the people.[27]

The reorganization made the corps accountable to the magistrate as well as to their local leaders, and in theory therefore less apt to cause chaos among the people. But the practice of the PFs ran directly counter to the theory. As county PFs, the pacification and defense corps had greater license than ever before to create havoc. A village calling upon a PF unit for assistance risked being pillaged by its supposed protectors, without any assurance that they could catch the fleet-footed Communist troops. According to reports received by the provincial government, the PFs, like the PSBs, molested innocent people, disturbed travelers, and generally "trampled on people as if they were grass" instead of maintaining law and order.[28] An extreme case was the PF unit commander of Yiyang county, Zai Chiwei, who was engaged in a feud with the county GMD bureau.[29] Fearing that some of its members were going to indict him before the provincial government, Zai murdered three of them. While the county magistrate stood by helpless to act, Zai then intimidated one witness into abject silence so as to avoid punishment.

The amount of actual protection the PFs could provide was severely limited. Only villages with their own means of self-defense could hope to fend off Red Army forces long enough for nearby PF units to assist them. The PF units were clearly inadequate for maintaining the security of Jiangxi's rural areas. Some units even gave the ultimate proof of their unreliability, by later mutinying and joining the opposition, probably as a result of Communist infiltration of their ranks.[30] For lack of any means of making the PSBs or PFs into truly effective local security forces, the government turned to the traditional enemies of rebellion in the countryside—the local militia.

The Baowei Tuan

The Nanjing government was ambivalent about the sudden proliferation of local militia units to oppose the Communists. On the one hand, it appreciated the features that made the militia an attractive security force. It was an inexpensive way for central governments, whether dynastic, republican, or warlord, to deal with the bandit depredations that were an endemic feature of the Chinese social landscape. Militiamen were nonprofessionals who sustained themselves through their regular occupations and therefore required no salaries. Occasionally they had to be temporarily supported when separated from their home villages, as when helping to defend a neighboring village. But the major costs were for weapons and materials. All these costs were borne by the local areas rather than by the provincial or central government. Since the militia was one of the few organized bodies in the countryside, it also constituted a conduit through which the government could disseminate its own ideology, the Three People's Principles, to counter the ideas being surreptitiously spread by Communist-organized peasant associations.

On the other hand, the government was reluctant to enhance the power of the rural elite by sanctioning the militia organizations. It had originally intended the Western-style police agencies, the PSB and the PF, to render superfluous the rural elite's security activities and to minimize any threat they might have posed to state control. But as those agencies rapidly proved ineffective, the government found itself in the awkward position of having to encourage the elite-led militia to fight the Communists. It thereby risked further erosion of central government authority.

Some government leaders thought the benefits of rural elite support outweighed its costs. The elite's anti-Communist, if not necessarily pro-government, sentiments were guaranteed by the CCP's ideological and actual attacks upon them. Chiang Kai-shek, a proponent of using the gentry against the Communists, encouraged magistrates to follow the example of the self-strengtheners who had used "upright gentry" to suppress the Taiping rebels less than a century earlier.[31] The rub was that fewer and fewer upright gentry could be found in the rural areas.

The government's problem was to increase and coordinate the militia's defense capacities while preventing the less than upright militia leaders from abusing their authority. Its solution was to enact a "County Militia Law" combining the multifarious militia into an official militia system called the *baowei tuan*.[32] The *baowei tuan* was to provide the local basis for a centrally controlled force responsive to the government's military needs. It was within the purview of the Civil Affairs Department of the province and placed under the management of the county magistrate, who in his capacity as general chief kept track of its progress through appointed inspectors.[33] It was scheduled to be completely organized by the end of August 1930.

The *baowei tuan* conscripted all able-bodied men between the ages of twenty and forty into tactical militia units organizationally corresponding to the neighborhood, village, district, and county self-governing institutions set up by the government. Leaders and assistant leaders of the militia at all levels were selected by the magistrate and vested with police power. The neighborhood leader and village leader, for instance, had the authority to investigate households to detect criminals and anti-GMD elements. In the event of an attack by a hostile force, the appropriate level of militia would be called upon to handle it. If the district encountered a large bandit or Communist force, it was to request assistance from the county government. As general chief of the *baowei tuan*, the magistrate could mobilize manpower and funds throughout the county to assist any part of it.

To increase the defense capabilities of the militia units, all militiamen were to receive military training from instructors employed by the district officials. Village-level units were to conduct training exercises every three months; the district, every six months. Militiamen also received political training; instructors sent by the magistrate taught them GMD party principles and fundamental political knowledge. This may have been aimed at assisting the self-government movement; it also constituted an effort to cultivate popular allegiance to the GMD.

Although the establishment of the *baowei tuan* had a salutary effect on the security of some areas of Jiangxi, the system as a whole was stillborn. The majority of counties failed to organize *baowei tuan* by the August 1930 deadline, and those that were organized were of uneven quality, often lacking weapons and training. Moreover, many of them were dominated by *tuhao lieshen*, who manipulated them, as they did other local organizations, for selfish purposes. [34]

The county magistrate was generally responsible for the *baowei tuan*'s abysmal condition since he, as general chief, appointed the commanders and supervised the equipping and training of the militiamen. [35] Apparently, magistrates declined to exercise their authority to alter the existing militia or, at best, did so in a perfunctory manner, probably to avoid jeopardizing their relationship with the local elite. [36] If the elite's cooperation in militia development had been the only problem, this might not have been the case. But the magistrate depended on the elite for financial support of the county government, including other security agencies such as the county PF.

Even with greater exertion, however, magistrates might not have been successful in remolding the militia. They were responsible for administering the *baowei tuan*, but they had no direct tactical command of the militia units. A coordinated defense of any county still depended on the uncertain cooperation of individual militia units. Building up these units meant an increase in the security of the particular areas in which they were located, but not necessarily of a county as a whole. As long as the magistrate was dependent on the local elite there was little he could do to change the existing state of affairs; indifference at least reduced his administrative burden.

The Baojia System

Its trouncing by the Red Army during the First Encirclement and Suppression Campaign (19 December 1930 to 3 January 1931) made the Nanjing government acutely aware that the elimination of the Communists could be a protracted ordeal requiring a competent internal security system. It became quite evident that the available security forces were unequal to that task. The government therefore resurrected the *baojia* system, a centuries-old bureaucratically organized police

system built on the principles of mutual guarantee and collective responsibility, as a comprehensive method for buttressing existing security forces and extending governmental authority into the countryside.
This was, however, at the expense of the self-government movement,
since it displaced the self-governing institutions below the county level
in the so-called bandit-suppression provinces.[37] The Nanjing government readily abandoned its commitment to Dr. Sun Yat-sen's program
of national integration through participatory democracy and replaced it
with a coercive system of mass mobilization in order to combat the
Communists. It sacrificed a political objective for a military one.

On 27 January 1931, less than a month after the first encirclement
campaign, Chiang Kai-shek ordered the provinces of Hunan, Hubei,
and Jiangxi to put the *baojia* into effect. Three months later the Legisla-
tive Yuan ordered four more provinces in South and Central China to
do likewise and called for all seven provinces to complete the creation
of *baojia* systems by 31 August of that year.[38]

The PSBs, the agencies entrusted with implementing the *baojia*,
failed to meet this deadline. The understaffed and underfinanced PSB
found it too complex to execute the household registration, too expensive to prepare the required door placards and registers, too difficult to
provide protection for informers, and virtually impossible to recruit
suitable personnel to *baojia* headmanships.[39]

Nationalist leaders were undeterred by the initial setbacks. They
recalled that the *baojia* had been instrumental in the suppression of the
Taiping rebels, and more recently of the anti-Japanese insurgents in
Taiwan.[40] It would allow them to exploit their advantages over the
Communists. They had found, much to their chagrin, that the government's comparatively large economic base, extensive administrative
apparatus, and powerful military force were useless against the elusive
enemy. These assets were, however, useful when applied to a static
rural population.[41]

The *baojia* organized the people into decimal hierarchies, with every
ten households constituting a *jia* and managed by a *jiazhang*, and every
ten *jia* constituting a *bao* and managed by a *baozhang*. The headmen of
these decimal divisions were primarily rich peasants and landlords.[42]
Historically, *baojia* had been used both to maintain local security and to
mobilize the masses to combat perennial natural disasters and widespread illiteracy. During the soviet period, however, they functioned
primarily as policemen for the villages.[43] The principal purpose of the
baojia system was to control the population physically and to force its

submission to the will of the government. It was used to deter people from providing aid and comfort to the enemy, and to identify and neutralize the Communist infrastructure in the villages. The *baojia* performed such security work as controlling people's movement in an area and noting the presence of strangers, reporting overt and covert Communist activities, constructing blockhouses and other defensive works, and protecting telecommunications lines and roads through the area.[44]

This security work depended largely on the census the headmen compiled. A thoroughly compiled census served as a basic source of intelligence, since it showed who was related to whom, a pertinent piece of information because family ties were a means of recruiting people into the ranks of the Communists.[45] Knowing who owned property or who worked outside the village indicated who had legitimate reasons for traveling. Such data enabled the GMD to root out Communists and their sympathizers in the countryside.

In addition to serving as a rural police agency, the *baojia* also replaced the self-government system as the administrative basis for the *baowei tuan* militia units. The census served as the basis for conscripting men into the militia. In 1932 the headmen culled from the household registers all able-bodied men between the ages of twenty and forty, forming them into militia units.[46] The following year the ages were changed to eighteen to forty-five. By 1934 the government had an available manpower pool of 2,137,036 from which to draw militiamen.[47]

The census registers were not the only reason for administering the *baowei tuan* through the *baojia* system. One of the *baowei tuan*'s underlying problems had been its dependence upon a self-government system permeated with *tuhao lieshen* who easily secured for themselves or their ilk command of the militia units.[48] The *baojia* system explicitly excluded these unsavory elements from headmen positions. By linking the *baowei tuan* system to the *baojia*, the Nanjing government should have been (and no doubt intended to be) better able to control the caliber of its militia leaders.[49] But because the positions were so unattractive, being held in low esteem and considered dangerous as well, the GMD was compelled to accept anyone who was willing to become a headman. Chen Gengya, who had made an official visit to Jiangxi and three other "bandit-suppression provinces" in the summer and fall of 1933, discovered that corruption was widespread in the *baojia* system. The majority of officials in Yichun county, for example, were illiterate gangsters.[50] They were simply carpetbaggers who saw the position as a convenient way to gain a modicum of political power. They used their positions to collect fees for performing routine services such as issuing travel passes and good conduct certificates, both of which were required if people wanted to make any journey.[51] In Nancheng county, the cost of travel and identity documents was prohibitive, preventing peasants from visiting the city except when it was absolutely essential (the documents had to be presented at the city gates). To say the least, this made it difficult for peasants to sell their produce.[52] But in a perverse sense this particular abuse actually helped the GMD by restricting people's movements and making it difficult for anyone to assist the Communists.

Considerably more burdensome were the assorted *baojia*-related assessments levied on the people. During the harvest season in Wanzai county, the peasants were forced to pay a substantial portion of their produce for the maintenance of the *baojia* organization and militia.[53] Such assessments were so heavy that people had to mortgage some of their property and curtail their annual festivities.[54]

From the establishment of the Nanjing government in April 1927 until the end of the Fourth Encirclement Campaign in April 1933, GMD attempts to control the countryside were ineffectual. What control the GMD did have continued to diminish because of provincial security forces' proclivities for milking the countryside of resources. The area under CCP control was growing. From the perspective of the GMD, the circumstances in the countryside were bleak indeed.

The Sanbao Policy, 1933–1934

Even as the fortunes of the Nanjing government fell to their nadir, a confluence of changes in the condition of the rural elite resulted in a watershed in the GMD struggle against the CCP. Changes in both CCP and GMD policies were responsible for a turn in the tide of Communist expansion.

The Communist Party ushered in 1933 with a call for intensification of the revolution. That summer it launched a land investigation movement to check up on and extend land reform. Its aims were to complete the land revolution in the 80 percent of soviet areas where it was still incomplete, and simultaneously to suppress counterrevolutionaries. As a result of this campaign, some thirteen thousand rich peasants and landlords in the Central Soviet Area were denounced and their lands

Map 2.2. **Communist-Controlled Counties in Jiangxi, 1933.**

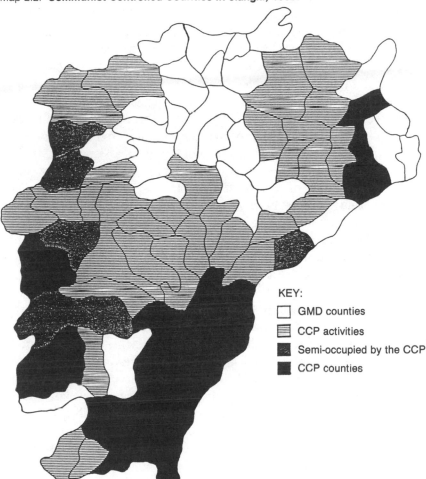

KEY:

☐ GMD counties

▤ CCP activities

▨ Semi-occupied by the CCP

■ CCP counties

redistributed, sending shock waves throughout the province. The growth of the Red Army and the consolidation of the soviet bases demonstrate that such radical CCP policies met with considerable success. The Jiangxi Peace Preservation Office (Baoan Chu) concluded on the basis of local reports that by the fall of 1933 the Communists completely dominated nineteen Jiangxi counties, had partially occupied six, and were active in thirty-five more (see map 2.2).[55]

Yet a year later the Communist movement collapsed like a house of cards. In retrospect, it is evident that the CCP policies were shortsighted. They mobilized peasants, but they also drove the rural elite into the open arms of the GMD.

The rural elite's indifference to the GMD began to crumble as successive Communist military victories made their situation extremely precarious. The Fourth Encirclement and Suppression Campaign (1 January–29 April 1933) provoked a Communist offensive outside the Central Soviet Area, convincing the elite that they were about to be engulfed by their implacable enemies.

In the meantime, the Guomindang had changed its tack to the deliberate conciliation of the rural elite, offering them greater benefits from the political, economic, and social changes in the province. In addition, the government tried once again to obtain their assistance, this time through the *sanbao* strategy adopted in April 1933. This policy called for the integration of security forces into the Communist-suppression effort through an expansion of the *baojia*, revitalization of the *baowei tuan*, and the construction of blockhouses (*baolei*) to blockade the soviet base area. By the time that policy was introduced, the elite had begun to realize that a position of neutrality was untenable and that their interests dictated arriving at a modus vivendi with the government, at least for the duration of the Communist presence. The government may have threatened their local autonomy, but at least it offered them a role in its bureaucracy rather than calling for their extinction. Besides, as low-level members of the government, the elite gained a modicum of legitimacy and access to higher levels of government power, potentially reinforcing their local position. Considering what a CCP victory held in store for the elite, the GMD was now making them an offer they could hardly refuse. They could ignore it only at their own peril. Reluctantly, the rural elite chose to side with the government. This made a formidable alliance, one strong enough to destroy the soviet bases in 1934.

Security Forces: Baojia and Baowei Tuan

Significant changes in the security forces followed upon the appointment of Xiong Shihui to the chairmanship of Jiangxi province in December 1931. Xiong tried to halt the security forces' deterioration and to restore order to the countryside. To assist him in accomplishing this task he was given responsibility for civil affairs, education, and peace preservation in the province.[56] Xiong thought that security forces had several advantages over the regular army.[57] They were potentially larger than regular armies, because their size was limited only by the number of able-bodied men in the population. They were more reliable because they operated in their home areas. Unlike the Hunan Army, for example, local security forces would not abandon the struggle against the Red Army in Jiangxi to quell disturbances in their home province. Also, soldiers in the regular armies were invariably poorly paid and stole from the local populace. The farther they were sent from their native provinces, the worse they behaved, and the more deleterious their effect on the security they were charged with preserving.

Xiong considered the proper management of the *baowei tuan* one of the most important counterinsurgency measures to be taken by his administration. The "County Militia Law" remained a dead letter, but the idea of using local militia as an anti-Communist agency was still viable. With this in mind, Xiong endeavored to increase the number of units in the *baowei tuan* and improve their training.[58] He did in large part succeed. By June 1934, there were 343 militia units of varying sizes working within the system.[59]

The militia's expansion was due mainly to new incentives provided the magistrates, the major stimulant being money. Beginning in September 1933, counties began to receive provincial subsidies as part of the militia program, the amount depending on the extent of a county's Communist problem.[60] The subsidy was unnecessary for the *baowei tuan* itself. In its original conception this was an inexpensive organization with most of its costs paid by the local area, a responsibility that was continued under the auspices of a local finance committee.[61]

The subsidies thus were tantamount to a bribe to implement the *baowei tuan* system. The GMD also became increasingly strict with the magistrates. Penalties for poor performance could be extremely harsh. For example, Nanchang headquarters ordered the execution of the Anyi County Magistrate Xiao Yehui and PSB chief Xu Tengshi for allowing the county seat to fall into enemy hands.[62]

Partly due to the increased intensity of the Communist threat, and partly to changes in Nanjing's pacification strategy and approach to the elite, the vicious war waged early in the soviet period between the rural elite and Communist-led self-defense groups reemerged with a vengeance in 1934. In 1932, the elite-led militia had fought more than two hundred engagements with the Communists. From July 1933 to April 1935 they fought some six hundred, a substantial increase in activity largely attributable to the *sanbao* strategy.[63] According to monthly county reports, there were 260 recorded clashes during the thirteen months from December 1933 to December 1934, resulting in the capture of 1,788 assorted weapons and 1,402 prisoners, and in 3,495 casualties.[64] Almost three-fourths of these engagements were fought by *baowei tuan* units, which reflected well on Xiong Shihui's efforts to improve their performance, and the remainder by volunteer militia groups (*yiyong dui*). The CCP's preoccupation with counterrevolutionary conspiracies notwithstanding, there was almost no armed resistance within the Central Soviet government's territory. The four recorded incidents there occurred in the autumn of 1934 when the Nationalist Army was rapidly closing in, and they were probably mopping-up operations conducted by militia groups emerging in the wake of the army's advance. The Communists were, until the last moment, in firm control of their central domain. This, however, was not true of the Northeastern Soviet, established in 1927 by Fang Zhimin and Shao Shiping, or of the Southeastern Soviet, the area of the former Jinggangshan base. Although the Communists had occupied these far longer than they had the Central Soviet, their control here was apparently far weaker. Both soviets, especially the Southeastern Soviet, experienced a high incidence of militia skirmishes.

A comparison of Communist activity in 1933 (map 2.2) and militia engagements in 1934 (map 2.3) shows that the CCP had made inroads into the GMD areas; there were at least sixteen violent confrontations in eight ostensibly government-controlled counties. The militia skirmishes were inconsequential compared to the battles fought by the regular army, but they were important evidence of the success of the new GMD military strategy. The tactical alliance between the Guomindang and the rural elite had come none too soon.

Although Xiong Shihui actively promoted the *baojia* system, it was unevenly organized in Jiangxi, existing only in those counties firmly under the control of the Nationalist Army, a pattern that is reflected in table 2.1.[65] Substantial progress in setting up *baojia* organizations was only made in 1934 and 1935, or during and after the successful Fifth Encirclement and Suppression Campaign. Without Nationalist Army protection the *bao* and *jia* were vulnerable to reprisals and subversion from local Communist organizations. Moreover, the earlier exodus of rich peasants and landlords from the countryside had created a dearth of reliable candidates for the headman positions. As each county was recovered from the Communists, the military authorities instituted the *baojia* system, employing the returning refugees who inevitably followed in the army's wake. The *baojia* could then begin to root out Communist soldiers, cadres, and sympathizers under the protection of

Map 2.3. **Incidence of Militia Clashes, December 1933 to December 1934.**

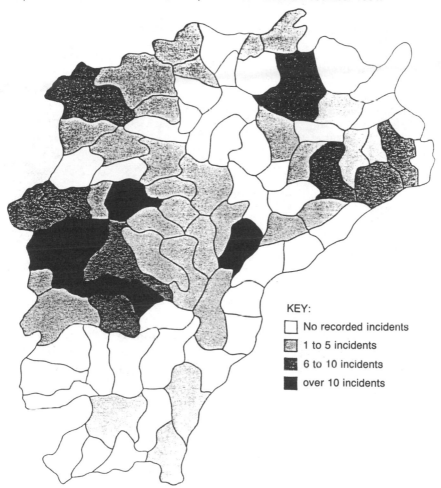

KEY:

▢ No recorded incidents

▨ 1 to 5 incidents

▩ 6 to 10 incidents

■ over 10 incidents

nearby garrison troops. As a security agency it was mostly effective only after the campaign had been fought and won. Its usefulness, however, was short-lived. As Gregor Benton points out in this volume, the Communists who were stranded in the province following the collapse of the Central Soviet developed what was described as a ''double-edged'' policy that co-opted *baojia* officials in order to survive the postsoviet pacification process. The most significant contribution of the *baowei tuan*, *baojia*, and other security forces to the struggle against the Communists was their participation in the communications and economic blockade of the soviet areas.

Table 2.1

Statistical Survey of *Baojia* in Jiangxi, 1932–1935

Date	Bao	Jia	Households	Population	Able-bodied males
1932[a]	21,018	211,646	2,245,558	11,217,799	1,905,613
1933[b]	21,872	219,454	2,349,248	11,650,160	1,971,454
1934[c]	23,089	231,818	2,539,460	12,860,353	2,137,036
1935[d]	26,584	269,066	3,055,251	15,690,403[e]	2,665,065

Source: *Gan zheng shinian*, chap. 15, p. 16.
Notes:
a. Based on reports from sixty-seven counties.
b. Based on reports from sixty-seven counties and two special districts.
c. Based on reports from seventy-seven counties plus two cities and six special districts.
d. Based on reports from all eighty-three counties and two cities.
e. This figure differs considerably from the estimate of 18,638,559 recorded in the *Shen bao nianjian*, 1935, p. (B) 88; and the 27,563,000 cited in the *Report of the Technical Agent of the Council on his Mission in China*, p. 21.

The Blockade-Blockhouse Strategy

The foundation of the blockade-blockhouse strategy was a well-developed communications system. The dearth of communications lines had had an adverse effect on the accomplishment of government policies. The failure of the first three encirclement campaigns had focused attention on the need to improve the existing communications system in the province. Nationalist leaders realized that the rugged and unfamiliar terrain of southern Jiangxi gave the Red Army a major advantage over the Nationalist Army. The ponderous Nationalist Army with its heavy equipment had found ingress into (and eventual and embarrassing egress from) the Central Soviet Area a debilitating experience. Its logistics, mobility, and coordination were seriously impaired by the lack of adequate communications lines.

There were few lines of communication in Jiangxi before the encirclement campaigns. In 1928 there were only an estimated 312 miles of highway and 80 miles of railway in a province of 69,498 square miles.[66] Telecommunications were limited to the important cities and towns.[67] Efforts to improve and expand existing lines of communication were thwarted by a shortage of funds and by the military insurrections that preoccupied the Nanjing government during its early years.[68] As map 2.4 illustrates, only parts of the proposed Jiangxi-Fujian highway (points 1 to 2) and the Jiangxi-Guangdong

Map 2.4. **The Blockade-Blockhouse Strategy.**

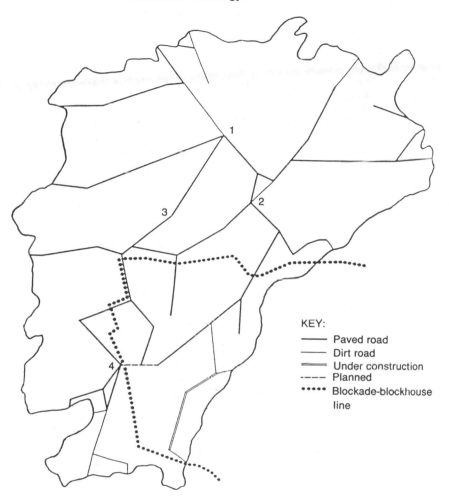

KEY:

——— Paved road
——— Dirt road
═══ Under construction
----- Planned
••••• Blockade-blockhouse
line

highway (points 1 to 3) had been completed.

Xiong Shihui endeavored to solve this problem by rapidly expanding the lines of communication in the province.[69] A telecommunications system was set up embracing the entire province.[70] The Peace Preservation Office reorganized the Telephone Unit and improved its ability to service telephone lines between the military administrative agencies and the city's defense units.[71] Three major airports were built in Nancheng, Ji'an, and Nanzheng, with a dozen other depots along the frontlines to enable planes to land for refueling and other purposes.[72] Most important of all was the construction of an extensive road network centering on Nanchang that converged on the Central Soviet Area.

Xiong's policy anticipated a major resolution, to develop a comprehensive inter- and intraprovincial road construction program, passed at the Military Affairs Conference held in June 1932.[73] That resolution saw roads as a stable defense measure and as a means of facilitating the flow of commerce, an idea that was probably added to justify the use of National Economic Council development funds for road construction. Detailed plans were developed several months later at a Seven-Province Highway Conference in Hankou. There, delegates from seven provinces in South-Central China agreed to build a twelve-thousand-mile road network to connect their provinces through six main arteries and forty thousand miles of supplementary trunk roads.[74] By March 1934, nearly fifteen hundred miles of road had been built in Jiangxi, with another six-hundred-odd miles either under construction or planned for the future.[75] Table 2.2 gives figures showing the tremendous jump in road construction in Jiangxi from 1930 to 1933.

A quarter of Jiangxi's budgetary appropriations for 1933–34 were spent on road construction.[76] The central government helped to defray part of the costs with a small monthly subsidy, and the National Economic Council loaned the province slightly over a million dollars for its road construction.[77] But the people of the province had to absorb the lion's share of the construction costs. Beginning in March 1932, the Jiangxi population paid approximately $1.2 million annually through a tax levied on each *dan* of salt sold.[78] Furthermore, they were forced to contribute land and labor for the construction of the roads. Local road construction committees used the *baojia* registers to conscript the necessary workers for each segment of the roadway.[79]

Though the people paid most of the costs for the road system in Jiangxi, they derived little economic benefit from it; the motor roads were being built in a land where motor transportation was almost nonexistent.[80] Even the Jiangxi Highway Office itself had difficulties in securing enough vehicles for road building.[81] Bicycles were equally scarce. Consequently, people continued to transport commodities on foot, and the roads were little more than expensive footpaths. Moreover, the road system was not integrated with existing water and rail transportation. From an economic perspective, the roads should have been built as feeders to water and rail transportation.[82] Instead, they often merely duplicated routes already available on water or rail. A case in point is shown on map 2.4, where the road constructed from Nanchang to Ganxian parallels the Gan River (points 1 to 4).

Table 2.2

Road Construction in Jiangxi

Year	Miles built
1928	14.40
1929	73.50
1930	24.90
1931	201.00
1932 (before October)	676.20
1933 (before October)	819.08

Source: Rui Wei, "Jiangxi gonglu jianshe gaikuang" (The general situation of the construction of Jiangxi highways), *Xiandai shehui* (Contemporary society), 3, 14 (5 September 1934): 28.

But the road network did serve its primary purpose, that of making the Central Soviet Area accessible to the Nationalist Army. Military units from the surrounding provinces were able to reach Nanchang and then South Jiangxi easily on the newly built roads. To prevent the Red Army and its guerrilla detachments from severing the roads, thousands of blockhouses were built along them.

County blockhouse committees were formed, consisting of the county magistrate, the local military commander, and local gentry.[83] They were charged with underwriting the costs of blockhouse construction and supplying the necessary workers and materials. Like the local road construction committees, the blockhouse committees conscripted workers by using the *baojia* registers. The overlap of membership on these two different committees, and of the work forces conscripted, was probably virtually complete.

Approximately fourteen thousand blockhouses were built in Jiangxi by the end of 1934.[84] Old temples were torn down and the material reused to save on expenses.[85] Depending on the style and size of the blockhouse, two shifts of laborers might complete one in three days.[86] Competitions were held to speed up the work, and some blockhouses were completed within twenty-four hours.[87] The bigger and better built structures were of brick and stone, three to four stories high, resembling medieval European towers.[88] Each level had a number of gunports, and the blockhouse was armed with at least two machine guns.[89] A fortification of this sort could serve multiple functions, housing a company of men and serving as a supply depot and communications center. Blockhouses were protected by a perimeter of trenches and barbed wire. People living in the immediate area were relocated to prevent them from assisting the Communists.

Along the main roads the blockhouses served as observation posts, checkpoints, and forts. They were built at convenient distances from each other so that occupants of one could go to another's assistance if necessary. Nanchang headquarters wanted one built at least every ten *li* of highway.[90] They were erected at strategic points such as hill tops that commanded a good view of the countryside. The local *baojia* headmen were responsible for manning them with militia units supplied with provisions to last at least two weeks.[91]

On the battlefield, the blockhouses were used as gun emplacements for interlocking zones of fire that were as much as six kilometers wide.[92] Under their protection, Nationalist Army units could prepare for attacks against the Red Army in comparative safety. They could effect a penetration on a narrow front without fearing ambush from another direction. After advancing a short distance, usually no more than five to ten kilometers, they extended the roads and built new fortifications. Each belt of blockhouses served as a stable base and staging area for the succeeding one. Wounded soldiers could expect to receive medical attention at these minibases, which raised troop morale immeasurably.[93]

The protected road network ensured that the Nationalist Army had reliable and well-defined logistical lines. Perhaps more importantly, the blockhouses disrupted Communist logistical lines and denied them supplies, thus effectively enforcing the blockade of the Central Soviet Area. The blockade subjected the Central Soviet Area to slow economic strangulation and a total communications blackout. Except for Nanchang and Xinjian counties, which were excluded from the blockade, the rest of the province was divided into four categories: secure zone, semi-bandit zone, adjacent-to-bandit zone, and complete bandit zone.[94] Nationalist Army field commanders were responsible for determining which of these categories applied to the area they occupied and for enforcing the blockade accordingly. No information or material could enter or leave a complete bandit zone, and in the other two bandit zones they were tightly controlled.

Blockade Bandit Area Management Offices were established in the semi-bandit and adjacent-to-bandit zones to censor all communications such as letters and telegrams.[95] They were directly under the authority of the Administrative Inspectorate System commissioner and were managed by the magistrate, district head, or *baojia* district headmen. With the assistance of military inspectors, they interrogated anyone leaving the complete bandit zone and issued permits to those travelling within their areas. Offices were located at every important communications point to inspect these permits.

Certificates from the highest local military authority were required for the transportation of all military material, which included materials used in the manufacture of weapons and uniforms, and articles with potential military value such as radios, gasoline, machine oil, and electrical components.[96] Articles of daily necessity such as oil, salt, and food being shipped from the secure zone to either the semi-bandit or adjacent-to-bandit zones required a certificate issued by a local civic association or monopoly committee, which was made up of gentry and merchants.[97] County-level monopoly associations distributed these items through branch associations, which in turn sold them to the *baojia* headmen. Allocations were calculated for a ten-day supply for the local population. The amount that could be sold to a person was rationed according to family size; for instance, a family of ten was allowed to have eight ounces of fuel, a family of five half that, and a family of less than five no more than two ounces.[98] Anyone caught with over ten kilograms of salt or fuel was immediately suspected of war profiteering.[99] People discovered hoarding material for resale were liable to severe punishment, including execution.

The blockade was enforced jointly by the Nationalist Army and local security forces. As a further precaution, the Special Movement Corps checked up on them to ensure that they operated the blockade effectively.[100] It had sweeping powers and acted independently of the regular army, being directly responsible to Chiang Kai-shek. Numerous inspection stations were placed along the roads (usually in blockhouses) and waterways. In those areas with partially built blockhouses, local crops were shipped to a secure zone rather than circulating freely in the immediate area. A Waterways Supervision Office patrolled Jiangxi's extensive river system to control the movement of goods.[101] Inspectors who discovered and confiscated contraband were rewarded with 50 percent of the value of the goods.[102] Violators of blockade regulations such as those who secretly traded or communicated with the Communists could be summarily executed.[103]

Setting up the blockade involved innumerable problems such as the inaccuracy of reports on blockhouses built and the incompetence of inspectors.[104] Many inspectors were untrained and illiterate.[105] In a proposal to Nanchang headquarters, blockade inspector Deng Chiyi attributed the abysmal quality of the personnel to their low salaries (some were discovered moonlighting as teahouse waiters) and to capable people's refusal to remain in rural areas to serve as inspectors.[106] The government accepted Deng's suggestion that the magistrates summon district heads for a week of training in blockade management; afterward, they would return to their areas and pass this training on to inspectors and *baojia* headmen, creating a ripple effect that would upgrade the quality of blockade personnel. Other problems included widespread corruption and confusion. Corruption was particularly evident among the Monopoly Association members who were actively engaged in profiteering.[107] On the pretext of administrative expenses, they levied an unsanctioned tax on salt, further increasing its price. The Nanjing government tried to curb corruption by ordering the abolition of illegal levies, and to lessen the impact of the salt taxes by lowering salt prices. Confusion over the application of regulations inadvertently impeded the circulation of noncontraband items such as grain in the government-controlled areas.[108] But confusion diminished as the blockade persisted.

Problems notwithstanding, the blockade achieved the main goals of the Guomindang. It had a fatal impact on the Central Soviet Area, undermining the economy and causing widespread suffering among the people. Sickness and death took on epidemic proportions. The blockade compelled the Communists to adopt stringent measures to emphasize frugality and increase production, which adversely affected public morale and alienated the people from the soviet government. Finally, it reduced the base area to an untenable position and forced the Red Army to abandon it and undertake the epic Long March. The failure to crush the fleeing Red Army would have profound implications for the future, but in the meantime the Guomindang savored the sweet taste of victory.

Conclusion

In its effort to control the countryside the Nanjing government organized a gamut of security forces, from the Western-style PSB to the traditional *baojia*. Still, it failed to develop an effective agency for internal security. Security forces, especially the urban-bound PSB and PF, were unable to prevent the Communists from roaming the countryside at will and from influencing the populace. What police power they possessed was used principally to survive the economic depression of the thirties, which they did at the expense of the people. Their extortionate practices alienated the people from the government and increased the general lawlessness of the period.

Only the militia, under the leadership of the local elite, offered a serious challenge to the Communists for control of the villages. If the militia could be brought under official supervision, then presumably its excesses could be curbed and energies directed exclusively to eliminating the Communists. Apparently with this idea in mind, Nationalist leaders sought to enlist the assistance of the rural elite. They wanted to take advantage of the elite's normative and coercive influence in rural society to mobilize the masses on behalf of the government. The rural elite, however, placed a premium on their autonomy and personally profited from their informal control of their local areas. Therefore, they initially rejected efforts to integrate them and their militia units into the government bureaucracy. They were averse to being held accountable to anyone other than themselves.

Under the combined pressure of the GMD from above and the CCP from below, the rural elite eventually threw their lot in with the Nanjing government. When the government renewed its efforts to enlist their support under the *sanbao* policy in 1933, they responded with an alacrity that was absent during the preceding three years. They felt compelled to make common cause with the Guomindang for the sole purpose of self-preservation. Thus the relationship was not organic in nature but rather an uneasy alliance of convenience.

The Nationalists were not the soulmates of the rural elite, as is so often thought. Throughout the entire soviet period, the Guomindang was never able to elicit from them a personal emotional commitment to the Nanjing government. Instead, the rural elite used the government programs as an opportunity to enrich themselves at the expense of the people and to increase their power. Besides profiting from the blockade through various illegal practices, the elite strengthened their control of the militia and therefore of the local areas.

Fortunately for the Guomindang, the rural elite's change in attitude dovetailed with its adoption of the blockade-blockhouse strategy, since the effective application of that strategy was due in large measure to their cooperation. As headmen of the *baojia* organizations, commanders of the *baowei tuan*, and leaders of other local organizations, they were instrumental in implementing all phases of the strategy from building the roads to guarding the blockhouses. Without their assistance, it is doubtful that the strategy would have worked. Thus it was the repressive policies of the Guomindang and the rural elite who helped implement them that were primarily responsible for the fall of the Central Soviet Area.[109]

3

Communist Guerrilla Bases in Southeast China After the Start of the Long March

GREGOR BENTON

When the main body of the Chinese Red Army set out on the Long March in the autumn of 1934 it left behind some thirty thousand troops entrusted with what must have seemed impossible orders: to harass and tie down the enemy, coordinate with the field armies, and restore and if possible develop the soviet area.[1] Three years later remnants of this "death legion" reemerged from the mountains and forests of Southeast China to form the nucleus of the New Fourth Army. Their reappearance astonished Communist leaders in Shaanxi, who had long since given them up for dead or irretrievably dispersed.

The three-year struggle in the South has been left in deep shadow by the legend of the Long March.[2] For the Long Marchers the break with Southeast China was also a break with a whole range of outworn political and military concepts of the early 1930s. In Northwest China they could reinvigorate their movement with new human and material resources. Not so the southern guerrillas, who lacked the advantage of a physical break with Jiangxi and were forced to endure the unmitigated consequences of the soviets' collapse. Their struggle began not as a new strategic venture, but as the last stand of a beaten army.

This essay examines the experience of the southern guerrillas, from

Since I completed research for this article, a small flood of books and articles has appeared in China that carry new information, mainly in the form of memoirs, on the three-year guerrilla struggle in the southern provinces. Since these new publications do not seriously affect my main findings, I let this article stand as written. But my work in progress will fully incorporate these new sources.

I wish to thank Kathleen Hartford and Steven Goldstein for their suggestions on this essay.

their apparent destruction in late 1934 to their regroupment as the New Fourth Army in early 1938. It finds that even after the "abandonment" of the southern bases, Communist forces could and did hold on in them and stayed loyal to the ideal of a Communist revolutionary movement. But their several years were a time of isolation from other survivors, from society at large, and from the central CCP leadership. This experience left them quarrelsome, independent-minded, and disunited—qualities that were to play no small role in the early problems of the New Fourth Army after 1938.

Background to the Three-Year Struggle: Guomindang Repression

By 1934 the failure of earlier encirclement campaigns against the soviet bases had convinced Chiang Kai-shek and his advisers of the need to "use a method of '30 percent military, 70 percent political' while combining government, Party and military resources in a new style of total war."[3]

The Nationalist Army conducted its military occupation of former Communist bases in late 1934 and early 1935 with far greater thoroughness than in earlier such campaigns. The Nationalist leaders knew from experience that even a small nucleus of Communists would soon grow if left to itself. "Although they are a motley crew," wrote one Nationalist official, "a single spark can start a prairie fire, so our armies could not let up for a moment in bandit extermination and pacification work."[4] Several full Nationalist divisions—twenty in all, according to Zhu De—occupied each former Communist base, and detailed pacification plans were carried out.[5]

The pacification forces sealed off areas containing Red units, crisscrossing them with grids of fortified lines and thus splintering them into innumerable small fragments.[6] Between December 1934 and March 1935, 2,454 blockhouses were built in Jiangxi alone.[7] Once strong units had secured key points, smaller ones were dispatched in all directions to search out and destroy the guerrilla forces. On the heels of the military came officials of the Provincial Highway Bureau to plan extensive new road networks.[8] Telephone lines connected villages to central military intelligence. In the reoccupied areas the Nationalists "drained the pool" in which Communist units swam by depopulating areas in which they were known to be active. Local people, reorganized according to the *baojia* system, were removed from mountain villages and concentrated into larger units, sealed off and guarded by troops. Salt, rice, and other essential commodities were strictly rationed and issued only to authorized residents. According to Communist reports, thousands of their sympathizers in the villages were killed or thrown into prison during this period. Reoccupying forces sometimes exacted terrible vengeance on local people in areas beyond outside scrutiny, wiping out whole villages. In evacuated areas houses and villages were systematically razed, and forests and vegetation burned or chopped down. Anyone remaining in these areas might be shot on sight.[9]

In the Nationalist vision, political measures were, in theory, to guarantee the preservation of military gains. In the wider perspective, Jiangxi was to be the workshop for fashioning the model for a new Nationalist China. In the weeks and months following the fall of the soviet, government rehabilitation measures may indeed have had a positive impact on war-weary peasants in some parts of Jiangxi. The economic blockade had created severe shortages, particularly of salt and medicines, in the soviet bases. Nationalist troops rushed salt, food, and implements into the recovered areas.[10] Government-sponsored health bureaus provided, in the words of one not uncritical foreign observer, "perhaps the easiest entrance into the confidence of the farmers."[11] Stricter training and better command of troops led to a reported improvement in military discipline and in the treatment of the peasants.[12] In parts of southeastern Jiangxi in particular Nationalist officers and officials made some effort to avoid unnecessarily alienating local people in the period immediately after the reestablishment of Nationalist rule. Reports of a new commitment to change among Nationalist leaders in Jiangxi appeared in foreign newspapers.

But the policy of sweet reason did not everywhere apply, and in the longer term government policy completely failed to address, and sometimes exacerbated, the root causes of peasant distress. As the Communists retreated, landlords returned to reclaim their rights over the land, while the government looked on with evident equanimity. The New Life movement, through which the government hoped to renew society in Jiangxi and areas like it, revealed itself as a reactionary irrelevance to the fundamental problems of poverty and deeply entrenched corruption. Government-led "rehabilitation" had brought basic change to former Red bases through the thorough militarization of rural life by government officials. Yet the extreme emphasis on military control and the proliferation of various types of security forces claimed resources that might otherwise have been used for social and economic rehabilitation, and laid huge extra burdens on local people. (These are discussed in some detail in William Wei's essay.)

The *baojia* system, the most widespread and successful policing measure of this period, relied almost entirely on landlords and rich peasants as local leaders.[13] These men were responsible not only for political surveillance and the organization and reform of local militia, but also for the recruitment of paid labor for public works and security tasks. Naturally these new responsibilities greatly increased the local power of the rural elite. "The underlying assumption," wrote one contemporary observer, "appears to be that the way to defeat Communism is to strengthen, both politically and economically, those classes of the population that have the most to fear from Communism. It is difficult to see at what point the program gives real help to the poor and landless. . . . Strategically considered, . . . the Government policy is directly opposite to that of the Communists, who sought to strengthen the poor against the rich."[14]

The persistence of old habits and attitudes among the Nationalist authorities and their failure to carry out reform were eventually to lead to the reemergence of many of the same tensions that had fostered revolution in earlier periods, offering new opportunities to the Communists in the former soviet bases. But the imposition of pervasive military and political controls posed difficult new tactical and strategic problems for the Communist rearguard.

Three-Year Struggle of the Southern Guerrillas

Nationalist military records claim that "the task of extirpating Communists in the twelve pacification areas was completed by April 1935."[15] According to one Nationalist historian the three-year struggle "amounted to nothing more than the desperate flight of a handful of defeated Communist remnants," in units at most a few dozen strong but usually smaller, among the rugged mountains.[16] Certainly the Nationalists had won a crushing victory, taking over sixteen thousand prisoners in the first six months after the start of the Long March.[17] Communist remnants were scattered over a wide area and had lost radio and other contact both with each other and with the field armies.[18]

Yet Red forces in the South were eventually able to reassert a small influence over parts of former soviet and some new guerrilla areas after 1934, belying Nationalist claims to have completely eliminated the Communist threat. Numerous small bands that had slipped through Nationalist lines strove with varying degrees of success to evolve new forms of struggle appropriate to the changed local conditions.

Scarcity of data rules out a systematic study of individual areas in which guerrilla units were active, or extensive comparisons between areas. (The most pertinent available comparative information is summarized in table 3.1 and keyed to the locations given on map 3.1.) The general dearth of information is unfortunate, since it would be interesting to know why some groups did markedly better than others in preserving their forces. Nevertheless there is a clear, common pattern in the experience of the various units. A few units were smashed so utterly in the first months after the evacuation of the Soviets that they were never able to recover from the blow. But most went through a broadly similar process of defeat, dispersal, localization, reorganization into smaller units, policy moderation, and eventual regrouping. It is useful and legitimate to consider them as a whole because of their common origins in the decisions of late 1934 and their eventual fusion in the New Fourth Army.

Defeat and Dispersal

The Chinese Communists have long maintained that bad military strategy was chiefly responsible for the fall of the Jiangxi Soviet in 1934. But in truth the crisis that unfolded in the soviet areas during the period of the Fifth Encirclement was as much political, social, and economic as it was military. Grain markets were shrinking. Capital goods were in short supply and the trade deficit with Nationalist areas was growing. These problems were increased, especially in 1934, by the Communists' deliberate and massive "overmobilization" of economic and human resources from a rapidly shrinking territory, and by the inevitable ravages of war.[19]

Even Communist sources hint at serious social unrest and peasant alienation from the soviet government in this period.[20] The collapse of soviet authority after the start of the Long March led in some areas to a state of "anarchic terror" in which people stole public funds, extracted grain at gunpoint, and used violence against Red Army dependents. Sweeping purges sapped party morale and the confidence of its peasant supporters. Several thousand cadres were said to have been removed from office and investigated during the buildup to the Long March, ostensibly to stop desertions and strengthen party organization and

Map 3.1. **Areas in Which Active Communist Presence Was Maintained, 1934–1937.**

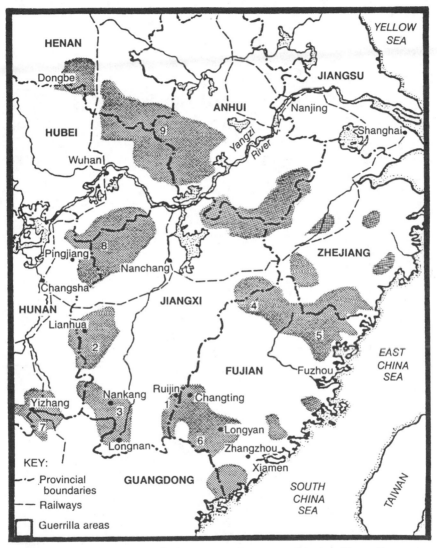

discipline. Executions of purge victims, particularly intellectuals, continued until a month after the start of the Long March.[21]

The Communist leaders planned and prepared the evacuation of the main force units in strict secrecy. Even some leaders learned only at the last minute that they were not to take part in the Long March.[22] Luo Mengwen, party secretary in the strategically placed Yanggan base,

Table 3.1

Summary of Information on Guerrilla Bases in Southeast China, 1934–1937

Area	Location	Number of soldiers	Leading personnel	New Fourth Army unit entered
1 Former Central Soviet Area	Fringes of Ruijin county, and area (esp. Gucheng Mts.)	100–700	None above regimental level in New Fourth Army	Zhang Dingcheng's Second Detachment
2 Hunan-Jiangxi Border Region	Centered on Jinggang Mts., around Lianhua county	3,000 regulars, 2,000 guerrillas; some units	Tan Yubao, Liu Peishan, Duan Huanjing, Zhou Li	Second Regiment, First Detachment
3 Jiangxi-Guangdong Border Area	Centered on Youshan in Dayou range, between Nankang and Longnan	200–300 local guerrillas, 500 assigned troops, 300–400 in rearguard units; total fell to 200–300, reexpanded to 600 by 1937	Xiang Ying, Chen Yi	Second Regiment, First Detachment
4 Min-Zhe-Gan	Northeast Jiangxi and Northwest Fujian	Several thousand, reduced to small handful by early 1938	Su Yu, Liu Ying	Second Detachment
5 North and East Fujian	Forty counties in North and East Fujian	3,000 later reduced to 1,000	Huang Dao, Ye Fei, Huang Ligui	Fifth and Sixth Regiments, Third Detachment

6 Southwest Fujian	Part of southern sector of of eastern flank of Central Soviet Area, plus area around Longyan	1,200–2,000	Zhang Dingcheng, Deng Zihui, Zhong Xunren, Tan Zhenlin, Fang Fang	Second Detachment
7 South Hunan	In and around Yizhang county	600+, later nearly wiped out	Gong Chu	New Fourth Army Headquarters Special Battalion
8 Hunan-Hubei-Jiangxi	Area around Pingjiang county, and to its east and north	2,000–4,000	Xu Yangang, Cheng Qiutao, Tu Zhenkun	First Regiment, First Detachment
9 E-Yu-Wan	Hubei-Henan-Anhui border area: Dongbe region, south Henan, Hubei-Anhui border	Variously estimated at between 1,000 and 5,000	Gao Junting	Seventh and Eighth Regiments, Fourth Detachment

Sources: For the former Central Soviet Area, see Renmin Chubanshe, ed., *Hongse fengbao*, vol. 3 (Nanchang: same, 1958), pp. 69–81; *Hongqi piaopiao*, vol. 11 (Beijing: Zhongguo Qingnian Chubanshe, 1957–58), p. 142; Ye Cao, *Sannian youji zhanzheng* (Hong Kong: Zhengbao Chubanshe, 1948?), p. 84; Warren Kuo, *Analytical History of the Chinese Communist Party*, vol. 3 (Taipei: Center for International Relations, 1966–1978), p. 353. For the Hunan-Jiangxi Border Region, see *Zhongguo gongchandang zai Jiangxi diqu lingdao geming douzheng di lishe ziliao* (Nanchang: Jiangxi Renmin Chubanshe, 1958), pp. 190, 195; Wuhan Night School, *Zhongguo gongchandang lingdao Hunan renmin yingyong fendou di sanshinian* (Changsha, 1951), p. 54. For the Jiangxi-Guangdong border area, see *Xinghuo liaoyuan*, vol. 4 (Beijing: Renmin Wenxue Chubanshe, 1961), pp. 169–70, 187; vol. 6, p. 376; *Zhonggong yanjiu* 4, 3 (March 1970), pp. 86–87; *Lishi yanjiu*, no. 6 (1977), pp. 36, 42. An account of the evacuation of the Min-Zhe-Gan base in July 1934 and the return to it by a few hundred survivors in early 1935 is in Miao Min (pseud.), *Fang Chih-min* (Fang Zhimin), *Revolutionary Fighter* (Beijing: Foreign Languages Press, 1962). For information on North and East Fujian, see Guofangbu, Shizhengju, *Jiaofei zhanshi*, vol. 3 (Taibei: same, 1967), p. 438; Hatano Ken'ichi, *Chūgoku kyōsantō shi*, vol. 5 (Tokyo: Jiji Tsushin Sha, 1961), pp. 43–44; *Hongqi piaopiao* 11:115–15; Kuo, *Analytical History* 3:56; *Xinghuo liaoyuan* 6:376; *Zhongguo gongchandang zai Jiangxi*, p. 276. On Southwest Fujian, see *Xinghuo liaoyuan* 4:200, 214–16; Ye Cao, *Sannian youji*, pp. 2–25, 54–55; Mao Tse-tung, *Selected Works*, vol. 2 (Beijing: Foreign Languages Press, 1965), pp. 73–74. For South Hunan, see *Lishi yanjiu*, 6 (1977), p. 37; *Xinghuo liaoyuan* 6:376. For the Hunan-Hubei-Jiangxi area, see *Jiaofei zhanshi* 3:438; *China Weekly Review*, 20 April 1935, p. 252; Hatano, *Chūgoku kyōsantō shi* 5:43–44; Hunan Shengzhi Bianzuan Weiyuanhui, *Hunan shengzhi*, vol. 1 (Changsha: Hunan Renmin Chubanshe, 1959), pp. 561–62, 694; *Xinghuo liaoyuan* 6:376; Kuo, *Analytical History* 3:357. On E-Yu-Wan, see *Xinghuo liaoyuan* 4:345, 354; Hatano, *Chūgoku kyōsantō shi* 4:424, 5:6–7; Kuo, *Analytical History* 3:357; Qiu Guochen, *Dabieshan banian kangzhan zhi huiyi* (Hong Kong: n.p., 1970), p. 12; Israel Epstein, *The People's War* (London: Victor Gollancz, 1939), p. 261n.

which formed the northwestern doorway to the Central Soviet, only learned of his precise military tasks more than a month after the start of the Long March. Chen Yi had no one capable of deciphering the code in which the Central Committee sent its final message to him in early 1935.[23] Even a major statement published some days after the start of the Long March carried no hint of an evacuation.[24] When heavy troop movements began, people still saw them as no more than "a plan to destroy the enemy's rear and release the blockade," and Jiangxi soldiers took money to buy salt and other provisions for their families from areas outside the Soviet.[25] The CCP leaders probably kept the breakout plans a secret for fear of organized peasant resistance to their campaigns to "borrow" huge amounts of grain.[26] Not surprisingly, many local people grew apathetic or even hostile toward the Communists when they finally realized that the soviet had been abandoned.

What of the morale and unity of the thirty thousand men and women of the rearguard?[27] Any picture of Red Jiangxi in this period that showed only apathy and despair would be one-sided. Communist idealism was not dead among the Red forces, and many peasants continued to identify with them. Although their network of support in the villages was heavily damaged, it was not completely destroyed. But the prospect was somber, and the prevailing mood must have been deeply pessimistic. Certainly, many saw their assignment to the rearguard as a sign of political disfavor or disgrace. This was a party that after years of victories had just suffered a massive strategic defeat and that was inwardly divided between bitterly opposed factions. Many of its lower cadres were demoralized by the evacuation and upset and alienated by the treatment they received during the preparations for it.[28] Some leaders had earlier been fiercely criticized for political errors, and as a result either harbored bitter grievances against the party or had lost much of their revolutionary enthusiasm.[29]

They would have found little to sustain it. The rearguard was made up for the most part of local and guerrilla forces hastily reorganized around a core of some six thousand regulars. Red Army leaders, wrote Edgar Snow, "did not wish to sacrifice in the rearguard any more first-line troops than the minimum necessary. Already surrounded on all sides, those who stayed faced total extermination."[30] At a later stage the largely local character of the rearguard was to prove an advantage, but at first lack of battle experience and poor discipline led to heavy losses. The rearguard forces were much more poorly armed and equipped than the Red field armies.[31] They had on average one rifle to three men. Bayonets, swords, and spears formed the bulk of their armory. Resources in soviet areas were insufficient to replenish losses. "There was no longer any manpower to mobilize," commented Gong Chu, "and only enough provisions to maintain 37,000 troops for two months." Soviet currency was no longer freely accepted, and the local market had collapsed.[32]

Sick and wounded made up a large part or even a majority of the rearguard forces at all levels. As many as twenty thousand wounded were said to have been left behind in mountain hospitals, with instructions to report for duty as soon as they recovered.[33] This placed huge additional strains on the rearguard's already greatly stretched resources. A population and economy worn out by months and years of all-out military mobilization; a party weakened by divisions and political terror; an ill-equipped, ill-prepared, and partly demoralized military cadre, overburdened with sick and wounded—these and other disadvantages weighed heavily against the rearguard leaders.

In the days and weeks after the start of the Long March the Central Soviet Area, where most rearguard units were assembled, was a scene of turmoil and confusion. Armies marched this way and that in largely futile attempts to escape the tightening Nationalist encirclement. Small groups of Communists roamed the countryside, especially around Ruijin, trying to renew links with the now underground party or with units of the rearguard.

In other parts of Southeast China where Communists were active the momentous events of October 1934 had less immediate impact. In southwestern Fujian, for example, where Nationalist military pressure was weaker than to the west, measures had already been taken to prepare guerrilla war. As early as April 1934 units were sent out in various directions to pierce the enemy rear as part of the complicated series of military movements preparing for a breakout by the Fang Zhimin expedition.[34] Only after the collapse of the Central Soviet and the defeat of its defenders did the Nationalists seriously turn their attention to southwestern Fujian. There, in February 1935, local guerrillas began a series of forced marches similar to those made by rearguard units evacuating southern Jiangxi.[35] But the consequences were not so serious as in southern Jiangxi. Not only were the Fujian forces better prepared for the sort of operations necessary under the new conditions, but the switch from relatively stable rule to chaos was not so abrupt in the Red-controlled areas of Fujian.

The immediate effect of the GMD's repressive measures against the population, backed up by strong troop concentrations, was to devastate Communist military organization. Detachments originally several hundred strong were reduced by casualties, hunger, and desertions to mere handfuls clinging to life in caves and on mountain tops. Weighed down by wounded and noncombatants, most rearguard groups began a long period of repeated migrations through remote mountains and forests, marching only at night and spending their days sitting back to back under giant umbrellas during the frequent rainstorms.[36] Constantly on the move, they were unable to restore links with the local people. They had no grain and instead ate leaves and wild plants. If they were lucky their diet was supplemented by wild pigs, frogs, grubs, fowl, and monkeys caught in the mountains. Illness wore down their strength. They had next to no weapons or ammunition. In one area guerrillas fought exclusively with spears (which, being noiseless, were apparently ideally suited to the new conditions) and claimed to have killed over fifty enemy at no cost to themselves.[37] These tiny groups were isolated not only from rearguard units in other areas, but even from other bands operating in their own areas. Lacking radio contact, some tried (always unsuccessfully) to restore links by sending out small search parties.

Morale among both civilians and guerrillas was at its lowest ebb in the first few months of the rearguard action. Communist accounts give many examples of continuing peasant support for the Red Army, but there is also evidence of anti-Red feeling among some peasants.[38] Even in southwestern Fujian, where Communist morale was still high,[39] peasants no longer opened their doors to the Red Army and women climbed the mountains to call their guerrilla sons and husbands home. According to Gong Chu, local people in southern Hunan viewed the Communists with hostility and loathing.[40]

Defections greatly eroded Communist ranks at all levels, reflecting a deep dissatisfaction with Communist policies as well as worsening military conditions. Gong Chu defected because of his opposition to the regime of terror that continued in the party even after the start of the Long March.[41] Other defections, for example that of Chen Hongshi on the Hunan-Jiangxi border, were triggered by criticism or by quarrels about strategy.[42]

Defeat and dispersal did not automatically lead to a rethinking of military and political positions, and the transition to a new strategy was accomplished sooner in some areas than in others. Events between October 1934 and March 1935, by which time the dwindling rearguard forces had retreated from more accessible areas, are passed over summarily by most Communist authors. The Chinese Communists portray this period as a continuation of the old "leftist" phase of the late Soviet period. They accuse rearguard leaders of pursuing a mistaken policy of "defending the soviet areas, awaiting the return of the main force," of concentrating local units into regular divisions to fight pitched battles, and of neglecting mass work and lacking political flexibility. [43]

The detailed Nationalist records of military campaigns during these six months provide ample evidence to bear out at least some of these criticisms. They describe frequent and mostly suicidal pitched battles fought by Red troops well into the spring of 1935. The military dogma of the late Jiangxi period, when Mao's views on the importance of guerrilla war were shared by only a minority in the leadership, may have helped to delay the switch to guerrilla tactics after October 1934. But it is hard to believe that this was the main factor in the delay. [44] More likely, the rearguard leaders thought it necessary to concentrate their forces along lines of defense abandoned by the Red field armies in order to conceal the full extent of the Communist evacuation. Within weeks if not days their former bases were saturated with enemy forces, so that the initiative passed completely out of their hands. By then they may have had no choice but to concentrate their forces at weaker points along the enemy line if they were to break through the encirclement and reach the remote mountains.

Some Communist leaders continued to fight pitched battles throughout the early period of the three-year struggle, neglecting to develop guerrilla war, of which they in any case lacked experience, and underestimating the overwhelming superiority of the enemy. Military mistakes led to even heavier casualties and defeats. Bitter disputes raged between supporters of "regularization" and supporters of guerrilla war. Some units, demoralized by defeat, adopted a "passive, wait-and-see attitude," hiding during the day and moving off elsewhere at night, in headlong and aimless flight. Others were said to have adopted a "pure guerrillaist" approach, neglecting to work among peasants or build bases. [45]

Reorganization and Localization

In and around the spring of 1935 heavily battered remnants of various rearguard units broke out through the enemy encirclement to take up new positions in less accessible areas along provincial borders. Some, like units under Su Yu and Liu Ying in northeastern Jiangxi and Huang

Dao in northern Fujian, broke through into the enemy rear to open up new areas of guerrilla activity. Others, like the units that had originally been operating in the four Communist military districts of Jiangxi, fought their way into mountain fastnesses where guerrilla forces of varying strengths were already active. By the early summer of 1935 the Nationalists, estimating that the Communist rearguard had been utterly smashed, began partial withdrawal from the pacification zone. This gave surviving rearguard leaders the chance to rest, reorganize their forces, and reassess their situation.

During this period, rearguard units held important conferences which, later Communist accounts say, corrected earlier "leftist" errors and outlined new strategic tasks.[46] The most important strategic decision made at these conferences was to switch to guerrilla war and mass work in rearguard areas.[47] The conferences resolved to improve guerrilla security and to keep the local population thoroughly informed of the changing political situation. The Communist leaders recognized that a realistic explanation of the extraordinary events of the previous few months was long overdue, if there was to be any prospect for restoring the party's links with local people. They decided that politics would henceforth play the decisive role in military planning, and that the guerrillas' immediate aim would be to preserve their forces, consolidate their organization, and build bases, rather than to press the enemy. In line with this new mood of realism at least one conference proclaimed the winding up of the Provincial Soviet (by then a dead letter in any case), and its replacement by a looser body. In some districts rearguard leaders established separate battle areas following a line of "independence and initiative," set up separate county committees to ensure that policies reached all levels and to prevent losses due to overcentralization of cadre, and restored communications systems on the basis of the old Worker and Peasant Correspondents networks of the soviet period. In a word, the accent was on extreme administrative and military decentralization. Finally, various steps were taken to reform and strengthen the old leadership and to organize short periods of study and training for cadres at all levels.

Although it was no longer capable of sustained military resistance, the rearguard enjoyed one major asset. In the words of one Guomindang official, its "various independent regiments, battalions, and guerrilla units are all made up of local elements who are well acquainted with local topography, and who can disappear among the people only to concentrate again as a bandit force." After reorganization Communist leaders put even greater stress on "localization" in its various forms. "Outsiders" were urged to study local customs, learn from local cadres, and integrate themselves as fully as possible into the local mountain communities.

In the Jiangxi-Guangdong border region, Chen Yi raised the issue of localization in early 1935. He distinguished between two groups. The first were the indigenous guerrillas, who had flesh-and-blood ties with local people, knew local areas intimately, and had many years' experience of guerrilla war, though they had little chance for study and tended to put immediate interests first. The second group were members of the Red Army from the Central Soviet Area, who knew little of guerrilla war and were not acquainted with the local people, language, or topography, although they had experience of large-scale mass movements and were politically knowledgeable. His conclusion was that although the two groups should learn from each other's strengths and weaknesses, "special emphasis must be placed on outsider cadres learning from local cadres, and outsider troops learning from local guerrillas." It is notable that most of those leaders accused of failing to adopt appropriate forms of guerrilla struggle during this period came originally from the Central Soviet Area, and that some were former Nationalist officers.[48]

In their effort to sink local roots, guerrilla leaders reorganized their remaining forces into tiny working parties and sent them into the villages after nightfall to set up peasant, youth, and women's associations. Underground soviet governments were even said to have been restored in some areas. One result of this localization policy was that the Nationalists, assuming that most guerrillas had been wiped out, further relaxed their military pressure on these areas. As Guomindang controls weakened, confidence in the CCP revived somewhat, and people previously relocated to lowland villages began to drift back to the mountains in small numbers. The by now extensively decentralized guerrilla units attacked the enemy only outside areas in which they were politically active, to prevent reprisals against the local population. They also maintained "gray areas" in which they ceased political activities completely in order to avoid attracting the attention of the Nationalists. They used such areas for collecting intelligence, training, sheltering the wounded and buying provisions. But even at their most successful the guerrillas were largely operating in areas with only the thinnest population. What they grandiosely called "mass work" often consisted of nothing more than Robin Hood-type raids on gentry families. In effect they were cut off from the mass links they considered so important.[49]

In some areas localization led to the forging of links with local bandit groups. At first rearguard units were ordered to destroy troublesome bandit formations,[50] but the collapse of their military positions led to drastic changes in this policy. Guerrilla leaders tried to win over bandit organizations by exploiting their grievances against local Nationalist authorities, and they won some notable successes. In northern Fujian, for example, Lin Ximing, local leader of some ten thousand Big Swords and a man with imperial ambitions, changed his standard from "save the people by following Heaven" to "save the country by resisting Japan" and fought alongside the Communists with his three hundred armed men. Some bandit leaders had links with officials right up to county level, and these links were also exploited by the Communists.[51]

But the Communist leaders insisted that it was necessary to maintain a clear distinction between themselves and the bandits in the eyes of local people. They tried to influence the bandits to treat ordinary villagers better, and on occasion Communist guerrillas won much local sympathy by destroying more troublesome bandits. They also stressed the need for constant vigilance toward bandit leaders, especially those with political connections in the local establishment. But such advice was not always heeded, with the result that at least one local Communist leader was betrayed by his bandit "ally" to the Nationalists.[52]

Communist cadres in some areas abandoned military roles entirely, taking on jobs as day laborers, carpenters, and even miners and dock workers, agitating around economic issues when the chance arose. In one area they chopped trees and sold firewood by day and made propaganda by night, secretly setting up a "Carrying Pole Society" and organizing a violent struggle against the firewood tax, which spread swiftly through the mountains. In other areas groups of party workers ran shops, which also served as liaison centers for local intelligence networks, or set up timberworks, paper factories, or other small industries in the mountains. A major problem of guerrilla support work was to maintain regular food supplies to economically blockaded areas that contained little or no cultivated land. Here mountain industries were of great value, not only as sources of finance but also as a pretext for buying food in large amounts and thus beating the blockade.

An extreme example of localization of this sort was the former Yanggan base in southern Jiangxi, where military activities ceased completely after 1935. Here Communists at first lived as woodcutters in small groups in the mountains, cut off from similar groups in neighboring mountains by distance and lack of finances. They adapted so well to local conditions that at one point there was nothing outwardly to distinguish them from ordinary mountain people. Later they switched to the more profitable trade of charcoal burning and were able to move their huts closer together. They also sent cadres to work in the villages, where they waged minor "legal" struggles. Their woodsmen's huts began to serve as tiny bases in which cadres received political education, pooled living resources, and organized mass work.[53]

Weakened and completely isolated by Nationalist military and political measures, Communist units thus drastically reduced the scope of their military activities throughout the southern guerrilla areas during this period and switched to a policy of localization. Rearguard units that survived the three-year struggle with fewest net losses were those in areas like E-Yu-Wan and parts of Fujian, where there was a strong tradition of semiautonomous local organization. In southwestern Fujian in particular a majority of the local leadership were Communists who had earlier been criticized as supporters of the "Luo Ming line," the Fujian-based party heresy that stressed the importance of responding sensitively to local moods and issues. Psychologically, politically, and militarily, such people were undoubtedly better prepared for the conditions that the isolated rearguard units faced than were military cadres evacuated from areas of stable soviet rule, who supplied most of the important defectors during the three-year struggle.

Localization was therefore an effective response to the problems that confronted the southern guerrillas. But it carried with it a danger as well: that the Communists might become so submerged in local life as to lose their distinct political identity.

Policy Moderation at the Local Level

During the early stages of the rearguard action, rearguard leaders' failure to adjust military tactics to the new mood and conditions was often matched by their dogmatic pursuit of wildly inappropriate political goals. At a time when all the towns and main Red areas had already fallen to the Nationalists, the soviets' leaders stubbornly refused to recognize the collapse of soviet power, continuing the pretense of soviet government up to and even beyond the spring and early summer of 1935. They issued grandiosely worded proclamations in the name of a nonexistent soviet government and forced their worthless banknotes, described as "valid world currency," on the shrinking core of peasants under their control.[54] *Baojia* heads were killed in large numbers in some areas, with the inevitable result that the Nationalist authorities stepped up their drive to exterminate the Communists and depopulate the mountain areas in which they were active.[55] Communist leaders still neglected to organize local people for "legal" struggle.[56]

Later Communist accounts depict a remarkably uniform transition to moderate policies in rearguard areas in the period after reorganization. Some of this claimed uniformity may be the post facto invention of local leaders intent on proving how orthodox they were during the period of the three-year struggle. But it is clear that political retreat was ultimately as indispensable as military retreat if rearguard remnants were to survive the new conditions. The trend toward moderation can be seen in the guerrillas' policies on finance and the land question, and in their treatment of the *baojia* system.

During the three-year struggle, and especially in the early period of guerrilla activities, the guerrillas obtained most of their finances by intimidating, beating, kidnapping, or selectively assassinating *tuhao* (local bullies). Many *tuhao* fled to Guangzhou from parts of southern Jiangxi to escape Communist assassination campaigns. But the guerrillas took pains to single out only the most prominent reactionaries for attack, and they later stopped the killings altogether as moves toward a united front got underway.[57]

Despite occasional lapses, Communist land policy tended to change from redistribution to more moderate campaigns for rent and interest reduction,[58] although steps were taken where possible to prevent landlords from returning to reclaim their rights over land that had already been divided. Different policies were pursued in different areas. In the Jiangxi-Guangdong border region, for example, a distinction was made between the intermediate or "red-white" areas of disputed control and the wholly "white" areas controlled by the Nationalists. In "red-white" areas guerrillas encouraged peasants to resist paying rent, providing grain, repaying debts, paying taxes, and conscription (the so-called Five Resists). When landlords attempted to collect rent or grain, guerrillas sometimes ambushed them and returned their takings to the peasants.[59] Tactics in "white" areas included distributing propaganda material, killing or kidnapping *tuhao*, and infiltrating the *baojia* system.

The newly established *baojia* system was a major target of Communist subversion in areas recovered by the Nationalists. After reorganization the Communist leaders developed what was described as a double-edged policy: struggling to isolate the reactionaries by winning over or transforming into "double-dealers" those *baojia* officials who occupied a "middle" position. As long as the Communists were not strong enough to restore the soviet, their slogan was to be "turn the enemy *baojia* into a Red joint defense organization."[60] *Baojia* heads under Communist control were expected to protect Red Army dependents and local people, give guerrillas information, warn them of approaching search parties, keep their visits to the villages secret until after they had returned to the mountains, and get them ammunition and provisions.[61]

In some villages and districts party members became *baojia* officials as part of their counterintelligence and espionage work.[62] Some *baojia* heads had earlier worked for the soviet government and were easier to influence. Others were made to cooperate either by kidnapping and threatening to kill them or by selectively assassinating the most reactionary among them.

This "red heart, white skin" tactic was a big success in many areas. "Double agents of an intermediate color" became valuable sources of intelligence for the Communists. In some mountain districts the entire *baojia* system was basically under Communist control, and in some villages Communists could parade openly with their rifles.[64] One official complaint, about *baojia* heads who had publicly "guaranteed" a local Communist leader, confirms this picture of widespread Communist subversion.

> One can say that [these *baojia* heads] have lost their powers of judgment. . . . Since they dare to stand guarantee for a notorious bandit, it is obvious that they must normally harbor, connive at, nurture, and aid bandits. . . . I think it is bad that troops engaged in bandit extermination rarely report bandits, and even more so that when they do catch them, many people come forward to guarantee these bandits. I am not complaining about the popular masses guaranteeing bandits, but I find it odious that *baojia* heads, who are the leaders of the popular masses, should do so. . . . It is not surprising that bandits abound in Pingjiang.[64]

Responses to New Openings

During 1936 and 1937 the Communist leaders in Northwest China gradually moderated their policy toward the Nanjing government and advanced a new program of national unity against Japan. In December

1936 Chiang Kai-shek was arrested by Communist-influenced officers in his northern armies. This and his subsequent release sped rapprochement between his party and the CCP, and the formation of a united front between them. For the southern guerrillas, the years of hiding in dense mountain forests were about to end. By early 1938 their scattered units would be reunited in the New Fourth Army.

The southern guerrilla leaders' direct links to the central leadership remained broken until mid- or late 1937, but most southern guerrillas continued to identify unshakably with the leadership in the North and tried constantly to restore links both with each other and with the party liaison offices in Shanghai and elsewhere.[65] Guerrillas in all areas searched local newspapers for news of the party and even fought battles to obtain them. They did their best to reconstruct the changing outlines of party policy from such sources, and they tried to implement this policy where conditions allowed: here they would ease their pressure on local landlords or *tuhao*; there they would try to take advantage of anti-Japanese feeling in the local Nationalist garrison or in the county government. Holed up in their remote hideouts, they stayed astonishingly loyal to the party.[66] In late 1937 and early 1938 they assembled at New Fourth Army staging areas in the lower Yangzi valley within only four months of being summoned, despite extremely bad communications, continuing Nationalist harassment, fear of reprisals against their dependents, and years of isolation in the remote mountains.

Although news of the resolution of the Xi'an Incident (especially the release of Chiang) and the adoption of more moderate land policies at first greatly angered the guerrillas, most guerrilla leaders loyally adjusted to the new line. The major exceptions were the weaker and more isolated guerrilla units in Hunan and Jiangxi, which made no noticeable movement toward united front policies in this period and stayed deep in the mountains until late 1937, living in dilapidated mountain huts and studying military, political, and cultural affairs. Although they heard vague reports of the new turn toward cooperation with the Guomindang, they saw these as nothing more than a ploy to lure them into the open, and they swore that they would "sooner die of starvation in the mountains than cooperate with that pack of dogs." When Chen Yi finally sought out one group with news of the united front, its sentries at first wanted to shoot him as a renegade, but fortunately they stayed his execution long enough to check out his story elsewhere and discover that it was true.[67]

In the bigger bases in Fujian and on the Jiangxi-Guangdong border, local leaders developed more nuanced and considered responses to the developments of 1936 and 1937, though they met with only limited success. Even before mid–1936 Communist leaders in southwestern Fujian adopted a whole range of united front-type policies after receiving some Central Committee documents via a liaison center in Shanghai. They pledged to cooperate with parties that resisted Japan, to attack only in self-defense, and to switch to more moderate forms of class struggle. These changes coincided with a clear trend toward reunification among the previously dispersed southwestern Fujian guerrilla units, a revival of some mass links, and a general strengthening of the party. Communist sources claim that by this time there was almost no rent or debt collection in guerrilla areas, that peasants previously evacuated to the lowlands were now returning to their villages, and that guerrillas could move freely and openly throughout most mountain areas.[68]

The trend toward moderation in this area was interrupted in June 1936, when long-simmering rivalries between Nanjing and the military elite in Guangdong and Guangxi came to a head in the Liang-Guang revolt. During the ensuing military clashes between Chiang's and the rebel generals' forces, military pressure on the guerrillas in southern Fujian and northern Guangdong was temporarily lifted. Guerrilla recruitment shot up during the crisis and the Communists expanded their political activities to the plains and the nearby towns, and even laid plans to agitate in cities like Zhangzhou and Xiamen (Amoy) for resistance to Japan. But in taking advantage of these openings, Communists in southwestern Fujian made a number of mistakes later criticized as "leftist." They forced *mintuan* units that were already secretly under their control to destroy their pillboxes and defect to them. They carried out land revolution in some mountain areas, and they even killed some *baojia* heads, landlords, and gentry.

By doing so, they not only violated their own earlier pledges but also left some of their supporters dangerously exposed. Nanjing rapidly resolved the Liang-Guang crisis to its own advantage. In October 1936 Central Army forces were sent to garrison southern Fujian; prominent among them were troops from three crack Guangdong divisions, who fought hard and flexibly in small dispersed units and were specialists in counterinsurgency methods. By late 1936 the Communists were in crisis and had lost many of their leaders. The guerrillas were forced to abandon their newly acquired positions and rethink their plans. During this period news of the arrival of the Red Army in Shaanxi belatedly reached southern guerrilla units, boosting their morale enormously. But their conditions remained harsh, and hunger, isolation, night marches, mountain bivouacks, and constant fear of enemy pursuit remained the rule rather than the exception.[69]

The guerrillas had no choice but to switch their emphasis once again to the political struggle. The Guangdong units in Fujian lacked local ties, could not speak local dialects, and aroused local hostility by burning down bamboo groves and crops in their efforts to hunt down the guerrillas. The Communists strove to exploit the resulting tensions by organizing protests against the damage to the local economy. Many Guangdong officers and troops opposed Nanjing's policy toward Japan, having been exposed to anti-Japanese propaganda during the Liang-Guang incident. So the Communists addressed open letters both to them and to local merchants and gentry, calling for a united resistance. They abandoned the name "soviet" and once again renounced more violent forms of class struggle. Soon they began to make small inroads into the Guangdong Army and the local Fujian elite, and some Guangdong troops even resisted orders to attack the guerrillas. Local gentry and owners of tobacco and paper factories made contact with the Communists and backed their unity proposals.[70]

In late 1936 and early 1937 guerrillas in southern Fujian and on the Jiangxi-Guangdong border learned from the Hong Kong press of Chiang Kai-shek's arrest at Xi'an. Overjoyed that Chiang was "going to have his head chopped off," they could not believe their ears when they heard of his release and his safe return to Nanjing. For a while their morale sank. Shortly afterward they learned from party documents received via Shanghai and from newspapers that the party slogan had changed from "oppose Chiang" to "unite with Chiang to resist Japan." It is hard to imagine that this new policy did not encounter at least some opposition among the guerrilla leaders, but if there were such, it is passed over in silence in the official record of these events. This mentions only that emergency conferences were held that expressed unanimous support for the new line of the party center and issued unity manifestos calling for an end to the civil war, unity against Japan, and the right of the southern guerrilla force to proceed to the resistance front.[71]

Large-scale military operations were said to have resumed against Communist guerrillas throughout the southern provinces after the Xi'an crisis and Chiang's release. Communist sources claim that over 250,000 troops in more than thirty divisions were mobilized in April

1937 in a campaign to bring about the "final annihilation of all traces of the Red Army in South-east China." This offensive, which the Communists in the North tried to ward off through negotiations, resulted in losses that were said to have amounted to up to half of the southern Communist troops. It is likely that Nanjing's aim was to destroy the Red nuclei in the South before they could restore firm links with the party center.[72]

In the Jiangxi-Guangdong border area, Communist efforts to develop the anti-Japanese movement at first had little impact, although their unity manifesto was said to have been favorably received by some Guangdong troops and by country magistrates in Dayu, Nankang, and Xinfeng, who issued a call for peace talks.[73] Of the areas for which information is available, it was in southern Fujian that the Communists most effectively took up the issues of resistance and national unity, developing policies closely in line with those of the central leaders and partly breaking out of their isolation. Their situation was in some ways more favorable than that of other southern guerrillas. Nanjing had never placed as much strategic or symbolic value on Fujian as on neighboring Jiangxi, and put relatively less effort into "pacifying" it.

The Fujian Communists' success in developing an effective anti-Japanese line may have been due in part to their at least intermittent contact with the Shanghai party office in this period, and to Japanese military and political pressure on the area and fears of Japanese landings in Xiamen and Shantou (Swatow). Local scholars, well-known local people, and fellow townspeople's associations in Zhangzhou and Xiamen lent support to Communist proclamations, wrote to Guangdong officers backing the call for local peace talks, and even gave the Communists money. Guerrilla leaders concluded nonaggression pacts with local officials and set up joint peace bodies with them. Even a vice-head of the Fujian legislature "began to have second thoughts about his ten-year-old Communist extermination policy, and agreed to contrive peace."[74]

Negotiations between Communist guerrilla leaders and the provincial authorities in Jiangxi and Fujian began soon after the fall of Shanghai but got off to a bad start because of mutual suspicions and hostility, and a number of difficulties and incidents arose during the talks. Intensive education through study sessions and mass meetings was necessary to overcome resistance to the new policies among the guerrilla ranks. Even after successful peace talks many guerrillas objected violently to wearing the Nationalist uniform. Their leaders insisted "that whatever the circumstances, alertness toward class enemies should never be relaxed." In August Chen Yi voiced the same sentiment in a simple poem:

> *After the ten years' war*
> *Guomindang and Communists collaborate again.*
> *On recalling past fallen comrades*
> *Tears of grief stain my sleeve.*
> *Our central task is to resist Japan,*
> *But our salvation needs democracy.*
> *We must insure ourselves by swearing that*
> *We won't behave like Chen Duxiu.*[75]

Although some Communist leaders, notably Xiang Ying, are accused (perhaps unjustly, and for factional reasons) of conducting negotiations in a weak and excessively compromising way, the sources show most adopting a tough approach. In the southern Fujian case some were even prepared to "go back into the mountains and fight" unless their demands for full independence were met.

The Nationalists did their best to portray the Communist presence at negotiations as a surrender, and they continued to wage selective "suppression campaigns" against the guerrillas even while they were transferring from their mountain bases to central assembly points. In one incident Nationalist troops disarmed over a thousand guerrillas under He Ming, who had imprudently and against party advice assembled his troops at Tanpu. The Tanpu incident hardened attitudes both in Fujian, where Communists launched a strident campaign of protest, and in Yan'an, where Mao used it as an example of the dangers of "excessive accommodation" to the Guomindang. To guard against repetition of the Tanpu incident, and perhaps also to keep their real strength secret until it had reached the levels they had claimed during negotiations,[76] guerrilla leaders insisted on assembling their troops at points deep in the heart of the mountains. They emerged only gradually and with extreme caution onto the plain, avoiding towns and cities, moving mainly at night, and making no attempt to win new recruits. Even so they were repeatedly ambushed during their march north to the central New Fourth Army staging area and as a result had to make lengthy detours along byways and mountain paths.[77]

Guerrilla leaders in South and Southeast China were largely isolated from the outside world and lacked an overview of national (let alone international) political processes. They were therefore not in a position to formulate new political strategies relevant to the national political situation, although they were quite capable of developing new local initiatives. But once in possession of the analyses and facts set out in the party center's documents, they responded sensitively and flexibly to the new political openings of 1936 and 1937, even though they lacked the resources to exploit them to the same good effect as the party in Northwest China. Anti-Japanese feeling was as passionate and deep-rooted among them as among Communists in the Northwest. The events of this period gave them the chance to articulate that emotion politically, to widen their audience, and to retrieve some of the ground they had lost through military weakness in the preceding years.

Some Achievements

The extraordinary feat of the southern guerrillas emerges most clearly from a comparison with the Long Marchers during the same period. The latter ended up in a part of China where local Communists had already established a firm base, where peasants were highly receptive to revolutionary propaganda, and where the Nationalist garrisons, infected by anti-Japanese sentiment, were weak, ineffective, and susceptible to Communist influence. The southerners, in contrast, were tied to an area socially and economically devastated by war and faced a mainly unified enemy. All the provinces in which they were active (including Guangdong after mid–1936) were firmly within the Nanjing camp.[78]

At the start, the southern guerrillas' morale and internal organization were also vastly worse than those of the Long Marchers. The emergence of a unified collective leadership at Zunyi strengthened the resolve of the Long Marchers. Factional problems persisted, but the Long March was an essentially unifying experience and generated a mood of optimism and confidence in the marchers. "The Communists realised," wrote Edgar Snow, "and apparently believed, that they were advancing toward an anti-Japanese front, and this was a psychological factor of great importance. It helped them turn what might have been a demoralized retreat into a spirited march of victory."[79] The Long March was a branching out into new political as well as geographical terrain. It made the anti-Japanese line real. It set the scene for the CCP's later reemergence as a main force in national political life.

The rearguard's situation could hardly have been more different. It was physically scattered into numerous unconnected fragments and cut off from the outside world for two years or more.[80] Its leaders knew little of national political developments and often were even unaware of major political crises as they unfolded.

Despite these big disadvantages, the southerners' feat measures up well against that of the Long Marchers. In 1938 Xiang Ying listed the four main achievements of his forces as the preservation of many foci of guerrilla war in the south; the preservation of armed forces with ten years' experience; the tenacious upholding of CCP proposals for resistance to Japan; and coordination with the main body of Long Marchers to propel the Chinese revolution forward.[81] On 13 December 1937 the CCP Politburo expressed similar views in a resolution praising Xiang and other southern leaders.[82]

By and large, the evidence supports Xiang's claim that the southern guerrillas preserved foci of resistance and an experienced military cadre. Guerrillas sometimes exercised intermittent control over mountain districts said to have spread for several hundred *li*. Their control never extended to possession of a fixed, stable territorial base except in some small and remote areas. Still, a much reduced but very experienced guerrilla nucleus survived, becoming increasingly skilled in the flexible adaptation of guerrilla tactics to local conditions. These guerrillas posed enough of a threat to persuade Nanjing to maintain large garrisons in some of the areas in which they operated and to mount yet another major ''Communist extermination'' drive in the South in the wake of the December 1936 Xi'an crisis. Thus southern guerrillas did go at least some way toward fulfilling one of their chief tasks: to relieve pressure on the main body of the Red Army by pinning down Nationalist forces in the south.[83]

They also furnished the bulk of the New Fourth Army. The ten to fifteen thousand soldiers at whose head Xiang and Chen Yi emerged in early 1938 represented in net terms between one-third and one-half of the original rearguard contingent, which slightly betters the performance of the Long Marchers during their year's trek.[84] These guerrillas had survived conditions of great harshness and had battled poorly armed and in complete isolation against forces up to fifty times stronger than they. ''Those who remained,'' said Xiang Ying, ''were hardened warriors, and they were disciplined and iron-willed revolutionaries. Our ordeals had cleared out the fainthearted and the traitors. Nearly every man was capable of leading others in battle.''[85]

Through certain new directions in their work, the southern guerrillas were able to develop new skills and insights for the party and perfect some useful new techniques for subversion of the *baojia* system, for combining legal, semi-legal, and illegal means of struggle, and for "localizing" cadre. From the depths of defeat they had regrouped, rallied stragglers, rethought strategy and tactics, and gradually reestablished a military and political presence, though never a large one. And yet their experience during the three-year struggle in the South was not all positive, and it left them in some ways ill-equipped to cope with the difficulties and crises of the early period of the War of Resistance.

The Three-Year Struggle and Problems in the New Fourth Army

Soon after the southern guerrillas' reorganization into the New Fourth Army in early 1937, serious problems arose in their relations with Yan'an. New Fourth Army leaders around Xiang Ying held different positions from the majority of central leaders on a number of key strategic questions. Although they were undoubtedly loyal Communists, three years of isolation in the South had nurtured a spirit of fierce independence in them. Xiang Ying in particular tended to see his New Fourth Army detachments as the product of a separate historical process, one that easily matched the Long March as a feat of revolutionary endurance. He was loath to yield control over them to anyone. At its most serious this New Fourth Army chauvinism became entangled with the wider factional struggle between Mao and Wang Ming. It was neutralized, however, by a second negative legacy of the three-year struggle—a tendency toward internal disunity and factionalism among former rearguard units, reflecting their extreme fragmentation after 1934. Xiang Ying's efforts to build on the separate identity of the New Fourth Army foundered on its basic lack of solidarity.

In late 1937 Mao made some largely unsuccessful efforts to influence the New Fourth Army's reorganization.[86] His attempted intervention was aimed mainly at countering the Guomindang, especially by rejecting its appointees to the reorganized forces.[87] But he may also have wanted even at this early stage to establish a counterweight to Xiang Ying in the southern leadership and thus to prevent the formation of an independent power base within the party.[88]

After reorganization Xiang Ying tried to build a cult around himself, based mainly on the achievements of the three-year struggle. In an understandable attempt to imprint the heterogeneous units under his command with a sense of corporate identity, he emphasized the special traditions of the New Fourth Army.[89] But he also implied that the three-year struggle was superior to other periods in party history, because the units engaged in it had had to cope with a stronger enemy than the Long Marchers and it "had more of a mass character than the Jinggangshan period." He argued that new and uniquely instructive "tactical principles" had been derived from the three-year struggle, which had "become a real model for the present war of resistance, of exceptionally important significance for seizing final victory in it."[90] At the same time he projected himself to foreign journalists as an authentic worker and associated himself with Wang Ming's factionally motivated campaign for the urgent "proletarianization" of the party.[91] In Yan'an his supporters boasted that he "ranks with Mao [Zedong] as a combination of military and political genius, and in the councils of the Communist Party is inferior in rank only to Mao."[92]

Xiang Ying was later criticized for seeing the New Fourth Army as a "third force" between Yan'an and Chongqing, and for opposing party hegemony in it.[93] In his speeches and writings Xiang referred to the need for Communist Party policies and "a correct general line," but he put noticeably less emphasis on the party than did the Yan'an leaders. This may have been partly due to his exposed military position along-side powerful Nationalist divisions in East China and his desire to avoid friction with the Guomindang. But it is also likely that he equated "party hegemony" with the subversion of "his" army by outsiders. Xiang particularly resented the appointment of Ye Ting as commander of the New Fourth Army, seeing it as a threat to his own position. Certainly he did his best to make Ye's position intolerable.[94]

Xiang's bid for more influence in the party leadership must have been greatly strengthened by the generous terms of the December 1937 Politburo resolution on the three-year struggle, which mentioned him specially as its main leader.[95] It was surely not just a coincidence that this resolution was passed immediately after the return to an active role in the China-based leadership of Xiang's old cofactionalist, Wang Ming. Neither Xiang nor Wang possessed sufficient independent authority to challenge Mao unaided. But Xiang's control of an army and his stature as a leader who had won his laurels in Jiangxi, combined with Wang's position as Comintern plenipotentiary, made them a strong team in an intraparty faceoff against Mao.

But unfortunately for Xiang the army in which he hoped to consolidate his base was riven with factionalism and disunity. Unlike the main body of the Red Army, which operated in large regular units under a unified command, the southern guerrillas had been splintered for three years into more than a dozen parts, each of which was usually decentralized into even smaller units.

"Guerrillaist" attitudes derived from the experience of the three-year struggle created special difficulties during the early period of the New Fourth Army. Its problem was in a sense the opposite of that of the Eighth Route Army, whose task Mao said was to switch from regular to guerrilla operations.[96] Although the southern guerrillas had kept the tradition of political organization, the New Fourth Army's political work was widely recognized to be very weak, and for a long time it had serious discipline problems.[97] The southern guerrillas had fought mainly in small autonomous units and tended to prefer informal to formal structures and "direct democracy" to military discipline. Ye Ting summarized the problems of regularizing these units thus:

> Our men had for years been fighting in small detachments which were run on a purely democratic basis. Everyone knew everyone else, plans were discussed in common, and there was practically no formal discipline. In the New Fourth Army, the partisans had to recognize different degrees of authority in people they did not know and to obey their orders. Their daily life was subject to strict military routine, something they had not been accustomed to before. Most of them were peasants, to whom the whole conception of large-scale organization was foreign. Among the old fighters, many were found who objected to these "infringements of democracy."

Despite extensive propaganda campaigns to explain the transition from small-scale guerrilla units to large mobile forces and to weld individual units into "one united army," Ye Ting confessed that "it is still not true to say that we have completely overcome the psychology of the old partisan period. We still have our problems."[98]

Small wonder, then, that the blocks began to slip away from under Xiang almost from the start. North of the Yangzi, problems arose with Gao Junting, who allegedly sought an independent arrangement with the local Nationalists and ran his detachment, then the strongest in the New Fourth Army, like an "independent kingdom."[99] Further divisions arose between Xiang and his subordinates as friction between the Communists and the Nationalists grew, with Yan'an insisting that Xiang adopt a more independent position and strike out into the Japanese rear beyond the reach of the Guomindang. Xiang procrastinated, for fear either of harming the united front or of losing his independent power base in an involuntary merger with superior Communist forces to the north. Not so the leaders of his detachments, who step by step transferred their troops to the east and north and linked up with forces controlled by Yan'an. Thus the lack of solidarity among the remnants of the southern guerrillas proved useful to the Maoists in persuading major parts of Xiang's command to go north across the Yangzi and implement Maoist strategy there.

Xiang Ying's refusal to move from the strip of territory that he shared with Nationalist divisions in southern Anhui was not determined only by his fear that Yan'an would gain control over his forces. There were other factors, bound up with his experience in the three-year struggle, that predisposed him not to accept the Maoist line of mobilizing the masses deep behind enemy lines.

During their three years in the southern mountains the Red Army guerrillas had held out with unsurpassed tenacity against an enemy that enjoyed overwhelming technical and military superiority. But they had also developed, for the most part well in advance of the Long Marchers, an ability to compromise with local officials, bandit chiefs, gentry, and other figures of authority. Without this, most of them would undoubtedly have been wiped out at an early stage. Their survival rested on an apparently paradoxical basis: their resolute refusal to submit to the military pressure and political blandishments of the Guomindang, and an ability to adapt and adjust to the local power structure.

What they lacked during their three years of separation in the South was an experience of mass struggle of the sort that erupted under Communist leadership in Northwest China in late 1935 and 1936. New Fourth Army leaders argued that the secret of the southern guerrillas' survival was their ability to retain close contact with local people.[100] Yet even during periods of supposed "stabilization" most guerrillas spent months on end flitting between mountain tops in almost complete isolation from society, only occasionally descending to attack traffic on the roads or to kill local reactionaries. Although some of their exploits may have won them popular admiration, they were on Xiang Ying's own admission "constantly moving and . . . unable to build a base anywhere," making their beds for the most part in the mountain forests.[101]

Even successful "localization" by no means enabled the guerrillas to restore their mass base. Only in exceptional cases were they able to mobilize local people in social struggle and organize them systematically in associations, and nowhere were they able to do this on a scale even remotely comparable to elsewhere in China. Their experience of mass-based revolutionary struggle was never renewed during this peri-

od, and those guerrillas who did not remain complete outlaws throughout those three years were forced to adapt more or less passively to
local conditions, rather than actively intervening in and transforming
village society in a radical way.

Xiang Ying's experience during the three-year struggle was probably the main reason why after 1938 he found it hard to appreciate the
need for a deep and extensive social mobilization. That mobilization
was possible only in areas beyond Guomindang jurisdiction. During the
early months of the war the New Fourth Army had to operate under
conditions in Central China that were particularly poorly suited to its
own special style of warfare. The flat terrain was densely crisscrossed
with waterways and offered little cover. There was no revolutionary
tradition among local people outside the large cities. Bandits and pi-
rates preyed upon the peasants; the population was swelled by refugees; and local morale was extremely low. Much of the area to which
the New Fourth Army was originally assigned was heavily garrisoned
by hostile Nationalist units, which imposed major restrictions on its
operations, forbade its cadres to carry out social reforms or mobilize
popular support by setting up organs of political administration, and
kept it desperately short of funds and provisions. Many of the smaller
towns were tightly controlled by the Japanese from Shanghai and Nanjing, and organizations of collaborators abounded.[102]

Unlike Chen Yi and other New Fourth Army leaders, who broke
away to strike deep behind enemy lines in accordance with Yan'an's
instructions, Xiang Ying remained a prisoner of his past and found it
easier and more natural to fight a predominantly military war in this
milieu, where necessary in loose technical coordination with Nationalist forces, than to develop that taxing combination of political and
military skills required by Maoist strategy.[103] The methods he came to
adopt had little in common with guerrilla war in the sense that Mao
understood it, as the extensive arousing of peasants on social as well as
"national" issues, the setting up of base areas, and the building of
broad-based organs of political power. Because of this lack of strategic
vision and the sectional jealousy with which he viewed the forces whose
nominal commander he had been since October 1934, he obstinately
clung to his base south of the river and refused to follow Yan'an's
orders to go north. As a result, he lost not only his army (or rather, that
small part of it that still remained under his direct control after the
"defections" of its main detachments), but his life, when strong Nationalist divisions swooped down and destroyed him in the famous New
Fourth Army Incident of January 1941.

4

Repression and Communist Success: The Case of Jin-Cha-Ji, 1938–1943

KATHLEEN HARTFORD

The War of Resistance against Japan witnessed the massive expansion of Communist power in North China. Shortly after the Japanese military invasion had swept most of the indigenous armies and governments out of the area, small units of the Communist Party's Eighth Route Army spread out into rural hinterlands behind Japanese lines. Their aim was to spark a popular guerrilla-style resistance, to implement a series of socioeconomic and political reforms vital both to securing peasant support and to supplying the war effort, and to establish territorial base areas serving as nuclei for political, economic, and military expansion. By 1945 these base areas controlled the better part of North China's territory and population; they were essential foundations for the postwar struggle with the Guomindang forces of Chiang Kai-shek (see map 4.1).

Previous studies, in trying to explain the resistance bases' strengths, have stressed the role of peasant activism either in resisting Japanese aggression or in implementing reforms. In the prevailing view, only the concerted action of millions upon millions of organized, committed peasants braving all odds made possible the victory of the Chinese Communist Party. Whatever the particular explanations for peasant mobilization, most have assumed that repression of mass activism by either the Japanese or the Chinese rural elite was basically futile.

This essay has benefited from comments by Rod Aya, Thomas P. Bernstein, Steven M. Goldstein, Chalmers Johnson, Lincoln Li, Pavel Machala, Craig Malone, Michel Oksenberg, and Elizabeth J. Perry, and from discussion in the Workshop on Chinese Communist Rural Bases and the Columbia University Modern China Seminar.

Map 4.1. **Shanxi-Chahar-Hebei Border Region.**

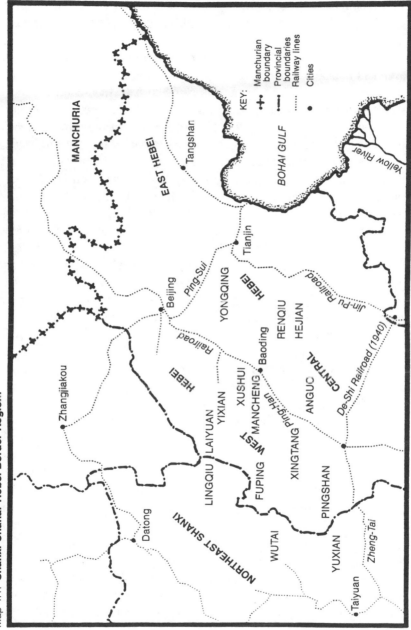

Repression either boomeranged, directly intensifying activism and determination, or was offset by the popular support engendered by base areas' economic and political reforms.[1]

My argument is that, to the contrary, repression reduced the mass activism considered indispensable to the CCP's success in the Resistance War period. While peasants came to hate the Japanese and to support base area reform policies, these *affects* were insufficient, either alone or in combination, to counteract the fear that inhibited *action*. In trying to limit the negative effects of a continually intensifying repression, resistance-base leaders employed a series of ad hoc measures to reduce fear and create courage, sometimes incrementally, usually piecemeal, and often only temporarily. Inelegant as the process was, it was essential to the eventual victory against Japan.

In developing this argument, I will concentrate on the Shanxi-Chahar-Hebei (Jin-Cha-Ji) Border Region. This was the earliest and largest Communist Party-led border region during the war, and it served as a policy model for other resistance bases. It is the ideal case for illustrating how seriously repression could affect a revolutionary movement, even when the revolutionaries did just about everything right.

Repression within Jin-Cha-Ji posed both a material and a psychological threat. Repression could materially eliminate the resources and personnel necessary to build the base or prosecute the war. Potentially more far-reaching was the psychological damage wreaked by repression. Repression might cause prospective supporters to fear any involvement with the resistance organizers. Moreover, initially successful mobilization for resistance still could, and frequently did, provoke Japanese countermeasures severe enough to demobilize previously mobilized peasants.

The Japanese used two basic forms of repression in North China: contingent and generalized. By contingent repression I mean a quid pro quo, specific punishment for specific acts, visited upon specific individuals or groups. By generalized repression I mean actions that were taken either locally or regionally against an entire population, indiscriminately in the sense that they affected "guilty" and "innocent" alike, but discriminately in the sense that they were aimed at removing the resources that could be used against the Japanese in guerrilla warfare.[2]

Contingent repression was designed to achieve primarily psychological results. The main intention was not to seek out and slaughter every resistance cadre, burn every village housing snipers, or wipe out any settlement where sabotage took place. Rather, by making examples of a few unfortunates, contingent repression was to deter others from engaging in proscribed activities, in particular (1) to deter individuals' active participation in programs, policies, or organizations fostered by the Eighth Route Army, the Border Region Government (BRG), or the Communist Party; (2) to make the population unwilling to harbor resistance forces, organizations, or personnel; and (3) to induce the population to inform upon the activities or movements of Eighth Route Army regular or guerrilla forces.

The Japanese preferred this form of repression because it economized on manpower and minimized popular hostility toward them. But it did entail a number of problems. In the first place, it required a fairly widespread military presence in the countryside. Troop levels did not have to be high in any given place, but troops did have to be placed throughout the countryside for the threat to be taken seriously. Second, the Japanese had to have reliable local sources of information if they were to detect resistance organization early enough to nip it in the bud. This meant securing collaboration from people familiar with the villages, particularly from the traditional rural elite and their clients or hangers-on.[3] Usually these sources were available only in areas that, in the CCP's classification scheme, were "enemy-occupied areas" or fairly weak "guerrilla areas."[4]

Generalized repression commonly took the form of large-scale extermination campaigns. These required large but not necessarily long-term troop commitments, costly logistics operations, and complicated arrangements for coordination of troop movements. They were aimed primarily at the border region's secure bases or more secure guerrilla areas. The tactics used changed over time, but the aim was generally constant: to seize territory and clear it of all resistance forces. By the middle period of the war, this meant turning the base areas into virtual wastelands.

Although this mode of repression had considerable material effect, its results were, in the final analysis, probably more psychological than material. As the historical account in this essay will show, the strains of repeated extermination campaigns caused a tremendous loss of will among the general populace and brought the border region to the brink of disaster.

Obviously this interpretation implicitly rejects a peasant-nationalism explanation of the border region's power. The results of repression on another front—*within* rural society—also require more careful use of another popular explanation of the CCP's power during this era. Social reforms, particularly rent and interest reduction and progressive taxation policies, were the initial drawing cards for peasants' membership in mass organizations and participation in governmental affairs.[5] But a reaction by the traditional village elite, in the form of contingent repression against peasant activists, often reduced the organizations to empty shells and made a travesty of the reforms. In addition, when hard-pressed by radical government measures, members of the elite could and did actively undermine the internal security of the border region. Scattered secret society uprisings and depredations by marauding armies loosely affiliated with the Guomindang continued to crop up. Such incidents were by no means universal, but they caused severe local crises, especially when timed to coincide with Japanese campaigns against the border region.

Repression in Practice: The Early Period (1938–1940)

The Japanese troops arriving in North China after late summer 1937, preoccupied with shoving the Guomindang armies out of the entire eastern half of China, left only small reserves in the major cities of North China as they moved rapidly south along the major railway lines. Almost immediately, Eighth Route Army units dispatched from the central Communist Party base in Shaanxi began moving into the North China countryside.

By the fall of 1937, Nie Rongzhen, vice-commander of the 115th Division, had led some two thousand troops into the mountains of northeastern Shanxi and western Hebei, and these fanned out to make contact with local resistance forces already organized (many by local party members) in the area. (See map 4.1 for the railways and the major border region locations mentioned in this essay.) In Central Hebei, Lü Zhengcao, the commander of a former Northeast Army unit stranded behind Japanese lines after the invasion, rallied some of his forces to maintain resistance on the plains. He was soon in touch with local Communist Party organizers of resistance and with Eighth Route Army cadres sent from western Hebei. By late 1937 he had accepted Eighth Route Army command, his troops had received political training and were reorganized, and the resistance efforts on both sides of the Ping-Han railroad were growing apace. In January 1938 an assembly of regional and local military and political leaders declared the formation of the Jin-Cha-Ji Border Region. The Border Region Government, the Eighth Route Army, and the Communist Party then began introducing rent and interest reduction, "reasonable burden" (progressive) taxation, new village governments, more systematic guerrilla organization, and a coordinated resistance strategy.[6] As these efforts expanded, so too did the border region's experience of repression and its negative consequences.

Japanese Repression

The Japanese strategy in the early period of the war was to pacify large stretches of territory, garrison them with small forces supplemented by puppet troops, cut up guerrilla areas with a network of "points and lines" (fortifications and blockade walls and trenches), and rely on contingent repression to keep these areas pacified.[7] Their limited extermination campaigns during these years were aimed first (and relatively unsuccessfully) at eradicating Eighth Route Army troop concentrations, and later (more successfully) at providing the ground for their blockade system. They did not employ the scorched-earth measures in widespread use later in the war.

The weakness of Japanese repressive capacity in most of the North China countryside for the first year of war is usually overlooked. In reality the greatest threat to the lives and livelihood of most people in North China until the fall of 1938 came from roving bandit groups.[8] The Japanese units left in the cities as their main forces continued south were hardly large enough to keep the cities under control. Although they made forays out of the cities, these were few, small, and grossly ineffective in curtailing resistance activities. The laxness of their control is illustrated by the ease with which one Western correspondent moved into guerrilla territory in Central Hebei in the summer of 1938: he took a train south from Beiping, hopped on a bicycle, and pedaled off across the fields until he reached the border region sentries.[9] Until late fall of 1938, the border region was able to control nearly all the county seats in Hebei and Shanxi that were not directly on the railroads. Even some of those towns initially seized by the Japanese were recaptured and held without serious challenge for months.[10] Peasants hastily organized for "guerrilla" activities indulged, with a zest spiced by impunity, in repeated sabotage of communications lines and other targets of military use to the Japanese.

This is not to say that the Japanese army failed to react to these early activities. In the spring of 1938, in retaliation for massed guerrilla attacks on the Ping-Han and Jin-Pu railroads, the Japanese army brought twelve thousand troops against the mountain bases of the border region along four routes. The attack was poorly planned and executed, however, and fizzled out without doing much damage.[11] From late 1937 through the first half of 1938, various Japanese campaigns were conducted in the Central Hebei plains, also with little result.[12] The turning point came when additional Japanese troops were reassigned to the North after successful completion of the Wuhan campaign in late 1938.

The Japanese strategy for gaining control of North China was formulated in detail by December 1938. The pacification plans, strongly influenced by the Japanese experience in Manchuria, called for three principal steps: (1) "enforcement operations" (*shukusei sakusen*), which were to drive out the main Communist forces, to be followed by "decentralized deployment" of garrisons in fortified "base points" for rapid suppression of any remaining Communist units; (2) establishment of puppet governments and consolidation of control over communications lines and commerce; (3) formation of puppet Chinese forces to take over "pacification maintenance" in the countryside.[13]

From early 1939 to early 1940, Japanese military units conducted several "enforcement" campaigns in the Jin-Cha-Chi Border Region. All followed roughly the same pattern. The first large-scale campaign, for example, swept through Central Hebei in September 1938. After surrounding and occupying an Eighth Route Army base just south of Central Hebei, Japanese troops pressed north, leaving soldiers in the more important towns and market centers, and then conducted repeated sweeps to catch and wipe out Eighth Route Army units. Subsequent campaigns there and elsewhere in the border region lasted anywhere from several weeks to several months.[14]

After four months of pitched battles in Central Hebei, from November 1938 to March 1939, the Japanese army had not only failed to drive out Lü Zhengcao's guerrillas but had also prompted their reinforcement by much more seasoned forces under He Long.[15] Eighth Route Army forces in the mountains of West Hebei and Northeast Shanxi proved even more elusive. Only in East Hebei did most resistance forces succumb under the onslaught—and there, the units under direct Eighth Route Army command survived, while the Japanese decimated the more independent-minded groups.[16]

The greatest danger to the border region came not from these campaigns but from what followed in their wake: the introduction of the points-and-lines system. By May 1939 the Japanese had occupied all county towns and many other important towns in Central Hebei, and most of the county towns in the mountains west of the Ping-Han railroad.[17] By mid–1939, 173 fortified "base points" had been established in Central Hebei alone.[18] Having taken these points, the Japanese set about constructing and fortifying the roads ("lines") connecting them.[19] By the fall of 1939, the gaps between points and lines in Central Hebei ranged from forty or fifty to only five to fifteen *li* (a Chinese mile, approximately one-third of an English mile). Japanese garrisons numbered from one hundred to four hundred troops in the more important towns, and in the secondary towns, from thirty to one hundred. Other "points" might have from twenty to fifty Japanese troops. These were supplemented by possibly more numerous Chinese puppet forces.[20]

The decentralized deployment facilitated rapid Japanese response to any resistance-force activities; by the spring of 1939 the Japanese Army could concentrate troops for an attack anywhere in Central Hebei within twenty minutes.[21] Such rapid mobility was not possible in the mountains to the west, but there as well the points-and-lines system was bringing Japanese firepower uncomfortably closer to the resistance forces.

Having spread out the net in this fashion, the Japanese used contingent repression to root out resistance organizations in the interstices. Puppet governmental bodies were established in the fortified base points and sent spies into the surrounding villages.[22] As the net tightened, the surveillance efforts grew more systematic. The strategy worked earliest and most effectively in eastern Hebei. There, the Japanese blockaded all grain and other necessities from entering guerrilla areas, established a village mutual-guarantee and household register system, and introduced a "good people's guarantee" (*liangminzheng*) to check travelers.[23] These methods corresponded closely to the Guomindang measures described in chapter 2.

Contingent repression during the early period found its most potent expression in the mutual responsibility system. The most organized, and to the Japanese the most strategically important, form of this system was the "railroad-cherishing" or "road-cherishing" village. The railroad-cherishing policy was introduced in June 1938. Villages within five kilometers of the railways were made responsible for "cherishing" the railway lines, motor roads, and other communications lines. Each village had to supply several men to patrol the line at night and report any suspicious movements.[24] If sabotage occurred, not only those guarding the line but also their families and sometimes the entire village suffered. As the points-and-lines system and Japanese garrisons extended more deeply into the countryside, the enforced love affair with roads and telephone lines went with them.[25]

How effective were these repressive measures? In one respect, they were quite helpful to the border region: the Japanese "enforcement operations" eliminated some other Chinese contenders for anti-Japanese military power in the area and thus temporarily aided the expansion of Eighth Route Army forces.[26] But for the most part Japanese repression in the early period had deleterious effects on the border region. The points-and-lines system severely hampered the movement of Eighth Route Army forces and the transportation of grain and other supplies—the more so as, toward mid–1940, the points became more closely spaced and the lines' fortifications wider and deeper or higher.[27]

Most striking, though, is the early Japanese strategy's considerable psychological impact on the resistance forces and peasant activists. While some military cadres were prophesying that the situation would continue to worsen and that more would be demanded of the population,[28] the mass-based village self-defense corps had long since collapsed under increasing Japanese pressure, and a much smaller picked militia was all that sustained resistance activism in the villages.[29] The morale problem, moreover, had infected the regular and guerrilla forces as well. Desertion rates had skyrocketed when Japanese military attention focused on the border region in late 1938. This problem was solved temporarily in most units through intensive political education.[30] But it is doubtful that the troops held up well under the more difficult conditions developing through 1939. An Eighth Route Army cadre reporting on the problem of North China troop attrition in October 1939 provided some illustrative figures: in one newly formed guerrilla unit, 20.8 percent of the soldiers had deserted in the space of a year; in a seasoned main force (regular army) unit, 16.4 percent had deserted. In both cases the desertions accounted for approximately two-thirds of the attrition rate.[31] Nor did the troops always desert quietly and individually. In late 1939 and early 1940, the Eighth Route Army uncovered a series of plots in Central Hebei, allegedly inspired by "Trotskyite bandits and diehards," aimed at taking entire detachments over to the Japanese. Leaders of a mutiny in the Second Independent

Detachment, for example, sent word to the Japanese that they would defect if they could wait for the right moment and offered to seize some political cadres as proof of their sincerity. Other conspiracies or actual mutinies occurred among three other units, including an entire battalion.[32]

As numbers dropped, so too did the activism of resistance forces. Voluntary engagements by army units probably declined sharply. Before late 1938 nearly all clashes had been of the resistance forces' own seeking; increasingly from early 1939 the resistance units were placed on the defensive. Authors of early reports in the Eighth Route Army journal chortle over the ingenious stratagems that made it possible to evade, ambush, or otherwise confound a bumbling enemy; as 1940 progressed, one finds a steadily lengthening list of the stratagems that no longer worked, the new precautions that had to be taken, the disasters that might (only with clairvoyance, one suspects) have been avoided.[33]

Although armed clashes may have increased due to involuntary encounters, acts of sabotage—the old forte of the village self-defense corps—appear to have declined dramatically. There are no figures for Jin-Cha-Ji alone, but we do have some Japanese figures for North China. Figures 4.1 and 4.2 illustrate the trends in sabotage, from 1938 through 1940, on railroads and communications lines. Both charts show activities peaking in 1938 and then tending downward except for a brief upsurge as part of the Hundred Regiments offensive in August–September 1940.

Yet Japanese repression, taken alone, was insufficient to eradicate all border region organization. Contingent repression of nonmilitary activities required more subtle detective work than finding a stretch of track gone or telephone wire missing. Despite the drop in resistance activism, despite the military difficulties, from 1939 to mid–1940 the border region nevertheless expanded its political and social power in the areas of early resistance organizing. It was during these months that popular village governments were chosen through general elections and rent and interest reduction and systematic progressive taxation were first implemented in more than pro forma fashion.[34] In the older resistance areas on the plains of Central Hebei, so vulnerable to Japanese reprisals, villages not under direct occupation often managed to maintain border region-affiliated governments, collect taxes, and implement rent reduction almost within rifle shot of Japanese garrisons.[35] In occupied areas, however, the effective implementation of reform

Fig. 4.1. **Statistics on Sabotage of Main Communications Lines of the North China Area Army.**

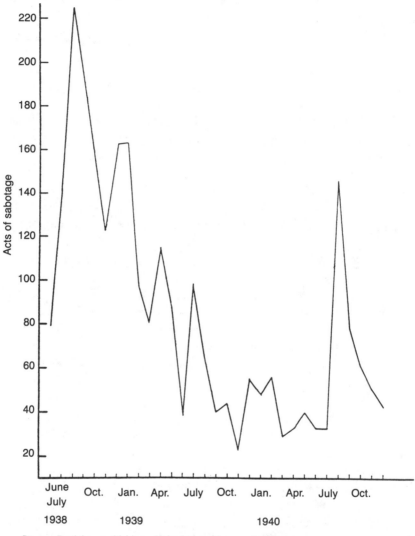

Source: Boeicho senshishitsu, *Hokushi no chiansen,* 1:409.

policies dropped as resistance forces and mass organizations went underground. Areas in which organizing started in earnest only after Japanese garrisoning began seemed to find the implementation of policies like rent reduction extremely difficult if not impossible.[36]

Fig. 4.2. **Damage to North China Railroads**

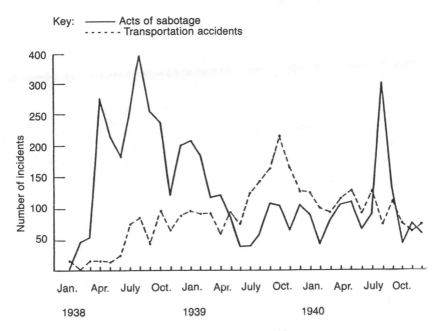

Source: Boeicho senshishitsu, *Hokushi no chiansen,* 1:407.

The effectiveness of contingent repression thus apparently varied in direct proportion to the proximity of the repressor and inversely with the duration of prior border region organizing, other things being equal. One other thing was not equal: the stance of the traditional rural elite, who could and did practice their own forms of repression against the border region.

Elite Repression

The traditional rural elite of landlords and rich peasants[37] proved more adroit than the Japanese in striking at the underpinnings of the border region's political and social power. The region's ability to collect taxes, recruit soldiers and cadres, and exercise control over the villages rested on the implementation of its socioeconomic reform policies. These reforms, particularly rent and interest reduction, progressive taxation, and popular elections, frequently provided the opening wedge for organizing in the villages. Over the long term, certain reforms tended to improve the economic productivity as well as the social and political power of the peasant majority. Both of these functions were essential in the long-run construction of the border region's own power.[38] At the same time, however, the reforms threatened to undermine radically the living standards, social standing, and power of the traditional elite. The elite reacted with their own variants of contingent repression.

Landlords could use contingent repression most effectively against tenants demanding rent reduction, for the tenant had to confront the landlord individually to insist on payment at the new rates. In the early rent reduction campaigns, landlords often retaliated by renting the land to new tenants. The old tenants therefore frequently signed new, public contracts with landlords in order to satisfy cadres but concluded secret rental agreements at the old rates.[39]

The elite could also use contingent repression against those supporting the new taxation system. Here they were more often pitted not against an individual but against a group of villagers pressing for "reasonable burden" tax assessment by a village assembly, which could usually be counted on to place the burden exclusively on the rich.[40] In this kind of situation the elite could single out prominent activists for retaliation as a way of controlling others.

One example will suffice to illustrate the elite's tactics.[41] In Hejian county, anti-Japanese guerrilla organizing had begun in December 1937. The county and district governments affiliated with the border region had been founded shortly thereafter, by absorbing many anti-Communist Guomindang members. Most of them were still in official positions when the "reasonable burden" taxation system was introduced in August 1938.

In Hejian's West Book of Odes Village, 3 landlord and 17 rich peasant families, out of 380 households, controlled half the village's arable land. The leader of the village peasants' association, Ming Shuzhen, sparked popular pressure to force the village elite to comply with the reasonable-burden tax. After being faced down in direct confrontations, some of the elite bought the help of the district head, himself a landlord, Guomindang member, and opium addict. The district head, having failed to disband or discredit the peasants' association, finally arrested Ming on a pretext. The village peasants' association appealed to the leader of the county association, who secured an order to free Ming. Before the release order could be formally delivered Ming had been shot as a "traitor" by command of the district head.

That this incident could have occurred at all is indicative enough of problems for the border region. But even more startling (for one of the earliest and most active guerrilla areas in Central Hebei), it was eight or nine months before county investigators could assuage peasants' fears enough to get the full truth of the affair out of them. The elite were thus capable of undermining the political and social bases of the border region in a manner that could go long undetected, until almost too late to remedy.[42] This demonstrates the potential effects of elite repression not simply on the implementation of a specific policy but also on the organizational strength the border region could build within the villages. If such cases of repression could occur in a place like Hejian, they could not have been rare.

Effective though these repressive acts might have been over the short run, they generally failed in the long run to stem a growing tide of peasant radicalism. The traditional elite began losing out in the repeated village elections and annual tax assessment meetings which pitted large groups of peasants against them. As they lost out there, more and more peasants were willing to insist upon rent reduction. As the number of emboldened peasants grew, the demands escalated into an insistence on perpetual tenancy rights or cancellations of interest, which amounted to refusals to pay rent or repay debts.[43]

Seeing these new developments as portents of their own doom, many of the elite turned against the border region in self-defense. They began to provide the Japanese with assistance and useful local information, or to organize anti-border region groups to attack activists during the particularly vulnerable moment of a Japanese extermination campaign.[44] The elite's individual or small-scale collaboration with the Japanese is usually not well documented. Contemporary Communist sources ordinarily make only the standard mention of subversive activities by "local bullies and evil gentry" (*tuhao lieshen*).[45] On a larger scale, the documented secret society organizations encouraged by the Japanese probably numbered many of the elite among their leadership. Over seventy different kinds of secret societies were active in Central Hebei in 1939–1940, many of them causing problems for the resistance forces.[46] One guerrilla leader in southwestern Central Hebei recalled the burgeoning of Big Swords and Red Spears groups there during the second year of the war. These groups, he reported, were incited by landlords and rich peasants and sometimes massed as many as fifty or sixty thousand followers to attack the resistance units in conjunction with a Japanese campaign.[47]

Traditional elites were probably also involved in some less localized cases of repression. One cannot help but strongly suspect the elite's role particularly in incidents where border region taxation officials or taxation policies were prominent targets. One such case concerned Meng Gechen, an alternate member of the BRG Executive Committee and commander of the Yixian-Mancheng-Xushui Military District. In early January 1939 Meng, according to the BRG, turned traitor, shot BRG tax personnel, and was later arrested and executed as a traitor.[48] It is probably no coincidence that Xushui's and Mancheng's county governments were the last in western Hebei to be formally constituted—two weeks after the incident.[49]

A second incident concerned the activities of Shanxi Peace Preservation Corps forces (forces under Yan Xishan's Second War Area and tenuously under Guomindang control) led by Bai Zhiyi.[50] These forces rampaged through Guangling county in Shanxi in mid-October 1939. On 20 October, numbering two hundred at the time, they surrounded the Lingqiu county government offices, seized documents, funds, and county government workers, and called for opposition to the BRG and to the collection of border region tax grains. On 24 October, a border region guerrilla unit arrived in Lingqiu. Bai left the county, reappearing in Laiyuan county in western Hebei, where he captured additional BRG cadres. On 5 December Bai's forces, now numbering some five hundred, surrounded a village and killed two BRG personnel. Three days later, in the wake of a Japanese attack, Bai's forces were in Tang county capturing yet more border region personnel. On 30 December Wutai county was making appeals for help against him. A few months later, he was reported to have substantially disrupted the resistance governments in Ying and Shanyin counties. By that point he was apparently rather openly collaborating with the Japanese.[51]

Although Bai was not part of the local traditional elite in these areas, he seems to have been considerably more effective than the Japanese in ferreting out and capturing border region personnel. It is inconceivable that he could have wreaked havoc to such purpose in unfamiliar areas without receiving information and assistance from disaffected locals. Moreover, an alienated local elite probably took many ordinary citizens over to the other side: Bai's forces seem to have grown as they moved through areas under secure border region control since 1938, and the local self-defense organizations were either powerless or unwilling to resist them.

Thus Japanese repression and elite reaction, singly and in combination, were proving a substantial threat to the border region, reducing the general level of security for local cadres and activists and causing a downward spiral in the level of local self-defense activism. However, they by no means completely eliminated the resistance organizations, nor did they completely block the implementation of policy. On the surface, by the end of 1939 and the beginning of 1940, the border region began to look extremely weak. Beneath that surface, it still had some hidden reserves of strength.

These were marshalled in the Hundred Regiments offensive in late summer 1940. Local militia and self-defense forces, which had been quiescent for months, secretly organized to coordinate with guerrilla and regular forces in a concerted assault on Japanese strong points all over North China. It was supposed to be a turning point in the war, and if it had succeeded in driving Japanese forces back out of the countryside, so it would have been. Indeed, it proved a turning point, but the turn was not that intended. A massive Japanese reaction exceeding all expectation came down upon not only the Eighth Route Army forces but the entire rural population.[52] This ushered in a new stage in the practice of repression within the border region.

Repression in Practice: The Middle Period (1940–1943)

From the end of the Hundred Regiments offensive until early 1943, the Japanese practiced a program of concentrated generalized repression in contrast with which their earlier measures seemed moderate indeed. "Enforcement operations" gave way to extermination campaigns. Savage, protracted, repeated sweeps of base areas and guerrilla bases were conducted. In the heartland of the border region these sweeps were designed to drag off, burn, shoot, bury alive, eviscerate, or otherwise eliminate any inhabitants of potential use to the border region. Any grain that could not be carried off was burned. Standing crops were burned or trampled. Villages were razed, livestock slaughtered or stolen, trees chopped down, irrigation works destroyed. In guerrilla areas, the extermination campaigns swept up any of the populace suspected of active cooperation with border region organizations and established strict controls over all movement by local residents. The Japanese termed their strategy "three clears": clearing all grain, draft animals, and people of use to the Communist forces. The resistance forces called it "Three Alls" after its all too fre-

Table 4.1

Largest Three Alls Campaigns in Jin-Cha-Ji

Campaign begun	Duration	Troop strength	Targeted area
August 1941	2 months +	100,000	Beiyue
Early 1942	3 months +	40,000	East Hebei
May 1942	3 months +	50,000	Central Hebei
September 1943	3 months	40,000	Beiyue

Sources: Renmin Chubanshe, *Kang-Ri zhanzheng shiqi jiefangqu gaikuang* (The Liberated Areas During the War of Resistance Against Japan) (Beijing: same, 1953), p. 31; Lu Zhengcao, "Chuancha zai gouxianzhong di youji zhanzheng" (Guerrilla Warfare Piercing Through the Blockade Ditch Lines), *Qunzhong* 8, 15 (16 September 1943), p. 415.

quent manifestations: burn all, kill all, loot all.

Four major extermination campaigns were conducted in Jin-Cha-Ji during this period; summary information on them is given in table 4.1. One example of the damage they caused should suffice. Pingshan county in western Hebei, one of the border region's model counties and therefore a prime target for the most vicious Japanese treatment, had suffered the following losses under the Three Alls up to the end of 1942: 60,000 sections of houses burned; 58,580,000 catties of grain destroyed; 50,000 *mu* of crops trampled (around 10 percent of the cultivated area); 5,000 fatalities; and 20,000 men and women dragged off. (The county's population in 1931 was 236,000.)[53]

Each extermination campaign was coupled with intensified construction of fortifications, and the new fortified base points served as staging points for renewed, smaller extermination campaigns. According to Lü Zhengcao, the Japanese conducted three kinds of "extermination" in Central Hebei:

One kind was an everyday, individual "extermination," i.e., each base point's or fort's enemy [soldiers], in the area they defended, regularly went out to surround and search villages. The second kind was to concentrate the mobile troops of large base points, conducting an "extermination" of one set area for a set time section by section, surrounding several or several tens of villages, searching village by village . . . . The third kind is a combination of the individual "extermination" and the section-by-section "extermination," using the garrison army . . . to draw in our attention and strength and to confuse our judgment, and later suddenly to change direction and coordinate with their main force to "exterminate" a different area.[54]

The fortifications greatly facilitated section-by-section extermina-tions as the sections grew steadily smaller. Highways, the backbone of the fortifications policy, were constructed rapidly. The figures for Central Hebei illustrate the effects of these developments. In 1939 there were 3,400 *li* of highway; by the first half of 1942, the total was 9,726 *li*. Blockade ditches were also extended. By June 1943 a total of 12,140 *li* of these ditches crisscrossed Central Hebei.[55] Often the ditches were twenty feet wide and thirty feet deep. The roads were flanked by blockade walls up to twenty feet high.[56] By the end of 1943, it was estimated that the points-and-lines network of forts and blockade ditches had divided Central Hebei into some 2,600 small chunks, further subdivided by roads and ditches. The gaps between the points and lines averaged around five *li*; none exceeded fifteen *li*.[57] Central Hebei was not the only part of the border region so carved up; the December 1942 totals of ditches, roads, and forts in the four major divisions of the border region are given in table 4.2.

Areas that had already been "exterminated" fairly thoroughly were then subjected to intensive political and economic controls: *baojia* organization, new investigations of the population in each area and the use of household registers, control of commerce, and grain and salt rationing. "Model areas" in each county served as nuclei for the expansion of puppet organization, using puppet self-defense corps and puppet army garrisons.[58]

Although the border region suffered considerable material damage and loss of life in the extermination campaigns, these losses were far lower than the Japanese had intended. Concealment of population, careful underground work, and prior removal of grain, tools, and farm animals limited the concrete damage suffered. The cumulative psycho-logical effect of the repression, however, was devastating. It was par-ticularly so in the former guerrilla areas or guerrilla bases in Central Hebei which were cleared of all Eighth Route Army forces and left to the very untender mercies of Japanese occupying garrisons. Without the assistance of larger forces and seasoned troops, the local mass organizations and resistance governments lapsed into near total inac-tivity, and a pall descended upon a population now vulnerable to Japa-nese labor impressment and grain seizures. Attempts to remedy the decline in mass morale met with repeated failures.[59]

A revealing example of the morale problem comes from Anguo

Table 4.2

Status of Blockade System in Jin-Cha-Ji, December 1942

	Beiyue	Central Hebei	East Hebei	Pingbei	Total
Base points and forts	1,219	1,635	329	175	3,356
Highways (in *li*)	9,238	11,987	3,062	2,618	26,905
Blockade ditches (in *li*)	1,779	5,000	924	282	7,885
Blockade walls (in *li*)	395	502	N/A	N/A	897[a]

Source: Mu Yi, "Jin-Cha-Ji jiefangqu di minzhu jianshe" (Democratic Construction in the Jin-Cha-Ji Liberated Areas), *Qunzhong* 9 (14 July 1943), pp. 550–51,
a. Typographical error in original corrected. Total includes only Beiyue and Central Hebei.

county, which had been part of the guerrilla base area of southwestern Central Hebei since the early months of the war.[60] The county-level guerrilla battalion, formed in July 1938, was led by old CCP members from the area. After the Hundred Regiments, the force fell first to a half and then, after May 1942, to a fifth of its original strength. According to documents captured by the Japanese, the guerrilla battalion was already on its fourth commander. The first had been captured, the second had surrendered voluntarily, and both, as of 1942, were serving in the county puppet army. The third had been captured and the report is unclear on his whereabouts. The nominal fourth commander was the Anguo county government head, but actual command was exercised by a special representative from the Eighth Route Army's military sub-region command. At about the same time, the former commander of the crack youth militia unit in a core (former) border region-controlled village was reported serving as an assistant *bao* chief in the Japanese-controlled *baojia* system.

Was Anguo typical? It is hard to tell for certain, but sending regular army cadres down to lead local guerrilla and even militia units became standard practice during these years. They were needed at least as much for morale as for practical military leadership.[61]

In the mountainous areas west of the Ping-Han railroad, the will to resist was maintained at a fairly high level, but the cumulative effects of repression nevertheless posed two serious problems for the border region. First, peasants' disaffection with resistance governments grew as landlords eroded previous peasant gains from reforms. Second, peasants proved increasingly reluctant to enter the guerrilla and regular army forces, which now required that they move out of their home areas.

In border region areas, the elite had been offered a stronger governmental position by the "three-thirds" policy initiated in 1940, and they were armed with some indirect admission of the importance of appeasing them in the form of moderation of BRG rent reduction and taxation policies. This may have encouraged many of them to take advantage of border region leaders' preoccupation with the all-important problem of survival, to recoup their earlier losses.[62] A sternly worded BRG directive in October 1943 underlined the dangers of these retrenchments. Even where rent reduction had been fairly thoroughly implemented before, landlords were raising rents or taking land back from tenants. A number of local government cadres had been confused over just where they stood in the tenancy disputes; some cadres had apparently even been collecting rent for the landlords.[63] Perhaps their "confusion" had been increased by apprehension over the potential danger to themselves if they championed the peasants' rights or interests too passionately. The first step in the one major secret society incident during this period, a Red Spears revolt in Yu county (northeastern Shanxi) led by elite elements, had been the systematic slaughter of border region government cadres.[64] The overall effect of the landlords' counteroffensive was, in the BRG's own assessment, to diminish the amount of activism or trust the government could count on from the peasants.[65]

The crisis in peasant morale was exacerbated by the new military situation. Even in its mountain redoubts the Eighth Route Army now had to transfer its troops to avoid extermination sweeps, leaving sections of the countryside "temporarily" undefended. Peasants in these areas worried about being left dead before the situation changed. In late 1941 a high political cadre of the Eighth Route Army observed that with the removal of these main forces, resistance work stopped in the undefended areas and peasant morale plummeted. Moreover, in anticipation of those transfers, hostility toward the military arose among local party organizations that were left minding the house. After relocation, soldiers frequently deserted to return home, circulating stories to justify their flight that damaged the army's reputation among the populace. Local party organs often opposed sending badly needed reinforcements to the main forces, contending that these militia or self-defense corps members were required for defense of home areas now left without regular military protection.[66]

The combined effects of repression against the border region during the middle period were threefold. The first was an enormous drop in the population's confidence in the ability of their governments, their military, or themselves to withstand continued Japanese pressure and win victory in resistance war. The second was a drop in the people's military, political, and socioeconomic activism because of both the material impact of repression (e.g., the loss of resistance cadres through attrition or transfer) and the psychological impact, especially the fear of reprisals or a general feeling of futility. The third, more indirect, effect was a resurgence in the traditional elite's power, evidenced by backsliding on reforms. Clearly, these three effects were related; together they threatened to cause a serious downward spiral in mass activism, policy implementation, resistance mobilization, and border region power.

Countering Repression: Heroes and Martyrs

E. P. Thompson once wrote: "Lest the reader should judge the historian too harshly, we may record Sir John Clapham's explanation as to the way in which [the] selective principle may order the evidence. 'It is very easy to do this unawares. Thirty years ago I read and marked Arthur Young's *Travels in France*, and taught from the marked passages. Five years ago I went through it again, to find that whenever Young spoke of a wretched Frenchman I had marked him, but that many of his references to happy or prosperous Frenchmen remained unmarked.'"[67] Up to this point, I have been marking the frightened peasants. Ordinarily when such examples in the materials on the period have been noticed at all, they have been cited as starting points, the problems that the CCP successfully solved through new policies or organizational approaches en route to the end point: support, heroism, success. The heroes, the daredevils, and the selfless martyrs, whose examples do abound in the literature of the era, are considered by most if not the norm, then certainly the key to the CCP's success.

My reasons for stressing the opposite examples are twofold. First, I would argue that while they do not refute the heroic examples, they are undoubtedly closer to the norm during the entire period in which the border region's existence was most imperiled. If the myth of mass mobilization in the Resistance War is valid, there were millions of heroes and heroines in Jin-Cha-Ji. But the internal documents of the CCP, the Eighth Route Army, and the border region government suggest that the number of willing heroes always decreased precipitously as the risks of martyrdom increased. They repeatedly assert the elusiveness of heroism. The heroes could be numbered at most in tens of thousands, and in the darkest and most difficult times barely that.[68]

Second, though I would agree that the heroic few were essential to the Communist movement's success, they were far from enough. The effort needed to withstand Japanese occupation and build the border region's power did rest upon the actions of more than a handful, though usually not a majority, of the population. The examples of the negative effects of repression signal to us, as they signaled to the resistance leadership, a recurrent tendency in popular reaction to repression. That the populace did not move much more drastically in the direction of that tendency must be attributed not only to the policies and organizational approaches that could increase mass "support," but also to the implicit strategy pursued by the border region in counteracting repression. That strategy involved reducing the material risks of martyrdom, reducing the demands of heroism to acceptable levels, and establishing a psychological climate in which group heroism could reduce the perceived and actual risk of individual martyrdom—in which millions of little and temporary heroes, through simultaneous action, simultaneously reduced the risks of action to themselves and performed tasks impossible for the handful of great and constant heroes to perform alone.

Reducing the Risks of Martyrdom

The material risks of martyrdom could be lessened by using counterrepression, by limiting the provocations for repression, and by concealing the targets of repression.

Counterrepression. Counterrepression, in the form of military action against Japanese forces or attacks upon the lives or property of the traditional elite, was aimed at reducing the opponent's capacity for repression. However, it might, by provoking a reaction, merely escalate the violence. But the border region could use both direct and indirect means of counterrepression that did not carry such heavy escalatory risks. One example of the direct approach was the treatment of puppet governments. The border region's early policy of "smashing" them meant assassinating their officials. For example, three puppet magistrates in Renqiu county in Central Hebei were disposed of in quick succession through this method.[67] This did not prevent the Japanese from establishing puppet organs in that county, but we may remain doubtful of the surviving magistrate's zeal in pursuing resistance activists.

The earliest assassinations were largely spontaneous affairs, even those performed by Communist Party members. In Anguo county, for example, resistance organizations in one large village had lapsed into inaction while under Japanese occupation from September 1939 to December 1940. As soon as the Japanese left the village in December 1940, some party members on their own initiative assassinated villagers who had served under the Japanese. Later, higher levels of the party or government exercised careful control over the assassination method. By 1942, the party's policy in Anguo placed the village party's traitor-elimination teams under direct control by the *district* party committee—not under the village party branch. Ordinarily the district level had to approve any assassinations beforehand.[70]

This later assassination policy grew out of meticulous attention to "enemy work." As early as July 1939, the border region had convened cadres from areas with particularly successful experiences in this field to compile materials on their work, debate the methods in detail, and train enemy-work cadres for other counties. Their materials included "descriptions of types of traitors, how to distinguish between them, how to approach them."[71] Later in the war, during the extermination campaigns, small cores of activists were organized into "guerrilla cells" of party members, mass organization cadres, and government workers. One of the major responsibilities of these cells, which operated underground, was surveillance of collaborators and elimination of those considered particularly zealous or dangerous.[72] This was an effective policy for motivating collaborators to strive for busy incompetence.

Direct counterrepression was almost exclusively aimed at puppet authorities or Chinese collaborators, not against the Japanese.[73] The reason for this seems obvious: the Japanese were more likely to respond to such attacks with reprisals of their own, whereas the border region's generally mild policy against ordinary puppet troops and lesser functionaries lowered their interest in reprisals. This left the higher-level puppets and collaborators highly vulnerable.

Indirect counterrepression was also used. One fictionalized account, which undoubtedly was based in fact, recounted the exploits of a guerrilla group of seven men charged with eliminating a puppet army officer. This collaborator had been sent by his Japanese superiors to ferret out the suspected infiltrators in a fortified village in Central Hebei. The guerrilla team managed to plant incriminating evidence on him; he was arrested by his superiors, while the real infiltrators enjoyed a reprieve from suspicion. An official border region source explicitly recommended frameups as second best to assassinations.[74]

Counterrepression thus significantly limited the effectiveness of contingent repression, either by reducing the collaborators' willingness to practice it or by turning Japanese repression against its own agents. It was not an effective weapon against generalized repression, and there is no indication that the border region attempted to use it as such.

Reducing Provocation. Reducing provocation was also effective in counteracting contingent repression. In resistance warfare this was commonly done by switching to other types of activities. A variety of schemes were used; their effectiveness is attested to by the Japanese Army's drastic underestimation of the border region's strength before the Hundred Regiments offensive. The Eighth Route Army's response to the railroad-cherishing policy is a good example of the technique. In the early months of the war, guerrilla units from western Hebei ordinarily approached the Ping-Han railroad in order to sabotage it, to attack a train or a station, or to launch an attack somewhere near the railway in Central Hebei. At the time, the Japanese had too few troops to punish ineffective railroad-cherishing villages. By the time they did have enough troops, it was more important to the guerrilla forces to penetrate deeper into Central Hebei than to sabotage communications or stage attacks along the way. They therefore sent advance scouts to these villages to explain that they would be just passing through. Usually they were permitted to pass unreported, and the villages' collusion went unnoticed.[75]

A second method of reducing provocation was to limit the number of fronts on which the border region had to fight. Basically this meant compromising with the traditional local elite to reduce opposition from within. The classic instance of such a compromise was the across-the-board moderation of socioeconomic and political reform policies that began in late 1939 and early 1940 and continued through late 1942 and early 1943. These included the provision of some palliative measures in the rent and interest reduction regulations, and the implementation of the three-thirds system of government, which reopened a place in formal governmental power to the rural ''moderates.'' The absence of many striking manifestations of elite discontent like those seen in late 1939 seems to indicate that these measures did work.[76]

The degree of moderation was keyed to the level of security in any given area. The approach was used by mid–1939 in eastern Hebei, where it had been impossible to maintain local resistance organization until the elite were placated. An Eighth Route Army cadre reported later that year that links between the guerrillas and the upper classes had been improved as one means of withstanding the Japanese "clearing the countryside" (*qingxiang*) methods. Guerrillas guaranteed the basic livelihood and property rights of the elite, maintained "social order," and refrained from harming the elite's basic interests. In more secure border region areas the moderate approach was pursued in earnest only after mid–1940.[77] Even as the party began to gear up for a more radical policy line in late 1942, its North China policy distinctly subordinated the reform policies to the interests of "unity against the enemy" in areas still subjected to the fortified Japanese grid.[78] The reasoning was clear: an elite threatened by reform programs in these areas could too easily provide the Japanese with enough information to eliminate *all* border region organization.

Thus policy moderation allowed the border region to avoid direct and devastating repression on more than one front. But it opened the door to landlord initiatives to force even greater concessions, especially in rent reduction. Therefore, although moderation helped to forestall elite attacks on cadres, it did not prevent their pressuring individual peasants.

Concealment. The third and final type of measure used to decrease the potential for repression was to conceal the targets. One obvious example of this tactic was the policy of "strong bulwarks, clear fields" in general use during the Japanese extermination campaigns.[79] Here, however, I will emphasize a method of concealment so effective that it is still generally overlooked. This was the guerrilla cell, a form expressly designed by the party to get the bases and guerrilla areas through the hard times brought by extermination campaigns. All party members and mass organization or government cadres were expected to arm and organize to defend themselves. They were to begin operating in groups of three to five persons, and to expand from that nucleus into larger forces. By the time that the Three Alls was in full swing, the greater part of these groups were led by the village CCP branch, and the majority of their members were party members or activist youths.[80] These groups were supposed to conduct activities in support of the whole range of border region policies, to help maintain mass morale as regular army forces withdrew, and to act as growth nodes for organizing militia to resist Japanese occupying forces locally.

The crucial importance of effective underground organization in providing a bulwark against the total collapse of resistance organizations is suggested by a Japanese intelligence report on the effects of extermination campaigns in eastern Central Hebei. This report compared the relative strength of resistance organizations in Hejian and Yongqing counties. Hejian had much the longer history of Eighth Route Army presence, political and socioeconomic reforms, and active resistance organizations. Yongqing's village governments were just being set up in late 1939, and only three of six reporting districts mentioned having accomplished any rent and interest reduction work. Yet it was in Yongqing and not in Hejian that the Japanese were finding resistance organizations more resilient against attack.[81]

Why? One would have expected Hejian to fare better, if past reforms or past Japanese repression explained the strength of border region local organizations. The explanation lies in the different organizational experience of the two counties. Hejian's organizing had started under fairly secure military conditions, and its activists, party members, and cadres had been out in the open, well known within their villages for what they were. When Lü Zhengcao's forces withdrew from the county, they left the local activists wide open to attack by Japanese forces or to retaliation by the traditional elite. Yongqing, on the other hand, having started organizing later and under much less favorable conditions, had had the opportunity to build secret cores of activists paralleling its open organizations.

Later party writings were to stress the crucial nature of such concealment efforts at the very outset of organizing. The better part of the January 1942 issue of the North China party periodical *Jianchi* (Perseverance) seems to have been devoted to outlining and stressing the importance of techniques of paramilitary organization under militarily disadvantageous conditions. Several of the articles included admonitions favoring early concealment measures, principally through the guerrilla cell form.[82]

One obvious contradiction in the role envisioned for the guerrilla cells must be noted. These were, on the one hand, organizational forms for taking the resistance underground; they were intended as concealment mechanisms. Yet, on the other hand, if they were to maintain resistance work and expand their membership, they had to remain active and thus reveal their existence. Many of the cells, facing this dilemma in the crisis situation brought about by the Three Alls campaign, seemed able at most only to practice some effective counterrepression against puppets and collaborators and keep themselves alive as an organizational nucleus for a time when the Japanese military presence might diminish.[83] Others remained hidden from the Japanese by melting into the general populace. A few cells, operating with only a handful of young stalwarts, conducted some daring—but limited—actions that gained them considerable local notoriety (and a few new recruits) among their fellow peasants. The sources suggest that the degree of openness in operation was determined by the relative security of any given area.[84]

Of the above methods, the provocation reduction worked most effectively against Japanese contingent repression; the compromise, against the rural elite's contingent repression of cadres; and concealment, against both generalized Japanese repression and contingent repression by elites or Japanese. Effective as they were in these respects, they were largely stopgap measures that might reduce the damage inflicted by repression but could not themselves reverse the tide in favor of the border region. Turning the tide required additional, largely psychological measures.

Reducing Demands for Heroism

One error in mass mobilization strategy committed by the CCP, most glaringly but not exclusively apparent in the Hundred Regiments Offensive, was to call on its supporters to run great risks for the sake of great victories. It was impossible to win great victories in one stroke against the Japanese military machine. When the inevitable Japanese reaction arrived, the result was loss of heart and loss of willingness to act on the part of those who had been so heroic—and so unsuccessful—shortly before.

The solution, used by the border region throughout the middle period, was to reduce both the demands for action and the promises of victories. The watchword was small promises, small rewards; large promises, no rewards. The tactic was applied to a wide variety of constituencies and in numerous concrete approaches. I will note just two specific examples by way of illustration.

The first was the border region's changed stance toward Chinese cooperation with puppet organs in occupied areas. Originally, the border region had taken an uncompromising attitude on the question of collaboration: anyone participating in a puppet organization was a traitor; hoodwinked or weak, perhaps, but a traitor nonetheless. During the middle period this attitude changed, and the border region accepted the existence of "double-sided" governments, which cooperated with the Japanese by day and the border region by night. More-over, it even encouraged its own activists to infiltrate puppet organizations so as to subvert them. At a point when the border region's ability to threaten these organizations directly was sharply on the wane, the change in policy made it possible to turn the puppet organizations themselves to good account. The policy permitted sympathizers to do a little bit for the resistance cause at fairly small risk—collect a little tax grain, help hide a few guerrillas for the day—rather than presenting them with the choice of doing a great deal (an all-out struggle) at enormous risk (to the death), or doing nothing at all. As the insistence on all-or-nothing gains for the border region increasingly promised to yield nothing, even something-gains were very welcome and helped sustain the border region's access to needed assistance in areas that otherwise would have fallen exclusively under Japanese control. The policy did work, to the extent that, in one area of Central Hebei, an explicit modus vivendi was worked out between puppet and resistance governments.[85]

The double-sided policy helped to undermine the reliability of Japanese intelligence, the essential underpinning of contingent repression. Defectors might begin to hedge their bets; even those with apparently impeccable quisling credentials might be underground party members assigned to infiltration work. Puppets stationed in their native areas might number relatives or friends among local resistance activists (while puppets stationed outside their native areas were as ineffective in acquiring information as they were adept at alienating the locals).[86]

The only assured proof of genuine collaboration was assassination by the border region, but such certificates of loyalty were of little use to the Japanese. The double-sided policy decidedly worked rather one-sidedly to the border region's advantage.

The second example of demand reduction pertains to the paramilitary and guerrilla forces. Early in the war, the need for demand reduction vis-à-vis the military recruiting system was sharply evident, as the desertion rates cited earlier suggest. Jin-Cha-Ji by early 1940 was being held up as a model for getting locally recruited guerrillas to enlist in, and stay in, regular army units stationed far from their villages. The usual political hortatory approach here had been supplemented by measures asking less of recruits' selfless fervor: ensuring that friends, relatives, or schoolmates were assigned to the same units, and incorporating local guerrilla units only gradually into regular army units, transferring them first from the district to the county level, and from there to the military subregional level. Such measures had helped stem the flood of desertions that had usually followed troop transfers.[87] Only about sixteen months later, however, as the Three Alls began building up, one of the principal Eighth Route Army political commissars in Central Hebei stressed a new slogan for the local armed forces: ''The county [forces] don't leave the county; the district [forces] don't leave the district.'' This, he argued, would sustain local forces' morale for fighting the enemy.[88] In short, in a time of intense military pressure, the closer to home the soldiers felt they would stay, the more reliable they would be.

For most of the middle period of the war, the policy of demand reduction applied even more to the guerrilla cells discussed earlier. Since these groups were designed to operate under conditions of extreme adversity, one might think that heroic efforts would be expected of them. Not so, or at least not immediately. It was more important to the border region that the guerrilla cells persist and continue to gather members than that they perform tasks that had already proved impossible for the regular and large guerrilla forces. The guerrilla cells had to be treated very gently and presented only with those tasks for which there was a reasonable certainty of completion. Small successes would gather more activists and more confidence for the next round, but the leadership always had to be careful not to ask more of the members than they were ready to deliver, or their confidence and activism would drop dangerously.[89] Moreover, the demand reductions applied to more than merely battlefield matters. The Central Hebei guerrilla cells and militia, for example, were not supposed to be ''divorced from production''—that is, they were to receive no recompense for the time and blood lost in protecting the villages. But during their early stages of formation, these paramilitary groups had been eating as much tax grain in Central Hebei as the entire Central Hebei Third Guerrilla Battalion. The first attempts to remedy the situation created enormous problems for local self-defense; with the source of food cut off, many of the militia put away their weapons and went home. Finally, a solution was worked out: the militia and guerrilla cells protected the masses from the Japanese, and the masses, in ''gratitude,'' voluntarily provided food for their saviors. Suddenly guerrilla cells' activism improved.[90]

Demand reduction was used throughout the border region in a multitude of forms. It did not produce spectacular victories, and it is perhaps for this reason that it has been so generally overlooked in analyses of the period. What it did produce was numerous small, local toeholds for the border region's activities and organizations, and a slowly growing core of increasingly experienced and bold activists who were to provide the foundations for the spectacular reexpansion of the border region in the final two years of the war.

Providing a Climate for Mass Activism: Making Little Heroes

This brings us to the final major tactic involved in the border region's implicit strategy against repression. It pertains primarily to the middle period of the war, when mass morale had declined to such a low ebb that it was almost impossible to rely on village organizations to get any policies implemented. Yet policies were implemented: tax grain was collected in greater amounts than ever before, rent reduction was actually launched for the first time in some areas, elections for new village governments were held, and resistance was maintained on an extensive if not an intensive scale. How was this possible if morale and activism were so low?

The answer is decidedly not that the border region managed to accomplish sustained mass mobilization. What it did achieve was mobilization of an intense but temporary nature, in which energies were raised to a suddenly high pitch, the village was suffused with a flush of optimism, and policies were in effect almost before anyone knew what had happened.

The successful method was new neither to the Communist movement nor to the middle period of the war, but it was used at an unprecedented level during those years of greatest difficulty. It was termed "blitzkrieg."[91] The blitzkrieg approach was based on two principles: first, the best time for seeking success was when another success had just been won, and second, doing everything at once took less energy and yielded faster results than doing things one by one. Ordinarily the process worked as follows. A blitzkrieg team from the district, county, or even subregional government, party, and mass organizations gathered, investigated conditions in the target village, devised a work plan, and moved into the village to launch mobilization for the implementation of policies. If the village was in an enemy-occupied or guerrilla area, the team often timed its arrival either to follow hard on the heels of a military victory nearby or to coincide with concentrated attacks upon surrounding enemy base points so as to take advantage of increased resistance optimism or local security. The team organized mass meetings, reorganized party, mass organization, and governmental bodies, and held tax assessment and collection assemblies and rent reduction meetings. Usually these efforts were successful in achieving their immediate objectives, and when the team left a few days later the village had all the trappings of a successful resistance and reform mobilization.[92]

The importance of prior success—particularly of recent military successes—in providing mass support was noted very early by the organizers in North China. It was not that people always chose the side that was winning, but that few would ever join a side they thought was losing. Even early in the war, a victory on the battlefield was generally considered the necessary first step in organizing. Here is how one of the CCP's leading military affairs cadres assessed the contribution of victories to success in early 1940: "Among the guerrilla units which we have organized, there is a saying generally current, 'victory decides everything.' That is to say, no matter how difficult it has been to recruit troops, supply the army, raise the masses' anti-Japanese fervor, or win over the masses' sympathy or help, after a victory in battle the masses all fall all over themselves to send us flour, steamed bread, meat, and vegetables; the masses' pessimistic and defeatist psychology is smashed, and many new guerrilla soldiers swarm in."[93]

One vividly detailed account of a successful blitzkrieg was given in an official BRG periodical in late 1941.[94] The fifth district of the newly drawn Shu-Ji county (parts of Shulu and Ji counties) in Central Hebei had been established in January 1941 as an area targeted by the county leadership to be taken back from under Japanese occupation. The effort began with a blitzkrieg in all but name: attacks on Japanese base points and communications, followed by the reform of village governments, anticorruption struggles, reform of village finances, and an "educational" effort that won the "masses" away from the local puppet-dominated Big Knives organization. Thereafter, however, village and district cadres had made "extreme-leftist" and "coercive" errors, and work came to a virtual standstill in the district. To remedy this situation, a blitzkrieg was planned for the "green curtain" season.[95] County-level organs and the county guerrilla corps coordinated for a "ferocious" blitzkrieg of the district. When they arrived in the district they called a conference of all cadres, discussed the question of work style and right and left deviations, and planned the "form and content for a good blitzkrieg." The blitzkrieg resulted in the purge of several villages' cadres, elimination of village puppet organs and of those maintaining liaison with puppet organizations, and the reestablishment or recovery of ten elementary schools. In three villages rent and interest reduction was conducted and the Unified Progressive Tax (a more sophisticated method than the reasonable burden) was collected. Fourteen villages collected the reasonable burden. Local paramilitary forces were formed and repeatedly attacked the local highway; the puppet garrisons of the district's two base points were afraid to sally forth to combat them. The results of this blitzkrieg were summarized: "Of the whole district's forty villages, we have already reformed nine; there are twenty-three in which we can conduct work and thirty-six in which we can hold meetings."

The same periodical issue features another, similarly cheery account of a successful blitzkrieg inspection of one village's work, a description of how a blitzkrieg campaign to level blockade ditches was coordinated with tax collections in Xingtang county, and an account entitled "The Failure of the [Blitzkrieg] Inspection in X Village" (success here pertaining only to immediate results).[96] Obviously the blitzkrieg was in frequent use; these detailed accounts all offered general pointers for successful conduct of a blitzkrieg campaign. At around the same time that this periodical appeared, a high border region cadre was complaining that the blitzkrieg had become the normal work for many areas, even in base areas.[97]

Ideally, the sudden jump in morale that made it possible to begin organizing, usually with the use of blitzkrieg teams, should have been necessary only once. After the "situation" was "opened," the newly formed governments, mass associations, and paramilitary groups should have been able to keep the villages at a steady simmer of activism. The sources do indicate that the blitzkrieg method could provide very useful immediate gains, in both mass morale and human and material resources available to the border region. However, the method was intended to break a psychological and organizational bottleneck so that border region organizations and policies could continue on normal lines within the village, but the principal long-term effect seems to have been that the use of blitzkrieg tactics became habitual. Strong continuing organizations were not formed, and continued doses of blitzkrieg tactics were needed to perform the necessary work of local resistance governments. Consequently the border region did not achieve the widespread and deep mass mobilization that was the preferred organizational result of this tactic. Nevertheless, there was a good reason why it continued in use: in some areas it produced just about the only results the border region could hope for other than those that were within the power of a few staunch local activists to provide.

Conclusion

By late 1934, the Jiangxi Soviet had experienced some four years of land redistribution, village elections, and mass organizing. There, with a population of approximately three million, the Communist Party managed to muster an army of one hundred thousand who embarked on the Long March to the Northwest. In 1942, the Jin-Cha-Ji Border Region had experienced four years of rent and interest reduction, progressive taxation, village elections, and mass organizing. There, with a population numbering somewhere between six and ten million, the party had a hard time finding a hundred thousand people willing to march into the next county. The Jiangxi Soviet collapsed. Jin-Cha-Ji survived. Success and victory are not necessarily coterminous.

Jin-Cha-Ji during the Resistance War did not represent an overwhelming victory for the CCP. Just as Steven Levine finds the margin of victory slender in Manchuria, so I have found it slender in the earlier period. The party in Manchuria chose a strategy of maximizing its (poor) peasant support in order to beat the margin. In Jin-Cha-Ji the more complex social environment and the united front strategy of resistance ruled out the radical programs that might have created more intense support and more reliable activism among the poorest strata.[98] There, the strategic choice was not to maximize poor peasant support but to minimize the negative effects of repression on the limited activism among different strata of the peasantry that could be generated by milder policies.

Here I do not mean to suggest that the border region's handling of repression provides a central explanation of the party's success or of Japanese defeat. My larger study of Jin-Cha-Ji provides a more complete explanation that investigates the role of numerous policies and organizations in building revolutionary power. Yet while the handling of repression may not be central to an explanation of Communist success, it is still essential. It provides an explanation on the margin, but where the margin of victory is slim, marginal explanations become crucial.

It might be objected that this essay, by breaking off just as the heyday of mass activism and border region expansion was on the horizon, does not convey an accurate picture of the process of the Chinese revolution during the Resistance War. What of the final period of the war, with the *zhengfeng* campaign, the production movements, the growth of mutual aid organizations within the villages, the more thorough execution of rent reduction? My answer is that although these factors have established the lingering image of the period, they did not *cause* the Japanese defeat; they were made possible by the onset of that defeat. The Japanese occupation strategy had basically failed by 1943,[99] and after that date Japan's activities in North China constituted largely a holding operation as the imperial armies fought viciously on other fronts.

What conclusions, then, can be drawn concerning the interaction of repression and response in the years from 1938 to 1943? The first relates to the uses of and solutions to contingent repression, the second to the matter of generalized repression, and the third to the issue of successful repression of a revolutionary movement.

The evidence suggests that in the first two years of the war, the border region was fairly successful in reducing the effects of contingent repression, so long as the Japanese capacity to apply that repression was confined to a limited territory. The border region's success in countering this repression hinged, in the final analysis, on its ability to avoid Japanese attention to particular targets. The minimal cooperation needed from the population of the guerrilla and occupied areas lessened their vulnerability as Japanese targets and therefore permitted the border region to continue securing that necessary minimal cooperation—silence on Eighth Route Army movements, information on Japanese movements, noncombatant support during battles, and so forth. The border region was in fact practicing an extended end-run around contingent repression in these areas. But as the Japanese extended the points-and-lines system, the situation developed into a strategic crisis for border region development: it was fast reaching the point where there were no more locales where contingent repression could be avoided. Ultimately the only way for the resistance forces to counteract Japanese contingent repression in this environment was to stop resisting, unless a breakthrough could be achieved.

The breakthrough, although it was not of the sort intended when Hundred Regiments was planned, was in part military and in part organizational. Militarily, the Japanese were provoked into a mop-up strategy of generalized repression which necessitated drawing troops away from many fortified points in order to attack an area of border region strength. In resorting to such measures, the Japanese put themselves precisely in the position in which Mao's strategy of protracted guerrilla warfare was designed to defeat them: a prolonged war of attrition in which, by moving to attack in one area, they weakened their troop strength in another area and rendered their supply position difficult everywhere. The Japanese practice of generalized repression became a bottomless pit into which they had to pile more manpower and more resources just to gain enough to sustain themselves.

With the threat of contingent repression temporarily removed in those occupied areas, guerrilla forces moved in and acted as both military and psychological umbrellas beneath which border region organizers could conduct elections, collect taxes, and mobilize military recruits. This strategy kept the Japanese running from one part of the landscape to another, always somewhat effectively repressing in one area (forcing resistance activism into quiescence) but never able to sit still long enough to use methods of contingent repression to extract the roots of that resistance. In this regard, it was not important for the border region that resistance be massive and constant in all areas. It was rather the ability to shift constantly from one pocket of active resistance to another to another that made its guerrilla war strategy successful. [100]

It is in this respect that the organizational breakthrough of the border region was so important. I consider that the use of the blitzkrieg method of mobilization and of the guerrilla cells was of vital importance in maintaining the border region's capacity to move back quickly into areas temporarily left nearly undefended by the Japanese, and to accomplish the necessary high (though short-lived) levels of mobilization. Far more work must be done on the uses of both these organizational methods and their relationship to each other before we can fully understand how resistance was successfully maintained.

Finally, we reach the issue that is of most significance to students of the revolutionary process in hindsight but was a crucial area of foresight for the revolutionaries. Could repression have defeated the revolution in North China? The record indicates that the CCP leadership thought it could, and was counting from the outset on the Japanese inability to notice the magnitude of threat posed by early resistance in their rear, or to recognize the only efficacious way of dealing with it. That would have been to counter with massive, focused repression against all pockets of resistance within the first year of the war.

Japanese repression, aided by repression exercised by the traditional rural elite, was extremely effective in curtailing the power of the border region, which had to rely on mass activism for any substantial growth in that power. If the Japanese had turned upon the embryonic resistance forces very early, when their numbers were still small and their local roots tenuous,[101] the results would have been fatal to the revolutionaries. The Communist Party leaders themselves recognized this danger and depended upon the Japanese focusing their military might on the battles further south to provide revolutionary forces with the necessary breathing space in which to spread out, sink local roots, and begin recruiting large numbers of partisans in preparation for the first sustained Japanese attack upon them. There is a sense of urgency in the documents on organizing during this period that is compelling when we keep these facts in mind. Expansion over large areas as quickly as possible was what mattered; quantity of adherents rather than quality. The Japanese reaction would sift out the chaff from these forces, and what counted for the revolutionaries was to have gathered enough followers beforehand that there would be something left after the sifting.

This is not to say that revolutionary movements could never take root in a setting in which repression was an immediate danger. It is crucial to note, however, that with the policy constraints within which the Communist Party had to operate at the time, the quick-expansion strategy was probably the only one that could have worked.[99] The effect, once that expansion succeeded, was to tie the Japanese down over a large stretch of territory and embroil them in a situation in which, in order to practice repression on one front, they had to relax vigilance on another, and the resistance forces grew in the interstices between repressive incidents. That they did not grow more, or more rapidly, that they did not develop the sustained mass activism for which they were always striving, is no fault of the revolutionaries and ultimately of no great moment. They survived, they built the infrastructure for later expansion and greater success, and they won.

5

Nationalist Guerrillas in the Sino-Japanese War: The "Die-Hards" of Shandong Province

DAVID M. PAULSON

Many journalistic and historical accounts have praised Chinese Communist guerrilla resistance to the Japanese invasion of 1937–1945, but the Nationalist guerrilla effort remains an obscure and largely unknown chapter of the history of this period. This essay examines the Nationalist guerrilla campaign in the area where it was most vigorous, Shandong province. I draw on new sources from both the Communist and Nationalist sides to analyze factors contributing to its ultimate failure, including charges of Nationalist collaboration with the Japanese, internal divisions in the Guomindang camp, and the lack of popular support for the Nationalist guerrilla effort. Finally I suggest reasons why this chapter of the war has remained in the shadows of modern Chinese history.

Collaboration: Origins of the "Crooked Path to National Salvation"

In the first year and a half of the Sino-Japanese War, as Chiang Kai-shek's armies fought conventional battles against the Japanese invader, guerrilla war held no prominent place in Nationalist strategy. After the fall of Wuhan and the Nationalist retreat into the interior, however, Chiang's thinking began to take a new direction. In response to Japanese Prime Minister Konoye's statement of 22 December 1938, which broadened Japanese objectives in China, the Generalissimo directed that "political efforts outweigh military efforts, guerrilla warfare outweigh conventional warfare, and the enemy rear be turned into the front line." By the spring of 1939 Chiang divided front-line areas in Hebei-Chahar and Shandong-Jiangsu into guerrilla districts and assigned units to conduct guerrilla warfare.[1] From this time the central government elevated guerrilla warfare to strategic significance.

Although Nationalist historians stress the function of their guerrillas in "wearing out the enemy and tying down his main forces," there was a second side to their activities. As the central government withdrew to Chongqing, Chiang Kai-shek began to see the implications of Communist expansion behind Japanese lines in North China and the lower Yangzi valley. Having already rashly sanctioned the creation of the Communist Jin-Cha-Ji administration during the early cooperative stage of the united front, Chiang turned around and introduced measures to limit Communist expansion.

In the March 1939 Fifth Guomindang Congress a document called "Measures to Restrict Alien Party Activities" (*xianzhi yidang huodong banfa*) circulated, and the central government began to apply political pressure to curb "illegal" Communist expansion. By the November 1939 Sixth Guomindang Congress military measures were stressed over political ones.[2] The Nationalist guerrillas were given an ambiguously defined mission to curb Communist activities. From this time they took part in a series of bloody clashes which the Communists called "friction struggles" (*moca douzheng*). Gradually this second mission came to assume greater priority than anti-Japanese resistance for the Nationalist guerrillas.

Shandong was one of the major collision points in the hidden war between Nationalist and Communist guerrillas. At first the Nationalists greatly outnumbered their rivals. At the start of the war, after Shandong's governor took to his heels and the Japanese defeated Nationalist armies at Xuzhou, small guerrilla forces proliferated. By one estimate, more than 260 self-appointed guerrilla commanders appeared on the scene.[3] The proliferation of guerrilla bands is shown by a Japanese intelligence map depicting Chinese guerrilla forces on the peninsula in December 1939 (map 5.1).

The local guerrillas were nurtured by Shandong's long-standing tradition of local militarization and the presence of disbanded soldiers whom Japan had expelled from the Northeast in 1932. Their leaders were of diverse backgrounds, running the gamut from retired military officers, students and teachers, local security officers, and militia captains to secret society chieftains, landlord bullies, and soldier-bandits.

Map 5.1. **Japanese North China Area Army Showing Guerrillas on Shandong Peninsula.**

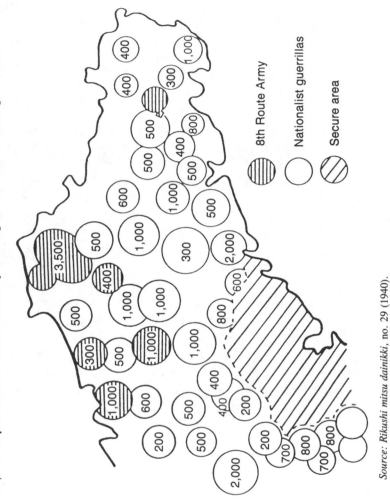

8th Route Army

Nationalist guerrillas

Secure area

Source: Rikushi mitsu dainikki, no. 29 (1940).
Note: Numbers in circles are estimated troop strengths of guerrilla forces.

A desire for legitimacy, prestige, and material gain led the overwhelming majority of them to accept offers of military titles from the central government.

Before guerrilla resistance became part of the Guomindang's strategic plan, the task of coordinating the local guerrillas was left to leaders from its two intelligence organizations. The first, Qin Qirong, a Shandongese graduate of the Whampoa Military Academy, recruited for the Guomindang military intelligence organization. The truculently anti-Communist Qin had made underground preparations before the Japanese invasion, and by 1938 his loosely organized Fifth Column claimed to lead as many as 300,000 local guerrillas.[4] The second, the urbane former mayor of Qingdao, Admiral Shen Honglie, recruited for the civilian intelligence organization under Chen Lifu. He led about 2,000 marines from Qingdao, the former governor's "pistol brigade," and thirty peace preservation forces (*baoandui*) claiming as many as 150,000 men.[5]

Both of these men recruited indiscriminately, even granting titles to notorious soldier-bandits. The Communists lampooned the Nationalist policy as "Anyone with guns and men can serve as a commander."[6] Still, although the uneven quality of the numerous guerrillas vitiated their effectiveness, they did succeed in preempting spontaneous mobilization in the province. The Eighth Route Army's Shandong Column, which was also formed locally at the same time, was vastly outnumbered, with only about thirty thousand men by late 1938, and had to act cautiously in the face of Nationalist pressure in the first eighteen months of the war.[7]

Chiang Kai-shek elevated guerrilla war to strategic significance in the spring of 1938, introducing regular armies to supplement the indigenous guerrillas in Shandong. The regulars were led by the Shandong-Jiangsu War District Commander Yu Xuezhong, with Shen Honglie as nominal vice-commander. In Shandong and Jiangsu together, Yu led a regular army of about fifty thousand men from the former Northeast Army. The 51st and 57th corps, made up of the 111th, 112th, 113th, and 114th divisions, were permanently stationed in the mountains of southern Shandong.[8] Since these troops were better trained and equipped than any of their allies or rivals, they appeared to be a serious threat to any Eighth Route Army expansion.

At the same time that these forces moved in and the central government began promoting its anti-Communist containment policy, the Communist Party center responded with new initiatives of its own. A

December 1939 order from the Central Secretariat observed: "The regions in which we can, at present, expand our armed forces, are limited principally to Shandong and Central China." Mao instructed his Shandong forces to embark on expansion on a huge scale. By the end of 1940, the Eighth Route Army's 115th Division was ordered to recruit at least 150,000 men and organize 1.5 to 2 million peasants into its auxiliary militia in Shandong alone.[9]

This instruction recognized that such large armed forces could not be created without a "process of serious struggle" and "political power." Since most of the territory behind Japanese lines was occupied by the Nationalist guerrillas, they were the main obstacle to this expansion. The instruction stated explicitly, "We must strike back at any reactionary forces or die-hard factions which obstruct the development of progressive anti-Japanese forces, and which launch attacks against us." Mao calculated that these "reactionary forces" and "die-hards" could be removed one by one through the means of cooptation and limited military conflict.

To provide the muscle to achieve these aims, in the spring of 1939 regular units of the Eighth Route Army raced into Shandong. In March parts of the 343d and 686th regiments of the 115th Division shifted from southern Hebei to western Shandong. Led by acting commander Luo Ronghuan, in June they moved to set up their headquarters in the mountains of southern Shandong. In the same summer Xu Xiangqian also led two regiments from his 129th Division in from Hebei. He proceeded to reorganize the native Shandong Column into regular brigades and assumed unified command of all Eighth Route Army forces in the Shandong sector. After the Eighth Route Army threw down this challenge, the contest for military and political supremacy began. Map 5.2 shows the disposition of the largest Guomindang and Communist military units in Shandong in July 1940.

A complex series of seesaw military clashes unfolded, as the Communist and Nationalist guerrillas were locked in a confused pattern that Mao compared to "dog's teeth gnashed together." While spurring his own guerrillas on, Mao vehemently protested alleged Nationalist violations of the united front and branded Qin Qirong a "friction specialist" (*moca zhuanjia*). He charged that the "Taihe incident," in which one of Qin's units laid a carefully planned ambush and executed about 200 cadres of the Shandong Column, was typical of Nationalist aggression. One Communist history claims that from June to December 1939, the Shandong Column lost 1,243 men fighting the Japanese, and 2,162

Map 5.2. **Japanese North China Area Army Showing Disposition of Major Anti-Japanese Forces, July 1940.**

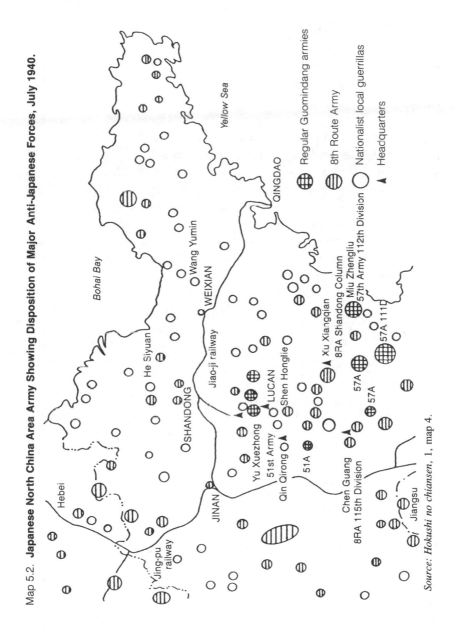

Source: Hokushi no chiansen, 1, map 4.

(including those captured) defending themselves against the Nationalist guerrillas. The same source alleges that in 1940 the Nationalists
halted their opposition to Japan completely and inflicted more casualties on the Eighth Route Army than did the Japanese "mopping-up"
campaigns.[10]

On the other side the central government's intelligence organs exhaustively recorded cases of alleged "illegal" attacks on Nationalist
units and claimed that its guerrillas were only acting in self-defense.[11]
Whichever side was the aggressor, in the course of these complicated
localized military clashes Nationalist strength steadily declined. By the
end of 1940 the Eighth Route Army had succeeded in eliminating about
half of the local peace preservation forces.[12] Nonetheless, the Eighth
Route Army fell far short of achieving the expansion Mao had demanded. As late as August 1941 the Shandong 115th Division could claim
only eighty thousand soldiers.[13]

Part of the explanation lies in the political realm. As Yu Xuezhong
sat on the sidelines, Shen and Qin were partially successful in preventing the Eighth Route Army from winning "dominant political power"
in Shandong, and in obstructing the development of the CCP's administrative and mass organizations. They used heavy-handed methods
against Communist cadres, including assassination and live burial, to
disband Communist organizations. At the same time they spread rumors to counteract the Eighth Route Army's propaganda. These rumors charged, in a play on the word "guerrilla" (*youji*), that the
"Eighth Route Army roves but does not fight" (*you er bu ji*). They
claimed that the "Eighth Route Army's anti-Japanese democratic regimes are illegal organizations. They are the same as soviets." They
complained that the Eighth Route Army's mass organizations were
"reddening the masses" and played on the fear that it would "commu-
nize property and wives."[14]

Due to this violence and political interference, the Eighth Route
Army could not guarantee enough security in Shandong to enforce its
rent and interest reduction policy. The development of its local infrastructure lagged about two years behind the Jin-Cha-Ji border region to
the north. In November 1940 Xu Xiangqian remarked to a journalist
that the development of the resistance in Shandong was "uneven."
Shandong was "still not a consolidated base area."[15]

The bitter conflict described above was the context within which the
Eighth Route Army began making charges of Nationalist collaboration
with the enemy. These charges pertained to Guomindang activities at

all levels in Shandong. In August 1940 Communist forces under Xu Xiangqian attacked the headquarters of the provincial government at Lucun in the central Shandong district. Nationalist sources claim that Xu's aim was to expel Shen Honglie's administration from the province.[16] On the other hand, Communist sources contend that this battle was fought in response to Nationalist provocation: the Eighth Route Army attacked Lucun in protest over Shen's alleged collaboration with the Japanese and attacks on Communist forces. After the Eighth Route Army occupied Lucun, Xu asked Yu Xuezhong to mediate. Shen used the hiatus to contact a friendly Japanese officer and persuade him to dislodge Xu's forces from his headquarters.[17]

Whether in response to Shen's request or by coincidence, the Japanese Army did attack Lucun shortly after this incident. After expelling the Eighth Route Army it withdrew. Shen returned to his original headquarters. Thus the Communist-Nationalist rivalry in the first phase ended in a hostile stalemate.

Guomindang collaboration might also take more direct forms. Eighth Route Army sources alleged that Chiang sent out a vaguely worded directive instructing his guerrillas to "act expediently according to conditions at a certain time and place" (*yinshi yindishi zhi yi*). In a speech to his cadre training school in 1939, Shen is alleged to have interpreted this as meaning, "To lose to the Japanese is only in form and temporary; to lose to the Communists is real and permanent," and "There are no traitors behind Japanese lines." Shen encouraged local guerrilla units to form "mutual nonaggression, joint anti-Communist" agreements with local Japanese garrisons. Some of his units sent men to join puppet forces and formed two-sided "heir to two family" (*jiantiao*) relationships with them. There was substance to these charges, and the way in which these relationships were formed has been described in at least one Nationalist guerrilla's memoirs.[18]

This form of collaboration existed early in the war, but it became especially widespread after the outbreak of the Pacific War. Now some units began to consider taking a step beyond mere exchanges of troops, to accepting puppet designations. As early as the spring of 1940 Japanese reports show that some of the larger Nationalist armies were already wavering. In Shandong, units in contact with the Japanese Army and seen as potential defectors were Yu Xuezhong's 57th Army under Miu Zengliu, and the 69th Corps under Shi Yousan. The southern Anhui New Fourth Army incident caused more wavering on the Nationalist side, and in January 1941 the Japanese Army reported that

Table 5.1

Nationalist and Puppet Troops in Shandong

Year	1940	1941	1942	1943
Puppet troops	80,000	122,000	155,000	180,000
Nationalist troops	166,000	120,000	80,000	30,000[a]
Total	246,000	242,000	235,000	210,000

Source: *Kangri zhanzheng shiqi jiefangqu gaikuang*, p. 90.
a. Including West Shandong, this figure would have been 50,000.

Yu himself was making "longing glances" to its side.[19]

The outbreak of the Pacific War was a decisive turning point in the attitudes of Nationalist commanders. At first the Nationalist guerrillas hoped for a rapid end to the war, and many puppet armies wavered or defected to the Nationalist or Communist side.[20] But as soon as it became apparent that the war would not end quickly, a defeatist mood set in. The idea of allowing their forces to be "temporarily" incorporated into Japanese puppet armies became more attractive to Nationalist commanders.

By 1943 when the tide of the war had clearly turned in favor of the Allies, Nationalist commanders saw that lenient terms for defection would permit them to stay in their home bases and wait for Allied victory. When victory came, they could help the Central Army to recover the province. They could claim that Guomindang intelligence organizations had authorized their puppetization in the first place, and they could point to their wartime opposition to the Communists to argue that, all along, they had merely been taking the "crooked path to national salvation."

This phenomenon was especially common in Shandong. Communist sources point to Nationalist defections as the explanation for the pattern of change in the ratio of Nationalist to puppet troops (see table 5.1). By mid–1943 this province had more puppet troops than any other province of North China.[21] These defections, besides damaging the morale of Nationalist guerrillas who remained true to the anti-Japanese cause, also made it difficult for them to survive. The defection of the provincial government's New Fourth Division in January 1943 robbed it of its main force. Its commander used his knowledge of the defense plans of the Shandong-Jiangsu War District to join in devastating Japanese attacks on its forces.[22] In another case, it was the defection of a subordinate of Yu Xuezhong that cost him twenty thousand men and forced the Shandong-Jiangsu War District forces to withdraw from the province in July 1943.[23]

After the withdrawal of Yu Xuezhong's regular army and the provincial government, the remaining local guerrillas were left without any center of leadership for two years. Virtually all were forced to compromise with the Japanese Army in order to survive. Even as puppet troops, however, these former Guomindang units continued to delay Communist expansion. Fighting between the Eighth Route Army and the puppet troops continued to the end of the war and was particularly intense in the spring of 1945 when an Allied landing on the coast seemed imminent. Even to the very end of the war, local resistance to the Eighth Route Army obstructed it from conquering all of the Shandong countryside.[24]

When the Japanese surrender came in August 1945, the two-sided guerrillas played out their last part in the Communist-Nationalist rivalry. Shandong Eighth Route Army Commander Luo Ronghuan ordered his armies to accept the surrender from the Japanese and to recover the towns and transport lines. Included within his objectives were the major cities of Jinan and Qingdao.[25] The two-sided guerrillas played an important role in the revanchist mission of helping the Central Army to steal the surrender and force the Communist armies to cancel their plans to take the large urban centers. Luo Ronghuan, to avoid confronting the Central Army prematurely, was compelled to abandon his plans to take Jinan and Qingdao "to take into account long-range considerations."[26]

When news of the surrender came, the puppet governor in Jinan assumed the title of Shandong Advance Army commander. He ordered all Japanese troops, puppet troops, and local administrators to stay in place until the Central Army could arrive. He let it be known that he had been an agent of the Guomindang military intelligence organization and had been in communication by radio with its Chongqing headquarters all along.[27]

The first Nationalist armies to enter Jinan were led by the newly appointed provincial governor, He Siyuan. He, a former guerrilla commander with shady ties with the Japanese Army as early as 1939,[28] allegedly met with the head of the Japanese 43d Corps to prepare for joint anti-Communist action before the surrender took place. When the day actually came, he raced to Jinan from the sole remaining enclave of Nationalist control near Weixian and assumed command of the 43d

Corps. He kept the provincial capital out of Communist hands until the Central Army could send reinforcements.[29]

In Qingdao, in similar fashion, a former two-sided unit under Li Xianliang assumed control until the Central Army could arrive.[30] Even the puppet New Fourth Division commander was given a commission in the Guomindang forces and helped the Central Army establish a foothold near Yanzhou. Although he had actually participated in attacks on Nationalist forces during the war, he unabashedly claimed that his defection too had been approved by the Guomindang military intelligence.[31]

The few Nationalist guerrillas who had clung to the anti-Japanese cause up to the war's end thus witnessed a demoralizing spectacle. Former puppet commanders joined in the victory celebrations and competed for rank in the new order.[32] Japanese troops wearily followed orders to defend the railway lines from the Eighth Route Army, and they even participated in some mopping-up campaigns. Until their final withdrawal in December 1945 it was not evident in many localities that the war ended at all.[33]

Whether or not Chiang Kai-shek actually condoned wartime collaboration, the outcome of the war did fit the "crooked path to resistance" scenario predicted by the two-sided guerrillas. In remaining on the scene to delay Communist expansion, the Nationalist guerrilla effort was a limited success. From a larger perspective, however, it was a failure. Besides tainting the nationalist image of the central government, the guerrillas failed to build a firm base for a Nationalist comeback in the countryside. The remainder of this essay will delve into the reasons for this failure.

Divided We Fall

In the three-cornered war among the Japanese Army, the Eighth Route Army, and the Nationalist guerrillas in Shandong, it was the last of these who were unable to stand up to pressure. Some Nationalist sources explain this failure by claiming that "Militarily, the Communists ganged up with the Japanese by signing secret treaties and adopting the so-called 'parallel movement' to launch converging attacks on our government forces."[34] Although the Eighth Route Army did occasionally attack the flanks of Nationalist units during Japanese "mopups," both evidence from the Guomindang side[35] and the well-known Japanese hostility toward the Communists make this charge of collaboration ring hollow. In any case, both the Eighth Route Army and the Nationalists were subject to two-sided pressure, and one must still explain how the Eighth Route Army survived whereas the Nationalists did not.

A Nationalist Defense Ministry review of its wartime record provides a franker appraisal: "The organization of our guerrilla districts was complex, and our party did not play much of a function in uniting them. It could not bring harmony in the four great relationships between army, government, officials, and populace. It was easy for the bandits [Eighth Route Army] to create divisions and exploit them, cause confrontations, and defeat us one by one. It was even less possible to speak of grasping the hearts and minds of the people, and carrying out a general mobilization. Gradually our armies fell into greater and greater isolation."[36] This analysis goes far in explaining the shortcomings of the Nationalist guerrillas.

A major factor contributing to the guerrillas' failure was the central government's inability to assume unified control of the autonomous former warlord and local armies comprising the guerrilla forces. Both the Japanese and the Communists skillfully exploited Nationalist disunity.

At the lowest level of militarization, the local guerrillas were a melange of factions and groups. Since the guerrillas enjoyed independent power bases and their outlooks were parochial, outside forces found it difficult to challenge their autonomy. This situation was vividly described by a writer on the Communist side: "Shandong's feudal forces have experience in armed struggle against bandits. Especially in southern and western Shandong, the gentry rule village alliances, security forces, and secret societies despotically. Every three *li* there is one corps, and every five *li* there is a fort. If they just have thirty or fifty rifles they can carve out their own territories and act as local emperors. In the Resistance War they seize the opportunity to lord it over the people. They close the stockades, put rifles up on the walls, resist the national army, and declare independence. When outsiders see this they think it strange, but in Shandong it is a common sight."[37]

Shen Honglie and Qin Qirong attempted to coopt these local forces by issuing commissions and integrating them into their command systems, but this did not induce the local leaders to rise above their parochial interests. They rarely engaged in coordinated operations or accepted even temporary assignments off their home turf. Moreover, the local guerrillas jealously guarded their territories against each other as much as against the Japanese or the Communists. Their conflicts often escalated into internecine clashes. This was one reason why these forces scattered when subjected to Japanese mopping-up campaigns. They could not take sanctuary in the territories of neighboring Nationalist guerrillas.[38]

Factional rivalries within the central government itself compounded local rivalries. The competition between the rival intelligence organizations with which Shen Honglie and Qin Qirong were allied complicated the effort to unify the local guerrillas. In the notorious Laiyang Incident of February 1939, an East Shandong unit affiliated with Qin Qirong actually opened fire and killed the East Shandong special commissioner and six other officials dispatched by Shen Honglie.[39]

At a higher level of militarization, the armies that made up the Shandong-Jiangsu War District under Yu Xuezhong were "miscellaneous armies" (*zapaijun*) not closely tied to Chiang Kai-shek. Such armies were the last to receive supplies from the center, and their losses in battle were usually not replaced with reinforcements. Yu and others strongly suspected that Chiang wanted to grind down their forces by locking them in mortal combat with the Eighth Route Army in order to strengthen his own hand against the regional armies after the war. From Yu's point of view, if this were allowed to happen both sides would lose and be injured (*liangbai jushang*). If he committed his troops to battle against either the Eighth Route Army or the Japanese, Yu knew that he would be unable to achieve the essential goal of "preserving his forces" (*baocun shili*).[40] For this reason, after participating in one desultory transport sabotage attack in the winter of 1939–40, Yu assumed a passive posture toward the Japanese.[41] A provincial government official who served under him observed: "From the time I arrived in Shandong until Yu withdrew, I felt that his strategy was this. He absolutely refused to take the initiative and attack or ambush the enemy. If the enemy attacked or mopped up, he would shift rapidly and avoid combat. After the enemy left he would return to his original position. In this way the area he controlled could only contract and could not expand the way the Eighth Route Army's did."[42]

Yu resisted Shen Honglie's effort to push him into a confrontation with the Eighth Route Army. Having participated in the famous Xi'an Incident of December 1936, when Chiang Kai-shek was kidnapped and held for two weeks, Yu was caught up in the spirit of the incident and favored a united front with the Communist army. He took an "impartial" stance in clashes between Nationalist and Eighth Route Army guerrillas. When Yu assumed the Shandong command in 1939, the Communist side observed that his attitude was "neither red nor blue, but a third path in the middle." He sought a modus vivendi with the Eighth Route Army while ignoring its nibbling attacks on the provincial government's peace preservation forces.[43]

Yu's differences with Shen on the question of Communist containment were sharp enough to inspire Shen to arrange an assassination attempt, according to Communist sources. A memoir of Yu's former secretary reports that Shen abhorred Yu's "stubborn" and "mechanical" attitudes and his lack of enthusiasm for opposing the Eighth Route Army. In the spring of 1941 Shen allegedly paid an assassin to make an attempt on Yu's life. As vice-commander of the war district, Shen expected that he would be able to take over his superior's post. The assassin missed, fled into the Eighth Route Army's base area by mistake, and was captured and returned to the war district. Shen feared that the truth would leak out and slipped away to Chongqing to resign his post. Later the assassin confessed in an open trial. Yu reportedly remarked to his secretary afterward, "Although I have not won merit in serving the Guomindang, I have not made any big mistakes either. How could things come to this?"[44]

Both the Eighth Route Army and the Japanese were aware of these internal resentments and profited from them. The leaders of the Eighth Route Army's Shandong forces (Xu Xiangqian and then Luo Ronghuan after 1941) applied the CCP's united front tactics to conditions in Shandong: "Develop the progressive forces, win over the fence-sitters, and isolate the die-hard forces." Early in the war this was encapsulated in the slogan "Win over the Northeast Army, eliminate Qin Qirong, and isolate Shen Honglie."[45]

The Eighth Route Army went through the motions of obeying orders from Yu Xuezhong and avoided clashes with him in order to keep his large force neutral. It openly cooperated with Shen Honglie until the August 1940 Lucun incident but reduced Shen's local security forces one by one. Since Qin Qirong was hostile from the start, the Eighth Route Army tried hard to eliminate his units. By keeping Yu out of the fray, the Eighth Route Army won breathing space to build up its own strength before seeking a final confrontation with the last Nationalist "die-hards."

This strategy worked until after the New Fourth Army incident of January 1941, when Yu was finally provoked to stop "sitting on the fence." With the simultaneous onset of several Japanese mopping-up operations, the three-sided war reached its peak of intensity. In this critical period the CCP's exploitation of dissension within Nationalist ranks again was a factor in the Nationalist decline.

The CCP's "friendly army" work inspired two mutinies within Yu's ranks, as described in a recent memoir.[46] Yu had been influenced by the Xi'an Incident, but after January 1941 he finally sided with the central government rather than the Communists. Other members of his officer corps, however, secretly joined the Communist Party. Some veteran Communist Party members also managed to infiltrate Yu's army without his knowledge.

The most prominent of these underground Communists were the 111th Division commander Chang Enduo, Yu's secretary Guo Wencheng, and the 111th Division's 333d Brigade commander, Wan Yi. The Manchu Chang Enduo had his first contact with the CCP in Xi'an while participating in anti-Communist suppression operations. After being sent to fight the Japanese in southern Shandong his thought "progressed" further, until he observed to a Communist contact, "In the three-cornered war each side has its own party. After we have defeated the Japanese, what party will I be considered as?" He asked to join and was admitted as a "special member" in the spring of 1939.

Wan Yi had also made contact with the party in Xi'an, and joined there. Before the outbreak of the war he was jailed by the Guomindang as a "dangerous element," and he rejoined the Northeast Army only after the Japanese invasion. Guo Weicheng had joined the party as a student in Shanghai in 1932, and as an inactive member he took a position as Yu Xuezhong's secretary without arousing his suspicions.

Together these three men attempted two mutinies, first against the 56th Army commander, Miu Zhengliu, and later against Yu Xuezhong himself. The first mutiny, which the Communists now call the "22 September Traitor-Elimination Campaign," took place in 1939. With Shen's encouragement, 57th Army commander Miu was attempting to negotiate an anti-Communist mutual nonaggression pact with the Japanese Army. Chang Enduo and Wan Yi got wind of this and decided to try to upset their superior's plans. Miu had ordered his troops to march on 21 September, so they decided to arrest him on the road. Miu unexpectedly delayed his departure to hold a drama performance and banquet for some officials who had returned from Chongqing. An attempt to arrest Miu at the foot of the stage failed, as an informer tipped him off and enabled him to make a hasty escape to 112th Division headquarters.

The plotters arrested some of the other officers and sent a telegram protesting Miu's agreement with the Japanese. Proclaiming that his aim was to "be loyal to the Guomindang and love his country, kill the enemy and eliminate traitors, unite to resist Japan, persist in democracy, and to return to the homeland in the Northeast," Chang Enduo asked the feckless Yu to mediate. Yu sent Guo Weicheng to represent him. Guo did what he could to protect his comrades, but eventually Wan Yi was put under house arrest. Protesting that Guomindang agents had urged the 57th Army commander to defect and that he had had no choice but to rebel, Chang was allowed to stay in his post.

In 1942 Yu Xuezhong's territory shrank under Japanese pressure, and since, as the Communist memoir put it, the "soldiers of the Northeast Army were unhappy shedding their blood fighting the Eighth Route Army rather than the enemy," morale was low. Chang Enduo, dying of tuberculosis, resolved to take advantage of the desperate situation of the war district to stage a coup and make Wan Yi his successor as head of the 111th Division. He urged Guo Weicheng to act.

Guo realized that he could not gain control of the 111th Division without using Wan Yi's influence on the officer corps, so his first step was to spring Wan Yi from house arrest. Toward sunset on a hot August evening, Guo and his wife pretended to go out for a stroll. When they passed by the place where Wan was detained, they saw that he was being watched by only one guard. This guard knew Guo and did not object to his approaching Wan. The two underground Communists exchanged a few casual words of greeting, and then Guo whispered, "Division Commander Chang is seriously ill. . . . We're going to take action. Be alert, and when the time comes we will send a man on horseback to come get you." Wan just nodded his head and said nothing in reply.

Impatient and doubting the feasibility of this plan, Wan decided to seek escape. Suffering from diarrhea, he made several trips a night to the outside toilet. The guards did not watch him closely when he went out. One night he used this pretext to climb a grape arbor over the courtyard wall and escape. Under the cover of tall gaoliang stalks he found his way several miles to the Eighth Route Army's base area.

Meanwhile Chang Enduo had decided that the time was ripe and called his officers to his bedside. The conservative officers hoped that they might be appointed his successor so they appeared, but they were rewarded by being arrested on the spot as "spies." Now Chang ordered an attack on Yu Xuezhong's headquarters to "sweep the Guomindang die-hards from the stage of history."

On the evening of 3 August 1942 Yu Xuezhong was startled to discover that his headquarters was surrounded by troops from the 111th Division. Guo contacted him over the telephone and offered lenient treatment if he would surrender. Yu, feigning a conciliatory attitude, replied, "I'm willing to hand over my rifles and return to my old home in the Northeast." Guo ordered his men to cease fire.

Meanwhile some of the Nationalist troops escaped, and Yu slipped away disguised as an old shepherd. Wan Yi returned to take control of three thousand troops of the 111th Division, which was incorporated into the Eighth Route Army and expanded into new territory in the Jiazi mountains. By this time Chang Enduo had already died, but as his last act he had dealt a serious blow to Yu Xuezhong's authority and stolen part of his strength.

Now it was the turn of the Japanese Army to take advantage of the Northeast Army's troubles. The Japanese, noting that Yu was vulnerable after the "3 August uprising," shifted the main force of their mopping-up attacks against the Northeast Army, with the 5th and 6th brigades launching the Third Central Shandong Operation. From 12 to 15 August they encircled Yu's headquarters in an attempt to capture him, but Yu was lucky enough to slip through an opening toward the south.

On 20 August the Japanese went into hot pursuit of Yu again in the Fourth Central Shandong Operation. This time they almost reached their goal. Catching up with part of Yu's headquarters, they took 733 prisoners including some staff officers and left 1,800 bodies on the battlefield.[47] Yu himself was trapped in a night attack and was wounded by machine gun fire.[48] Somehow he escaped and held out until the following summer, but by July 1943 further splits and defections made his position untenable.

When another Japanese mop-up chased Yu out of his home base, the Eighth Route Army moved in.[49] The Nationalist provincial government followed Yu out, and only Qin Qirong was left to struggle for the Nationalist cause. On August 6, the Eighth Route Army delivered the coup de grace to Qin. Cornered in Anqu county, he committed suicide to avoid capture.[50] Japanese forces and the Eighth Route Army had succeeded in destroying or eliminating the major Nationalist "diehard" forces one by one.

Hearts and Minds

It is obvious that in a guerrilla conflict popular support has some bearing on military success, but this support is very difficult to evaluate and measure. One way in which this can be done is through comparisons. Both Japanese and Communist sources agree that the Eighth Route Army was much more adept than the Nationalist guerrillas in surviving Japanese mopping-up campaigns. Although these campaigns dealt serious setbacks to the Eighth Route Army, they had a devastating impact on the Nationalists. When the Nationalist armies withdrew from their home territories, the administrative structures they had established collapsed. The Eighth Route Army often took advantage of this opportunity by waiting for the Nationalist guerrillas to scatter and then moving in to take over their territory. This occurred in the first large scale mop-up of southern Shandong, the June 1939 South Shandong Operation. A Communist report described the effects of this operation on the provincial government: "The Shen Honglie-Qin Qirong dichards scattered and fled. The old-style regimes which they had forced over the heads of the masses a second time also disappeared completely. Even the ruling strata of society lost confidence in them."[51]

The Shandong Column commander, Zhang Jingwu, analyzed some of the reasons why the mop-ups could shatter the Nationalist infrastructure:

> The base area and army should be inseparable. We must have base areas to mobilize our latent popular and material strength. . . . This is not what the die-hards do. They just take over a strategically situated mountain area or town, and call it a base area.
>
> Because they do not understand what a base area is, they mistakenly adopt a policy of "army noninterference in government." They do not have their troops do mass movement work, do not approve of the organization of guerrilla cells or the setting up of checkpoints, and limit their mass organizations to decrepit *baojia* and militia systems lacking the slightest vitality. They isolate the regular army and cannot even speak of practicing democracy, improving the popular livelihood, and mobilizing the masses to participate in the war. Thus when the enemy "mopped-up" South Shandong, many of their troops could not hold their own.[52]

A review of Shen Honglie's approach to base construction shows that Zhang's description was not far off the mark. Neither extensive mass organization nor reform was part of the Nationalist approach. In a July 1938 interview with the governor, Evans Carlson found that Shen was " 'unalterably opposed' to the organization of the people, especially along political lines. 'I have no objection,' he told me, 'to the organization of cultural groups among the people. But the [Guomindang] is the governing party and the people must abide by its dicta.' He went on to say that both political and military authority was vested in the magistrates and the governors of the districts. His plan was to build an army within each country and administrative district which would enable the officials of those districts to deal with the situation." [53]

Shen aimed to impose a bureaucratic structure on top of society as it existed. Insofar as he paid lip service to the idea of mass mobilization, he spoke in terms of relying on the local "intellectual class" to lead the masses. [54] In contrast to the Communist policy of combining reform and anti-Japanese resistance, he followed the central government's guidelines to postpone indefinitely reform and mass involvement in politics. Guerrilla war was seen simply as a problem of military and bureaucratic control.

Communist reports, no doubt exaggerated but still revealing, claim that Shen's approach to infrastructure building failed miserably. As a case in point, they document the charge that over a period of three years Nationalist guerrillas turned Shen's "model district" in Linqu county into a "no-man's land" (*wurenqu*). [55] When the Eighth Route Army moved into this area in late 1943, it found that about 80 percent of the population had either died or fled to avoid starvation. Wild grass grew so high in some villages that one had to part it with both hands in order to walk through. Half-starved survivors lived on tree bark, corn husks, and silkworm excrement (normally pig feed). Wolves settled into abandoned houses and became so accustomed to eating human flesh that they lost their fear of humans.

How did this condition come about? While the Nationalists side blamed the drought of 1943, [56] Communist sources maintained that the problem was larger than this. When Shen first arrived in the district and made it his headquarters, he had attempted to levy enough grain to support all his military and organizational personnel from this small area. His soldiers felt that since they were dying for the sake of the people, they should be the first to eat. One provincial government official is said to have commented, "No matter what, the soldiers must eat. We can sacrifice the common people, but not the army." There were no restrictions on the frequency or size of tax collections, and with venal officials lining their own pockets, the amount demanded sometimes exceeded the local surplus.

After August 1941, Qin Qirong's troops moved into the area and disturbed it further. Qin's Fifth Column was notorious for its high taxes and poor discipline. Since many of the wealthier villagers had relatives in Qin's officer corps, they were exempted from taxes while the poorer villagers bore a heavy burden. Peasants who did not pay were maltreated or arrested. The poor discipline of Qin's troops was even more obnoxious to the villagers. Qin's officers might demand attractive village women as concubines. If the parents were not receptive, the officers would take the women by force. The only way that they could be returned was by paying a ransom. Shen reportedly did not approve of this practice, but he could not persuade Qin to deal with the problem.

Eventually the Fifth Column had collected all the grain the regular *baojia* system could yield. When the 1943 drought hit, soldiers went into the villages to search for buried grain stores. When they found villages where bark remained on the trees, they concluded that there was still hidden grain and searched repeatedly. Soon the whole area was looted clean, all the domestic animals were gone, and even the dogs had all been eaten. Qin could no longer support his force in the area and moved away to Anqiu county, where the Eighth Route Army put an end to his career.

The modus operandi of the Nationalist guerrillas also included other well-documented abuses. Many officers indulged in gambling and opium smoking. The guerrillas issued paper currency without restricting the money supply, used their positions to take over land or property, and pressed unwilling peasants into the army. The worst of the Nationalist guerrillas—Liu Guitang of southern Shandong was the prime example—were simply veteran soldier-bandits who continued to prey on the population as they had done all through the Republican era.[57]

After the villagers had made great sacrifices, ostensibly for the cause of resistance, it was not clear who were Central Army and who were traitors. According to one story reported in a Communist source, one of Qin Qirong's officials, when asked where his men would eat after food supplies were depleted in the government-controlled area, replied, "We'll eat on that side [pointing to the enemy-occupied district]. Isn't it true that our men are over there too? Look what the 8th Detachment [a Qin Qirong unit that defected] did! Can't we be traitors too? As long as we have rifles we'll still have our share to eat!"[58]

Nationalist sources, corroborated by the testimony of outside observers, show that there were some exceptions to this rule. Even Communist sources occasionally concede that, in the case of the "native die-hards" (*tuwan*) rather than regular armies, some units were bound to the population through "feudal ties." A good example of this type of unit was that led by former school teacher Wang Yumin in Changyi county.[59]

Wang ruled part of his home county, and through the force of his puritanical personality he enforced strict discipline. By violently wresting control of taxation from the hands of his regimental commanders, he imposed a rational tax system. He issued his own currency but controlled the money supply so that stable commodity prices could be maintained. Material conditions were tolerable enough in his territory so that in late 1944 an emissary was shocked to discover that things were worse in Chongqing than in his home county. Wang's soldiers were eating better than those in the wartime capital.[60]

Almost every family in Wang's district had at least one member in his army or militia. His peasant soldiers fought to protect their homes from Japanese vandalism and to defend their right to till the land in peace. Families of soldiers killed in action received pensions. In this way the gap between army and populace was bridged.[61]

In the spring of 1945 the Eighth Route Army opened up an offensive against this force. Although Wang was ultimately unsuccessful in defending his home territory, the Eighth Route Army was not able to stimulate opposition within his own camp. There were few landlords in his villages, and class resentments did not surface. The *baojia* system and anti-Communist indoctrination were sufficient to discourage Communist infiltration. Wang had to be defeated militarily before he could be discredited politically.[62]

If it is fair to generalize from this case, it appears that if the Guomindang had made a serious effort to unify, reorganize, and discipline the local guerrillas, they might have been capable of building a popular base sufficient to support protracted guerrilla warfare. Under Wang's form of benevolent despotism, the minimally necessary level of popular compliance could be obtained with the introduction of a few simple administrative reforms and the enforcement of discipline.

Unfortunately, due either to inattention to the problem or to inability to influence the behavior of autonomous local commanders, the provincial government did not prevent widespread abuse of the population. The guerrillas exhausted the human and material resources of their territories. Without building extensive popular organization and support, they left no roots behind when Japanese mop-ups temporarily pushed them out of their territories. This made the Nationalist guerrilla effort difficult to sustain. The Ministry of Defense review cited earlier was correct in observing that the inability to win the hearts and minds of the population and effect a general mobilization was one factor explaining the Nationalist failure.

Conclusions

If we put aside charges of Japanese-Communist collusion, a plausible analysis of the rise and fall of the Nationalist guerrillas can be developed within the Nationalist frame of reference. This was because Chiang Kai-shek was caught in a basic dilemma. He saw that the Japanese invasion unleashed powerful centrifugal forces in Chinese society—the forces of regional militarism—which he had barely been able to tame during the Nanjing Decade (1927–1937). Chiang recognized that if the local guerrillas became too strong, after the conclusion of the war they might be back in a position to challenge his authority again. On the other hand, he needed them to obstruct Communist expansion behind Japanese lines.

Chiang's response was to make a half-hearted effort to control the local guerrillas by issuing commissions and coopting them without giving them much material or organizational support. The central government failed to find a workable formula enabling it to assert effective leadership over regional armies and local elites that jealously guarded their autonomy. This lack of internal coherence led to the inexorable decline of the Nationalist guerrillas and the failure of both their anti-Japanese and their anti-Communist missions.

Chiang's attempt to use the local guerrillas against the Eighth Route Army also proved counterproductive. When his guerrillas attempted to coopt puppet armies against the Communists, they were instead coopted. In the confusion that ensued, the nationalist image of the central government was tainted, and the military decline of the guerrillas who continued to resist Japan was hastened.

The impossibility of coordinating the guerrilla effort eventually made it difficult for the guerrillas to survive. Nationalist disunity permitted the Eighth Route Army and the Japanese to fight one guerrilla force at a time, keeping the others on the sidelines. Unresponsiveness at lower levels left the provincial governor powerless to regulate the relations of the guerrillas with the population. The human and material resources of the guerrilla territories were rapidly exhausted, alienating the population from the guerrillas who needed their support. The Nationalist inability to foster local initiative without losing control was at the root of its failure in prosecuting a guerrilla war.

The Communist Party's drastic solution to this problem was the destruction of the local armies and militias over which Chiang was unable to assert his authority. By removing the centrifugal forces in Chinese society from their point of origin, it became possible to put in place a new structure of authority dependent on leadership from the center. Whether this was the only solution, or whether—as Guomindang spokesmen asserted—a better formula for the reconciliation of control and autonomy could have been worked out by the Nationalists, is entirely speculative. The fact is that the Nationalists failed on this score, and the Communists succeeded.

In any case, it is the claim of both the Guomindang and the Chinese Communist Party to the mantle of nationalism that has kept this story in the shadows of Chinese history. Neither party is eager to recall how its wartime activities did not always fit with an image of single-minded, patriotic devotion to anti-Japanese resistance. For the Guomindang, it is not pleasant to remember the way in which the "crooked path to national salvation" was used in an attempt to save the country for the central government. The Communist role in hastening the decline of the Nationalist "die-hards" through "friction struggle" is also better forgotten. This will remain a political reality to be whispered about and discussed indirectly, but rarely exposed to the light of public scrutiny on either side of the Taiwan Straits.

6

Mobilizing for War: Rural Revolution in Manchuria as an Instrument for War

STEVEN I. LEVINE

> A great revolution must go through a civil war. This is a rule. And to see the ills of war but not its benefits is a one-sided view. It is of no use to the people's revolution to speak one-sidedly of the destructiveness of war.
>
> —Mao Zedong, *Notes on the Soviet Text Political Economy*

The Chinese civil war of 1946–49 remains virtually terra incognita to most students of the Chinese Communist movement. The paucity of work on this period suggests that most scholars assume that Communist victory in the civil war was foreordained by the developments of the preceding decades. By the end of World War II, the Communist movement in China had grown in less than a decade from a beleaguered band on the verge of extinction into a vital political-military force that claimed a party membership of 1.2 million, a regular army of 910,000 troops, and control over an archipelago of nineteen liberated areas containing a population of some 95 million persons.[1] Under Mao Zedong's flexible interpretation of united front policy, the Chinese Communist Party had pursued an aggressive strategy throughout the Anti-Japanese War aimed at maximizing its growth.

Yet despite their revolutionary optimism, CCP leaders entertained no illusions that the task they faced in 1945 was merely to ring down the curtain on a play whose action was virtually completed. They believed that they faced a long and difficult military and political struggle against an enemy that surpassed them not only in military power but in domestic political authority and external support as well. Mao's con-

Map 6.1. **Manchuria.**

cern that Chiang Kai-shek might wrest the fruits of victory from the hands of the people (read CCP) attests to his anxiety that the Communists' territorial "profiteering" during the Anti-Japanese War period might be undone by a sustained Nationalist offensive.[2]

In retrospect, of course, what is most astonishing is the rapidity of the Nationalist collapse.[3] In January 1947, Lin Biao's armies stood on the north bank of the Sungari River in China's northernmost province of Heilongjiang (see map 6.1). A year later they were investing the Nationalists' beleaguered garrisons in the urban centers of the Northeast (Manchuria). Yet another year later they were marching into Beijing, and before the end of 1949 the augmented survivors of these northern campaigns were in the streets of Canton.

The struggle for control of Manchuria was a critical phase in the CCP's successful contest against the Nationalists (Guomindang) in the civil war.[4] Both protagonists considered that struggle crucial to the outcome of the overall conflict, and they invested political and military resources in the region accordingly. In Manchuria, as elsewhere in China, a massive rural revolution accompanied the shift of power. In the predominantly rural counties from which the CCP drew most of its strength, a vast army of peasant lads was recruited to the Communist banner, sustained by the surplus of the agricultural sector, and led to victory in battle.

What was the relationship between the peasant revolution and the Communist victory in Manchuria? The image of the peasantry as an elemental force whose epic struggle for land and social justice is the very essence of revolution dates back to Mao Zedong's famous report on the Hunan peasant movement of 1927.[5] That revolutionary-romantic image, however, bears little resemblance to the processes through which peasants actually become involved in political, including revolutionary, activity. The transition from individualist or familist orientations to the intense social activism of the mobilized participant in rural revolution entailed a basic change in perception and individual and group identity, a transformation of the calculus of trust and commitment, and development of a new sense of the possible links between the village and the world outside.

That transition ordinarily requires a great deal of time. But in Manchuria the peasant revolution began and climaxed in the space of only eighteen months. For the CCP in Manchuria, time was the crucial limiting factor in its relationship with the peasantry, and the rapidity with which the revolution was initially carried out resulted in a pattern of change marked by abrupt shifts in party policy, a shaky foundation for CCP rule, and a process of revolution somewhat different from that in the old liberated areas of North China.

The region had no history of prior peasant activism, having languished under repressive—and quite effective—Japanese colonial rule until August 1945. The CCP's pre–1945 experience there consisted largely of a dismal record of failure and defeat. In Northeast China fourteen years of Japanese rule had left the legacy of a cowed and submissive rural population little inclined at first to respond to the CCP's revolutionary program, let alone to take the initiative for change into its own hands. Patriotic opposition to the Japanese, expressed in the early and mid–1930s in widespread local resistance, had failed to survive ruthless suppression by the Japanese and their Manchukuo collaborators. When the Soviet Red Army entered Manchuria in August 1945, the Communist underground was mostly in prison and the guerrilla fighters had long since been suppressed. Even after two years of intense efforts, the CCP's position in Manchuria was far from secure, and its margin of victory in the civil war was perilously thin. An only slightly better organized and better led opponent might at a minimum have fought the Communists to a standstill in the region.

Operating among peasants with a generally low level of political consciousness, forced by the exigencies of war to recruit and provision an army quickly or suffer defeat, the Communist leaders relied upon organizational techniques developed through years of work in intramural China. Enjoying local military superiority at first because of its forces moved into the region from North China, the CCP hastily brought into being new structures of power and rapidly organized revolution in the rural areas in order to harness the support it needed to fight a conventional war against the Nationalists.

But the Communist victory in Manchuria was not a triumph only of organizational superiority. The CCP secured the support of a significant number of rural dwellers in Northeast China through its revolutionary program. In return for their military and labor service, their contributions of provisions, livestock, carts, and so forth to the Communist armies, Manchurian peasants received land, movable property confiscated from the old elite, a share in the new organs of revolutionary power, and a new sense of identity as political actors. This much is familiar from earlier studies of the Communist movement in North China, but the revolution in Manchuria had its own distinctive features. Precisely how these two elements—organization and revolutionary program—combined to produce the Communist victory will be the focus of my analysis.

This essay, abstracted from a larger study of the Communist movement in Manchuria, will concentrate on only three out of the very complex interplay of organizational and programmatic factors that contributed to the Communist triumph in Northeast China. I shall examine, first, the relationship between local elites and the hierarchy of power; second, the mobilization of manpower in civil war Manchuria; and third, the methods by which the CCP secured peasant support. I shall begin by arguing that in Manchuria the Communist victory, far from being the ineluctable outcome of underlying socioeconomic forces, was very much contingent upon a variety of political, military, and organizational factors peculiar to the conflict in the Northeast.

Local Elites and the Hierarchy of Power

When the CCP entered the Northeast in 1945–46 it lacked a local organization, secure base areas, and the human and material resources to fight a conventional war against the Nationalists. Despite the heroic efforts beginning in autumn 1945 to recruit an army, establish governmental organs, and mobilize the population, the Communist position was still exceedingly shaky when the peace negotiations collapsed in the summer of 1946. Until that time, the Communist high command in Manchuria had been inclined to favor a policy of frontal resistance to the Nationalists. The regional Communist high command (Peng Zhen, Lin Biao, Lin Feng, and others) succumbed to the temptation of an urban power play. Taking advantage of the continuing occupation of the region by the Soviet Red Army, the Chinese Communists in the spring of 1946 tried to seize the main urban centers of Manchuria as a shortcut to power. Like earlier Communist efforts in the 1920s to control cities, these attempts failed.[6] The Nationalist victory at Siping in May 1946 led to the Communist evacuation of Changchun and retreat north across the Sungari.

At this critical juncture, when a series of well-aimed Nationalist military blows might have virtually eliminated the Communist Northeast Democratic United Army (NEDUA), party leaders decided to concentrate their limited assets in an effort to stimulate and organize revolution in the rural areas. They sought a reliable base from which to draw the supplies of manpower and provisions needed to sustain the war effort. In transforming the countryside into such a base, the party had to eliminate the entrenched power of local elites and to establish new organs of revolutionary power in the countryside. And that, it so happened, was not to be easy. The first wave of Communist-directed revolution in the Northeast countryside was characterized by widespread passivity on the part of the peasantry and consequent reliance on cadres, nearly all of whom were outsiders to the communities where they worked. Nevertheless, the CCP acquired an initial rural base which it subsequently strengthened through succeeding waves of revolution, land reform, and property redistribution.

Perhaps the most striking features of the revolution in the Northeast countryside were the local elites' capacity for protracted resistance to Communist pressures to oust them, and the concomitant reluctance of much if not most of the rural population to support the Communist attacks on local elites. Communist organizers complained about the misconception prevalent in many places that "Northeast landlords and peasants have a mutually supportive relationship."[7] How can we account for the phenomenon?

In his work on Manchurian social structure in the Republican period, Ramon Myers has suggested that considerable opportunities for economic and social mobility existed in the Northeast.[8] The expanding frontier economy promoted a relatively rapid turnover of fortunes and illustrated the aptness of the old Chinese saying, "Nobody stays rich for three generations; nobody stays poor for three generations."[9] The class cleavages that the CCP portrayed as the primary rural fault lines initially proved less salient in most villages than the countervailing cohesive forces that bound individual villages together against the outside world. Class relations were also much more complex and class divisions much more tenuous than the clear-cut lines the Communists drew for political purposes.[10] It was certainly not that pre–1945 rural social relations in Manchuria were idyllic, that intravillage conflicts were absent, or that violence was alien to the Northeast countryside. To the contrary. Nevertheless, it is clear that existing tensions would have produced nothing more than scattered and purely local agrarian disturbances in postwar Manchuria, had it not been for the CCP's determined and persistent efforts to establish its organizational presence in the countryside and bring about rural revolution.

Manchurian villages manifested a peculiar combination of open and closed characteristics.[11] In economic terms the commercialized character of Manchurian agriculture from the late nineteenth century on meant that villages were not closed corporate communities dominated by a traditional landlord class. Market relations, a well-developed transportation system, and considerable physical mobility in an expanding economy linked individual villages and individual peasants to the wider world.

But both politically and militarily, Manchurian villages exhibited the characteristics of what I would term *political encapsulation*. The endemic violence of a region preyed upon by bandits, regional and local militarists, venal politicians, and a variety of foreign imperialists encouraged a closed defensive response on the part of local communities. In times of turmoil local elites organized their dependents and clients into local defense forces to preserve order and minimize the depredations that outside forces could inflict upon their villages.[12] Such a reaction occurred, for example, at the time of the Japanese invasion of 1931–32. From the point of view of large property owners and the poor alike this defensive encapsulation was a kind of collective good because the exactions of outside forces in terms of military recruitment, confiscation of draft animals, carts, grain, and so forth fell upon all sectors of the village community, even if not equally.

In response, then, to outsiders demanding contributions of village goods and village men, the collective community in effect curled up like an armadillo and presented a forbidding exterior to the outside world. To be sure, intravillage solidarity was not absolute. Communist organizers were eventually able to work on the class and other intravillage cleavages to transform the village power structures. But this initial intravillage solidarity for a long time outweighed the fissiparous tendencies that the Communists sought to utilize.

The superior political resources of the local elites likewise made them formidable foes of the Communist revolution. Experience in local politics, possession of or access to wealth, control of superior communications systems, ownership of arms, the ability to manipulate networks of family members and personal retainers or clients, the deference they enjoyed and the fear they inspired all favored local elites in their resistance to Communist organizers. What party leaders condemned as the crafty efforts of inveterate feudal elements to resist historical progress can equally well be seen as the natural efforts of local elites to defend their prerogatives.[13] A veritable catalog of tricks listed by a county party committee suggests some of the tactics employed. The committee accused landlords of feigning enlightenment to lull the masses, bribing backward peasants, using beautiful women to corrupt cadres and activists, directing their agents to infiltrate peasant associations, encouraging factionalism, colluding with bandits to carry out assassinations, and so on.[14]

Many of the methods used by the elite were hard to detect, and yet threatened the very underpinnings of revolutionary power. An integral part of rural revolution is the creation of new networks of economic and political institutions to replace the existing institutions.[15] Yet, if one may trust the Communists' own accounts of class struggles in the Northeast countryside, the old elites were adept at entering and taking over control of precisely those peasant associations, local governments, and other new institutions that the party had established in the countryside by dint of much effort.[16] Many of the rural folk who responded to the party's revolutionary call were apparently members of the old elite, or even more frequently their clients, who sought to preserve the old distribution of power by controlling the very organizations the party had established to wrest power from their hands.[17] Veteran party cadres in the itinerant rural work teams often finished up work in one village and traveled on to the next with no inkling that the newly recruited activists and local cadres in many cases were far from disadvantaged and exploited class elements engaged in seizing power. The shortage of veteran cadres and their unfamiliarity with the local environment (initially most were from outside Manchuria) made it very difficult to assess the reliability of new recruits. Thus many villages had to be "struggled" and organized over and over again.

The first stage of the Communist-initiated land reform, beginning in the summer of 1946, was like a quick sweep through a broad field with a dull scythe. More than anything else it represented an act of desperation by a party leadership that judged that the Northeast might rapidly fall to the Nationalists unless rural bases of support were rapidly acquired. The results of the first phase of land reform were superficial in most areas. Understaffed rural work teams distributed the land and choreographed struggle meetings against the class enemy in which most of the peasants remained passive and uncommitted. Reports from the field indicated that a genuine revolutionary transformation had been effected in perhaps no more than 20 percent of the villages. About half the villages had undergone superficial transformation, with cadres themselves performing the work the masses were supposed to shoulder (*baoban daiti*). Fully 30 percent of the villages were as yet untouched by land reform. A report from Mingshui county suggests that an acute shortage of cadres may have been a prime reason for this unsatisfactory situation. That county, with an estimated population of 160,000 in

1947, had only 111 cadres in land reform work teams, or one cadre for every 1,441 persons.[18] With so few cadres available, work teams could not afford the luxury of squatting in one point for very long in order to make sure their work was carried out properly, but rather shuttled rapidly back and forth.

In the winter of 1946–47, the party undertook to eliminate this phenomenon of "half-cooked" villages (*bansheng bu shou*) by mobilizing the masses for another round of land reform. Cadres were adjured not to do the work for the masses but to elicit genuine participation in struggle.[19] Substantial progress was claimed in eliminating "half-cooked" villages, but additional rounds of land reform were still required in many localities. Many villagers continued to show marked reluctance to commit themselves wholly to the violent overthrow of those in their midst targeted for attack. This reluctance may have been due variously to intravillage solidarity, to uncertainty about the duration of Communist rule, or even to certain scruples against the sometimes gratuitous savaging to which landlords and rich peasants were subjected during the height of the campaigns. In any case, party exhortations to the cadres stressed the necessity of combining political, economic, and ideological struggle in the long-term process of revolutionary base-building.[20]

Given all the difficulties, how were the Communists able to displace the local elites in the countryside? The answer to this critical question lies in the relationship between regional, provincial, and local elites on one hand and the Communist counterelites on the other.

In the prerevolutionary society, the forces of order and stability had possessed one decisive advantage over the assorted rebels, bandits, and revolutionaries who challenged their authority. The disparate uprisings of the late nineteenth century or the anti-Japanese guerrilla movements of the 1930s lacked well-integrated and coordinated organizations that interlocked at the regional, provincial, county, and local levels. Lacking such vertical and horizontal ties, rebels or guerrilla patriots were isolated and vulnerable to attack.

Local elites by contrast were embedded in a hierarchical network of power relationships that stretched outward and upward from the villages through the market towns and county seats to the urban centers of economic and political power in Manchuria. The authority and security enjoyed by local elites derived in large measure from their position within this hierarchy of status and power. Their ability to maintain order in their communities depended not only upon the resources and support they could mobilize within their localities, but also on the coercive power they could call in from outside.[21] If local security forces were insufficient to cope with local challenges from either bandits or revolutionaries, mobile military power could be dispatched from higher-order administrative units to deal with local challenges. The prestige and aura of legitimacy that local elites derived from their membership in the nested hierarchy of power no doubt also enhanced their position within their local communities.

The fourteen-year Japanese colonial interlude had a shattering effect on the hierarchy of power. The Japanese conquest of Manchuria in 1931–32 failed to produce a Communist-led ''peasant nationalism'' or widespread networks of resistance organizations as later happened in North China, and during the Manchukuo period, centrally dispatched and coordinated military units amply demonstrated their efficacy in suppressing local Communist resistance forces.[22] However, Japanese rule was no less significant in preparing the ground for the postwar revolutionary movement. The Japanese occupation of Manchuria splintered the regional and provincial elite, some of whom fled southward into exile in Nationalist territory while others remained in Manchuria as collaborators with the puppet regime. Following Japan's surrender, the collaborators became targets for attack during the movement to settle accounts (*qingsuan yundong*). The exiled pre-1931 elite was unable to recover its lost authority. Chiang Kai-shek, fearing Northeast regionalism almost as much as he did the CCP, systematically excluded Northeasterners from the administration he established in the region. In sum, the old elite at the upper levels lost its cohesion, its legitimacy, and its ability to rule. This in turn profoundly affected the position of the local elite.

Although local elites retained much of their economic power and political influence into the postwar period, they became fatally isolated. The normal networks of power were disrupted. The local elite, which had normally been connected to higher-level administrative centers, now found themselves cut off and vulnerable. In North and North-Central Manchuria, where the CCP attacked local elites, carried out land reform, and established new institutions of revolutionary power in 1946–47, the Nationalists had neither the political organization nor the mobile military power to come to the rescue of their potential adherents. Thrown back upon their own resources, local elites ultimately proved unable to resist the repeated assaults directed by the CCP.

In this context, the scope and intensity of the Communist organizational and military challenge became decisive. In post-1945 Manchuria, the CCP was the only organization that operated successfully on a regional basis, coordinating and controlling political and military campaigns across a broad territory. The local rebels, those traditionally disadvantaged in organizational terms, were now the ones connected to outside organizations and able to enjoy the advantage of superior coercive power and growing ideological legitimacy. The CCP and the NEDUA functioned as the critical agencies bridging the gap between the villages and the larger world. Party cadres and soldiers became the political brokers who entered the villages to identify and then link up with villagers who were willing to make or support revolutionary changes.

In the struggle between revolution and counterrevolution, the Communists thus had a decisive advantage. They were able to overcome the initially superior position of the local elites because the CCP could choose the time and place for its revolutionary attack and could mobilize organizational and coercive power from outside the village to bring down its targets. That was only part of the process that led to victory. The CCP still had to solve the problems of supplying the war effort, and of gaining peasant allegiance in order to consolidate its authority in the rural areas.

Mobilizing for War

In the first half of 1947, Lin Biao's Northeast Democratic United Army launched a series of offensives across the Sungari River challenging Nationalist control in the central Manchurian plains.[23] Although the NEDUA suffered immense casualties (40,000 at Siping alone) and experienced a tactical defeat in the last and largest of these campaigns, the new initiatives of the Communist forces revealed major Nationalist weaknesses. The offensives marked a turning point in the civil war in Manchuria.

As the scale and intensity of the fighting increased, the demands on the rear area's economy multiplied. The civil war in Manchuria was a conventional war in the sense that large armies using conventional tactics and armed with modern weapons opposed each other on the battlefield. Lacking a modern industrial infrastructure and transportation network, however, the NEDUA was dependent upon a mobilized population to provide it with the goods and services it needed.[24] From the spring of 1947 until the nationwide victory in 1949, support of the war effort through increased production of goods and mobilization of labor became the primary goal of Communist leaders in the Northeast. Production supplanted further revolution in the scale of Communist values. Cadres were repeatedly instructed to oppose the widespread tendencies among the masses to consume the fruits of struggle (e.g., by lavish feasts and celebrations) or to curtail production for fear that by accumulating wealth they might make themselves vulnerable as new targets of struggle. As revolutionary goals yielded to production imperatives, there was no doubt that the initial stages of the agrarian revolution had provided the Communists with the base they had previously lacked in the Northeast. Lin Biao, commander of the NEDUA and first secretary of the CCP's Northeast Bureau, made this point in May 1947 when he announced that his army was beginning its strategic counteroffensive. Lin asserted that the dramatic change from the Communists' imperiled position one year earlier was due to the effective work of thousands of cadres who had gone to the countryside in the summer of 1946 to carry out land reform, mobilize the masses, and eliminate the problem of banditry in the rear areas.[25]

At the first Northeast Administrative Conference (18 July–9 August 1947), Lin Feng, chairman of the Northeast Administrative Committee (NEAC),[26] reviewed the accomplishments of the previous year and outlined the agenda for the future. After reeling off an impressive list of accomplishments, Lin admitted that serious shortcomings still existed in military recruitment and supply as well as the care of military dependents and wounded soldiers. Rural organizations, he said, were still characterized by commandism and formalism, departmentalism was rife, and too many cadres were ill-trained or corrupt. But Lin identified the main political task as material support for the front. Everything else had to be subordinated to this goal in order to achieve final victory in the Northeast and then to support the nationwide effort to defeat the Nationalists.[27] In meeting this need one of the critical economic problems facing the CCP in the Northeast was assuring an adequate supply of labor for both production and military purposes. Extraordinary measures were required to provide a constant stream of civilian noncombatants to support the war effort without at the same time crippling the rural and urban economy on which the war effort rested.

Labor Mobilization in the Agricultural Sector

The economic problems brought up by Lin Feng were discussed in detail at a lengthy regional meeting on finance and the economy convened by NEAC in August and September 1947. Before the assembled provincial chairmen and financial and economic specialists, Li Fuqun, speaking on behalf of the party's Northeast Bureau, asserted that the demands of the war had far outstripped the performance of the economy and the financial system. Li called for the implementation of planned economic development to bring order out of chaos and meet the urgent requirements of the war effort. He condemned a number of mistaken views: reliance on guerrilla warfare and neglect of the mainline forces, belief in the primacy of peaceful construction, egalitarianism, separation of the task of economic construction from that of supporting the front, slighting of the long-term nature of the war, and paying excessive attention to the immediate interests of the masses. Above all, he stressed the need for unity and coordination of economic efforts.[28] Li's central message, in other words, was that to ensure victory it would be necessary to get even greater contributions from peasants and urban dwellers alike.

The 1948 Economic Outline drawn up by NEAC's Financial-Economic Committee was endorsed by the Northeast Bureau on 10 October 1947.[29] It listed as the party's principal tasks for 1948 the development of agriculture, particularly of grain production; restoration and further expansion of war-related industries; protection of legitimate private enterprise; and control of external trade. Cadres engaged in mass work were instructed to make production the key link of their activity. Specifically, the outline set a target of a 12 percent increase in grain production (or an additional one million tons), along with expanded production of cotton, flax, sugar beet, tobacco, and livestock. In industry, the outline emphasized increasing coal production and developing the machine tool, textile, shoe, electric power, and chemical industries to serve the war effort.[30]

The outline pointed to the mobilization of additional supplies of labor as the key to achieving the agricultural targets. It claimed that the labor force could be increased by 1.2 million persons in northern Manchuria alone, by organizing labor exchange groups in the villages to embrace at least 60 percent of the labor force, and by mobilizing 40 percent of village women. In addition, 3 to 5 percent of the urban population were to be mobilized for agricultural production. After publication of the outline, individual provinces drew up concrete plans of implementation.

Increasing the labor supply was far from easy. Unlike other regions of China, the Northeast had no large number of unemployed or underemployed rural and urban workers who could be pressed into the military and military support services in time of war. In fact, first as an expanding frontier economy and later as an industrializing region, the Northeast had had a constant need for additional labor, met by migration from North China to supplement natural increase. [31] Although the disruption of industry by the removal of Japanese technical personnel and Soviet spoliation released a substantial number of urban workers, this occurred for the most part far from the areas where the Communists needed manpower. Thus it was primarily from the rural population (generally considered more reliable than the urban dwellers in any case) that the Communists recruited their manpower.

Military recruitment, by draining able-bodied labor from the countryside, had exacerbated an already serious agricultural situation. The rural revolution had disrupted the intricate pattern of agricultural production relations, and the government was as yet unable to restore production by allocating enough resources to agriculture. An urban food crisis of early 1947, the mounting demands of the front, and the agreement to ship Northeast agricultural products to the USSR in exchange for industrial and military equipment made it imperative to increase agricultural production. Only an increased labor supply could provide a short-term solution to the production problems in agriculture. Let us look briefly at three expedients for achieving that increase: the campaign to mobilize *erliuzi*, the transfer of urban labor to the countryside, and the establishment of labor exchange and mutual aid teams.

In the spring of 1947, NEAC began a campaign to compel *erliuzi* (loafers or idlers, i.e., nonproductive elements of the rural population), to join the agricultural work force. [32] The *erliuzi* were exemplars of what one sociologist has termed a "culture of shiftlessness"— persons lacking a work ethic, who survived by sponging on the labor of family, friends, and acquaintances. [33] Local peasant associations mobilized the wives and children of *erliuzi* to persuade their delinquent husbands and fathers to work. Meetings, remonstrances by model workers and cadres, and compulsory assigned labor were used to reform the village idlers. In one village, for example, a certain Wang Yongjiang was labeled a Special Class Idler and ordered to chop seven hundred catties of wood in two weeks and to gather one load of manure every morning. *Erliuzi* were forced to confess their errors and were given two weeks in which to mend their ways or face further struggle meetings, confiscation of their land, and banishment from the village. [34]

In some places *erliuzi* were made to perform menial tasks for army dependents while being supervised by public officials. Various articles in the press estimated that perhaps 1 to 3 percent of the rural population were *erliuzi* whose sloth could no longer be tolerated in a period of revolutionary warfare.

Potentially a more important source of labor power was the 3 to 5 percent of the urban population deemed surplus by the Communist authorities. In the autumn of 1947, a population census and registration was conducted in the Communist-governed cities. On this basis NEAC decided to shift large numbers of people from the cities to the countryside. The shift of population also served the important secondary purpose of easing the strain on the urban food supply. However, unlike the *xiaxiang* campaigns of the 1960s and 1970s, the primary objective of this shift was not to alleviate urban problems but to provide additional labor power for the countryside. Regulations published to implement the decision focused on teamsters, carters, hawkers, petty tradesmen, and the like as major targets for relocation. Where persuasion failed to evoke compliance, compulsion was used.[35]

County governments were directed to set aside land and settlement areas for the migrants, but the expenses of moving were to be borne primarily by the migrants themselves with some assistance provided by local governments and peasant associations.[36] Scattered evidence suggests that many of these unwilling peasants (just how many there were is impossible to say) encountered grave difficulties in their new rural environments, not the least of which stemmed from their lack of agricultural implements, livestock, and seed as well as from their inexperience. One wonders how much these unfortunates were really able to contribute to solving agricultural problems. If they reaped enough to keep themselves alive they may have been doing well. In any case, from the point of view of the regional and municipal authorities, even a small reduction in the urban population would relieve pressure on the urban food supply and reduce strain on the hard-pressed transportation system. Incidentally, the Communist authorities did little if anything to impede the flow of urban refugees from the liberated areas to the GMD-held cities because this flow eased the strain on their food supplies while contributing to inflation and ultimately to famine in the Nationalists' territories.[37]

It is worth noting that draft animals were as urgently needed as human labor in the rural areas. Many horses and other draft animals had been requisitioned for military service, and the toll on the beasts was heavy. The rural revolution had brought a redistribution of livestock, but many peasants lacked fodder to maintain the animals they received through land reform. A large number of livestock died or were too weakened to work. Therefore, county and urban public security and tax offices registered urban livestock (particularly horses) and shipped surplus animals to the countryside. Horses and oxen were needed more urgently to plow fields than to service Harbin's taxi industry!

Still more important as a source of additional manpower was the exchange of labor and the formation of mutual aid teams. Traditionally, the exchange of labor was more prevalent in Manchuria than elsewhere in China because the short growing season and the greater use of draft animals in agriculture predisposed peasants to develop labor exchange relationships.[38] A number of different arrangements were used, including the mutual exchange of human labor and the exchange of human labor for animal power. Perhaps a third of the peasants—mostly poor and middle peasants—were involved in these exchanges, which tended to be among family and friends and were limited in duration and scope.[39]

The party sought to broaden the scope and prolong the duration of the old-style labor exchanges by expanding them beyond the boundary of family and friends and using them for more and different kinds of agricultural tasks. Labor exchange teams were deemed particularly important in cultivating the lands of military dependents whose menfolk were off at the front or had fallen in combat. There is evidence that the more well-to-do peasants, particularly those with healthy animals, often got the better of the labor exchanges since draft power was at a premium. But in any case the exchange of labor was widely promoted to rationalize the use of human and animal resources to alleviate the labor shortage.

It is difficult to assess just how much labor power was made available to agriculture through each of the preceding means,[40] but the fact remains that the economy was able to meet the expanding needs of the war as well as supply agricultural exports to the USSR. Organizational controls and social pressures emanating from the network of new mass organizations, combined with the support the party enjoyed as a result of its redistributive policies, enabled the Communists to meet the manpower needs of a wartime economy.

Labor Mobilization for the Front

Unlike the Nationalists, whose infrequent attempts to tap Manchurian manpower were unsuccessful, the NEDUA recruited most of its soldiers from within the region.[41] In addition, the Communist armies depended upon hundreds of thousands of *minfu* (noncombatant laborers) to serve as carters, stretcher-bearers, porters, nurses, and so forth. CCP success in accomplishing this difficult task derived from the party's ability to link protection of the land revolution to the requirements of the civil war. Peasants who had benefited from the redistribution of land and other property were told that they could defend the fruits of the revolution by labor service at the front as well as by volunteering for combat duties.

The Communist effort to recruit *minfu* was based on the principle of an equitable distribution of the burden of military support service while ensuring an adequate supply of manpower. The party made a serious attempt to avoid press-gang techniques of recruitment, a common feature of both warlord and Nationalist armies and a sure way to alienate the peasantry. The central principle was to assign manpower quotas to the local levels and to see that these were filled without resort either to outright coercion or to mechanisms that could easily be manipulated by the well-to-do.

Recruitment was often done through labor exchange groups, but those who were not thus organized were also subject to service. Alien class elements such as struggled landlords or refractory persons like the *erliuzi* were used as mobile labor to replace peasants recruited as *minfu*.[42] The desire to ensure that *minfu* were politically reliable, however, had to be balanced against the overwhelming need for manpower, and thus cadres were advised not to be as choosy about the class status of the *minfu* as they were about actual military recruits. Even landlords' sons could be used in stretcher corps if properly supervised.[43]

Elaborate regulations, which could not always be adhered to, of course, defined the length and conditions of service for *minfu*. Those who had already served were given certificates exempting them from further service. Peasants who provided horses and/or carts were similarly protected and were to be compensated for loss or damage to their property.

Cadres and activists tried to achieve a high level of voluntarism in the mobilization of *minfu* through propaganda appealing to both patriotism and self-interest. With the nature and purpose of the war explained, it was hoped, peasants would give their labor willingly and loyally to the Communist side. One article in the *Dongbei ribao* touted the use of popular slogans such as, "Good men should join up or else they're not heroes," and "If everyone will shake a leg, then that's the end of Chiang bad egg!" (A free translation.) Inevitably, the stress on voluntarism was often jettisoned as harried cadres pressed unwilling peasants into service to meet their quotas.[44]

Once they had been recruited, attention was paid to organizing the *minfu* into appropriate units, giving them adequate supplies, making provisions for their dependents, and instilling them with an esprit de corps so that they would not desert en route or break under attack.[45] A rather idealized portrait of the *minfu* is presented in the following free translation:

> *Song of the Stretcher Bearers*
> *by Fang Xing*
>
> *On our heads felt caps,*
> *On our feet plaited shoes.*
> *We are liberated peasants*
> *Bearing stretchers for our soldiers.*
> *We carry without a jolt,*
> *We walk lightly*
> *And won't allow the wounded*
> *To suffer cold or hunger*
> *We help the NEDUA wipe out the central bandits*
> *So we need never again be Nationalist soldiers.*[46]

Understandably, many peasants were reluctant to serve as *minfu* not simply because they were separated from their families and their land, but also because of the grave dangers *minfu* encountered. To counter this, propagandists were instructed to spread news of Communist victories to bolster *minfu* morale, to hold appropriate send-offs for the volunteers and also to welcome back those returning safely from the field, to refute enemy rumors about the devastation wreaked by Nationalist bombers, and so forth.[47]

In the areas where the Communists had had time to initiate the agrarian revolution, the peasants who were called upon to contribute their men and their wealth to the revolutionary war could perceive a stake in the outcome, because they had already benefited from the distribution of land and movable property. Yet as the war moved southward in Manchuria at an accelerating pace, the party was increasingly compelled to recruit soldiers, mobilize labor, and requisition supplies in areas just behind the front lines, where it had not yet had time to carry out land reform or redistribute the enemy's wealth. It was forced to impose heavy burdens on the local population before it had conveyed any advantage by its presence. Nor did it have sufficient time to organize and motivate properly the men who were pressed into service as the military machine ground forward. In July 1947, for example, right after some active campaigning in Jilin, twenty thousand people from the newly liberated areas of Xifeng, Dongfeng, Qingyuan, and Kaiyuan were pressed into service as *minfu*.[48] Under the strain of campaign conditions, it is unlikely that peasants found such mobilization very different from the burdens previously imposed by the militarists, the Japanese, and the Nationalists in their turn. Yet from the party's viewpoint the only alternative to such politically premature mobilization was certain defeat.

Despite the shortcomings in the implementation of its mobilization policies occasioned by the pressure of ongoing military campaigns, inadequately trained cadres, and the general atmosphere of revolutionary fervor, the Communist Party's approach to the problem of manpower recruitment probably went far to neutralize peasant suspicions of the party and to win a substantial number of active supporters in the villages, particularly once it became evident that Communist power was there to stay. Yet it would be a mistake to minimize the burden the party placed upon the peasantry in Northeast China or to exaggerate the enthusiasm most peasants probably felt for the CCP.

Toward a Theoretical Understanding of Communist Power in Manchuria

The large-scale conventional war fought in Manchuria in 1946–48 imposed its own requirements upon the participants. Unlike the guerrilla-style Anti-Japanese War of the North China base areas, which was fought on a shoestring,[49] the fighting in Manchuria devoured huge supplies of men, weapons, war matériel, provisions, horses, and transport equipment. An endless supply of military recruits and hundreds of thousands of civilian noncombatant support personnel had to be raised for the most part from among the Manchurian rural population. Grain, fodder, cooking oil, fuel, shoes, clothing, and numerous other items had to be supplied to a large army that lacked the leisure to grow its own supplies or produce its own goods on the model of Nanniwan.[50] In addition, the several tens of thousands of officials, cadres, local organizers, and others administering the revolution were also consumers dependent upon requisitioned supplies. In sum, the Communists, lacking foreign benefactors[51] or well-established mechanisms for taxing the rural population, were compelled by force of circumstance to procure what they needed from a population that at least initially viewed them with suspicion and no little hostility.

Manchurian peasants were inured to being squeezed to support military and administrative machines. Zhang Zuolin in the 1920s and the Manchukuo government in the 1930s and early 1940s had imposed heavy burdens on the Northeast countryside.[52] How is it, then, that while these earlier regimes had alienated the peasantry and were widely perceived as exploitative, the Communists were able to achieve decisive support from among the rural population? The key distinction between the Communists and these earlier power holders was not that Communist levies were less severe or even that different strata of the rural population bore the chief burden. Although part of the property confiscated from landlords, rich peasants, collaborators, and other enemies was funneled directly into the war effort, most of it was first distributed to the peasants, who were expected thereafter to contribute to defraying the costs of the war. The costs of the war were far too great to be borne by confiscated wealth alone, and the middle peasants, poor peasants, and laborers who were the beneficiaries of Communist rule also bore a very substantial part of the total economic burden as well as most of the manpower burden.[53]

The essential Communist innovation in the course of the Chinese rural revolution consisted of instituting an exchange relationship with the peasantry marked by reciprocity and justice. Taxation, military and labor service, provisioning, and other obligations were not unilaterally extracted by the Communist Party from the peasantry in exchange for nothing, but rather were one side of the equation of revolutionary transformation. Without an understanding of how this exchange was instituted and functioned, it is impossible to grasp the process that led to the CCP victory in Manchuria.

In recent years a growing number of scholars have addressed the question of how and why peasants become participants in revolutionary activity. A few basic points in the literature may serve as the starting point for analysis of the Manchurian case.[54] Modern rural revolution (as distinct from sporadic, traditional peasant jacqueries) typically originates in an effort by an urban-centered revolutionary movement to develop contacts with rural dwellers. In this process, ideologically based appeals for political action stand little chance of success for, as Migdal notes, "The revolutionary looks no different from all the other city folk who have taken advantage of the peasants' weaknesses."[55] The most successful approach is likely to be one that speaks directly to needs perceived by rural dwellers and offers them something tangible in return for their political participation.[56] Revolutionary action, then, begins as an exchange relationship in which both elements in the exchange pool their resources or values to their mutual advantage. Cooperation yields an increase in available power.[57]

The peasant's decision whether or not to enter into exchange relations is contingent, however, upon a calculation of risk. Popkin notes that such calculation involves weighing the resources expended against the possibility of punishment in case of failure, estimating the anticipated rewards, gauging the probability of success, and judging the quality of the leadership of the joint enterprise.[58] The probability of a positive decision to participate is increased to the extent that the scope of the project is narrow enough to provide for a short-term payoff. If the initial commitment turns out to have been justified and trust in the revolutionary leadership increases, it becomes progressively possible to substitute longer-term and more abstract goals requiring successful collective action for the short-term, individual goals that first elicited participation.[59]

Exchange theory (as presented by Race, Migdal, and Popkin) explicitly addresses the question of how revolutionary organizations get started in rural areas previously lacking a tradition of collective peasant political activity. In its emphasis on the problem of "starting up" the revolutionary machine and on individual decision-making as the proper focus of analysis, exchange theory is to peasant revolution as liberal social contract theory is to the origin of the state: provocative but somewhat abstract and excessively individualistic. Nevertheless, a modified version of exchange theory will help us to understand the connection between the Communist Party and rural dwellers in civil war Manchuria.

As applied to the development of peasant revolution, exchange theory asserts the need for a prolonged investment of effort passing through several stages before peasant participation in revolutionary organization becomes institutionalized. As Migdal says, "Revolutionaries create power through a painstaking, step-by-step process of social exchange, a process which routinizes behavior, rather than trying to foment unpredictable and uninstitutionalized action.''[60] Such efforts take a great deal of time. Among the major empirical evidence for this notion of accumulative revolutionary participation is the development of the Chinese Communist movement, particularly in North China. The logical corollary of this proposition is that political movements which for one reason or another try to accelerate the pace of recruiting rural dwellers into the ranks of the revolution will run afoul of peasant conservatism, suspicion of outsiders, low political consciousness, and so forth. How does exchange theory help us understand the particularities of the rural revolution in Northeast China?

In Manchuria Communist rural organizing began in earnest only in 1946, under the intense pressure of the burgeoning civil war. The party lacked the time necessary to cultivate relations with peasants step by step. It could not wait. The civil war, then, greatly accelerated the process of forging links between the Communist cadres and the peasants, but it did so at a price.

The growth of the Communist Party in rural Manchuria is unlike the problem of initially emerging organizations analyzed by exchange theorists. The CCP came to the Northeast as an existing organization with a large number of trained cadres, a well-articulated program of social change, and extensive experience in rural organizing. The problems it faced differed substantially from those of a fledgling revolutionary organization attempting to start up operations for the first time. Here, the major problem was that of organizational growth in a new territory under wartime conditions. Its major difficulties were encountered in recruiting enough reliable local leaders to supplement the core of outsider veterans (an estimated twelve thousand) who had been shifted into the region, and in overcoming the reluctance of many rural inhabitants to become involved in revolutionary activity.

The party's handling of these problems entailed less innovation than marginal adjustment to the standard operating procedures that had stood the test of time and circumstances in the North China base areas during the Resistance War. It already had three existing assets. First, its established organizational structure provided an internal system of command and coordination whose smooth functioning ensured both centralized direction and local flexibility. Second, precisely because it was an already established organization, the party had rewards to distribute to those willing to join its ranks or work for its goals. Since the party and its auxiliary organizations expanded at a particularly rapid rate in the civil war years, it could offer inducements of prestige, power, upward mobility, and status to recruits willing to assume local leadership positions. Third, as the possessors of a large, well-organized and well-equipped military force, the Communists could offer protection and security to those willing to join them (both individuals and villages) and could also impose sanctions on those who demurred or resisted. This system of rewards and sanctions structured the environment in which individuals and entire communities responded to Communist revolutionary organizing.

The establishment of exchange relationships between villagers and a revolutionary organization is a complex phenomenon even though the essential notion of exchange is a simple one. If decisions whether or not to join the Communist revolutionary enterprise or participate in local activities such as land reform and struggle meetings represent a calculated weighing of costs and benefits, it must be stressed that rural inhabitants do not make such decisions in a value-neutral atmosphere. The choice is perhaps typically made in a highly charged atmosphere of crosscutting pressures generated by a local elite that is trying to preserve its power and by the outside organization, which is trying to oust them. The decision, obviously not a trivial one, may entail enormous consequences, not all of which can be anticipated. Yet the villager confronts not the Gestalt of revolution but a concrete choice, such as whether or not to attend a meeting called by revolutionary organizers, to provide or conceal goods wanted by the revolutionary army, to serve or to seek to evade labor service or conscription.

The cost of participating must be weighed not only against the potential or actual benefits derived therefrom, but also against the possible sanctions for refraining from participation. In sum, the local coercive balance may be decisive in structuring the participatory choice. Finally, it may be observed that choice may be the prerogative not of the individual but of a group such as the family or the village leadership. For example, local elites faced with a demand to provide men and matériel by a Communist (or other) military detachment operating in their vicinity may decide to comply without consulting more than a small number of those individuals who will bear the burden of conscription, labor service, or provisioning.

In northern and central Manchuria, where rural revolution occurred in 1946–47, the Communist military presence provided a more or less secure environment in which the political transactions between villagers and party organizers could take place. Even if peasants and village leaders doubted the long-term viability of the Communist cause (rumors about the imminent return of the Nationalists were disseminated by the CCP's opponents), it was difficult to say no in the short term to Communist commanders and organizers who physically controlled a particular territory. This makes it difficult if not impossible to assess the mixture of voluntary response versus grudging compliance with demands in any given locality on the basis of available information.

If Communist success in northern and central Manchuria originated in the local military superiority enjoyed by the Communist armies, it was certainly consolidated and expanded as a result of the reciprocal benefits exchanged in the course of developing the Communist-villager ties. Through the rural revolution many peasants received land, a portion of the wealth confiscated from the old elite (landlords, rich peasants, moneylenders), and the right to participate in the new institutions established in the countryside to exercise power. Those who made an active commitment to the revolutionary side were also provided with opportunities for mobility outside the village as well as increased status and power within their localities. Peasants who had often before borne the burden of conflict without getting anything in return were now being rewarded for their efforts. This was a profound change that undoubtedly generated significant popular support for the CCP in the Manchurian countryside. Perhaps no less important in shaping villagers' attitudes toward the revolution was the principle of equity incorporated in the Communist system of taxation and corvée labor (the latter to be sure disguised as voluntary contributions). Instead of the arbitrary and capricious methods of the past used to recruit soldiers and civilian support personnel, levy taxes, and secure carts, livestock, food, and fodder, the CCP initiated an equitable and fairly predictable system that spread the burden quite evenly across the rural population and protected villagers from repeated labor service or overly onerous contributions to the military effort.

In sum, Communist success derived from a number of interlocking factors—organizational superiority, a program that elicited popular support through a genuine exchange relationship, and an equitable system for distributing the burden of conflict.

Conclusion

The civil war in Manchuria was not rooted in the Communists' attempt to secure or to defend revolutionary gains won by previously dispossessed peasants under party leadership. Rather, the CCP, seeking the high road to power, organized a rural revolution, attacked the old elite, and distributed land and other goods in order to gain the base of support without which their hope of victory was doomed. From the perspective of the Communist high command, revolution in rural Manchuria was a means by which the party could tap the supplies of manpower, grain, livestock, carts, and fodder it needed to wage the war. The conventional war that the Communists fought in Manchuria rested on a broad popular base, and in this sense—and this sense only—the party fought a people's war in the region. The rural revolution became, in effect, the Communists' supply train and recruiting station.

The Chinese civil war of the late 1940s remains insufficiently studied by students of modern Chinese history. Vast research areas remain to be explored. Regional variation alone provides fertile ground for many monographs. This essay has simply probed at the edges of one large topic—the civil war in Manchuria. It is likely that detailed study of the civil war years will reveal many variations in the pattern of Communist victory. I have made no assumption that the explanation of the victory in the Northeast is a model for understanding events elsewhere in China. At this tender stage of our understanding of the Chinese revolution let us at least accept the possibility that the victory of the CCP may have involved very diverse paths to power in different regions, provinces, or even localities on the complex gameboard of Chinese politics.

NOTES

Chapter 1

1. Gunther Stein, *The Challenge of Red China* (New York: Whittlesey House, 1945), p. 54.

2. Tang Tsou, *America's Failure in China 1941–1950* (Chicago: University of Chicago Press, 1963), p. 223.

3. Edgar Snow acknowledges that his view of the base areas would have been quite different had he come directly from the United States rather than via Guomindang China. Edgar Snow, *The Long Revolution* (New York: Vintage Books, 1972), p. 177. Archibald T. Steele, who visited Yan'an, makes the same point. *The American People and China* (New York: McGraw Hill, 1966), ch. 2.

4. See, for example, G. E. Taylor, "Reconstruction After Revolution: Kiangsi Province and the Chinese Nation," *Pacific Affairs* 8, 3 (September 1935): 302–11, and Dorothy Borg, *American Policy and the Chinese Revolution, 1925–1928* (New York: American Institute of Pacific Relations, 1947).

5. O. Edmund Clubb, *Communism in China: As Reported from Hankow in 1932* (New York: Columbia University Press, 1968), pp. 71–73, 81–87.

6. See, for example, Evans Carlson, *Twin Stars of China* (New York: Dodd, Mead, 1940); George Taylor, *The Struggle for North China* (New York: Institute of Pacific Relations, 1940), p. 101.

7. A good statement of this view can be found in Michael Lindsay, "The North China Front," *Amerasia* 8, 7 (31 March 1944): 105.

8. Edgar Snow, *Red Star Over China* (New York: Grove Press, 1961), p. 299. Snow perceived this apparent bond between the people and their political organizations as "something new in rural China" (p. 237).

9. Lyman P. Van Slyke, ed., *The Chinese Communist Movement: A Report of the United States War Department, July 1945* (Stanford: Stanford University Press, 1968), p. 1.

10. A good statement of this view is Taylor, *The Struggle*.

11. See, for example, Harrison Forman, *Report from Red China* (New York: Henry Holt, 1945), and Stein, *The Challenge*.

12. Taylor, *The Struggle*, p. 78. Emphasis added.

13. Edgar Snow, *Random Notes on Red China, 1936–1945* (Cambridge: East Asian

Research Center, Harvard University, 1974), p. 37.

14. This was also clear in Snow's later *Battle For Asia* (New York: Random House, 1941). Our thanks to Christine Torre for this insight. The view that the Communist movement was in the mainstream of an ongoing Chinese revolution against domestic ills was an important factor causing Snow to minimize the influence of the Soviet Union on the Chinese Communist movement.

15. Theodore H. White and Annalee Jacoby, *Thunder Out of China* (New York: William Sloane Associates, 1946), pp. 201–202.

16. See White and Jacoby, *Thunder Out of China*, ch. 20 and 21.

17. Tang Tsou suggests this in his *America's Failure*.

18. On the mood in Chongqing, see Steele, *The American People*, ch. 2.

19. An eloquent statement of this view can be found in Lin Yutang, *Between Tears and Laughter* (New York: John Day, 1941). See also his exchange with Edgar Snow in *The Nation*: Snow, "China to Lin Yutang," 160 (17 February 1945): 180–83; Lin, "China and Its Critics," 160 (24 March 1945): 324–27; Snow, "China to Lin Yutang—II," 160 (31 March 1945): 359. For a discussion of pro-GMD elements within and without the government, see Michael Schaller, *The U.S. Crusade in China, 1938–1945* (New York: Columbia University Press, 1979); Schaller, *The United States and China in the Twentieth Century* (New York: Oxford University Press, 1979), ch. 4 and 5; and Ross Y. Koen, *The China Lobby in American Politics* (New York: Macmillan, 1960). Walter Judd's 1945 speech to the House of Representatives is in *Congressional Record*, vol. 91, pt. 2, 79th Congress, 2d session, pp. 2294–2301.

20. Koen, *The China Lobby*, pp. 156–58.

21. See ibid., and Kenneth E. Shewmaker, *Americans and Chinese Communists, 1927–1945: A Persuading Encounter* (Ithaca: Cornell University Press, 1971).

22. H. Arthur Steiner, "Foreword," *The Annals of the American Academy of Political and Social Sciences* 277 (September 1951): vii.

23. The first term is W. W. Rostow's and the second, Lucien Pye's. W. W. Rostow, *The Stages of Economic Growth: A Non-Communist Manifesto* (Cambridge: Cambridge University Press, 1960), p. 162; and Lucien Pye, *Guerrilla Communism in Malaya: Its Social and Political Meaning* (Princeton: Princeton University Press, 1956), p. 349.

24. Sigmund Neumann, "International Civil War," *World Politics* 1, 3 (April 1949): 346.

25. Philip Selznick, *The Organizational Weapon: A Study of Bolshevik Strategy and Tactics* (New York: McGraw Hill, 1952); Ivo Duchacheck, "The Strategy of Communist Infiltration: Czechoslovakia 1944–1948," *World Politics* 2, 3 (1950): 345–71. See also Josef Korbel, *The Communist Subversion of Czechoslovakia 1938–1948: The Function of Coexistence* (Princeton: Princeton University Press, 1959), and Stefan Possony, *A Century of Conflict: Communist Techniques of World Revolution* (Chicago: Henry Regenry, 1953).

26. Isaac Deutscher, "The French and Russian Revolutions," *World Politics* 4, 3 (April 1952): 378. The best overview of the Eastern European takeovers from this period is Hugh Seton-Watson, *The East European Revolution* (London: Methuen, 1950).

27. See, for example, Ronald Schneider, *Communism in Guatemala, 1944–1954* (New York: Frederick A. Praeger, 1958).

28. Eduard Heimann, "Marxism and Underdeveloped Countries," *Social Research* 19, 3 (September 1952): 322–45; Robert V. Daniels, *The Nature of Communism* (New York: Random House, 1962), ch. 6; Eugene Staley, *The Future of Underdeveloped Countries: Political Implications of Economic Development* (New York: Harper and Brothers, 1954), part 2; A. V. Sherman, "Nationalism and Communism in the

Arab World: A Reappraisal," in *The Middle East in Transition: Studies in Contemporary History*, ed. Walter Z. Laqueur (New York: Frederick A. Praeger, 1958), pp. 452–61; and Walter Laqueur, *Communism and Nationalism in the Middle East* (New York: Frederick A. Praeger, 1956).

29. The above is based on Koen, *The China Lobby*.

30. Selznick, *The Organizational Weapon*, p. 318.

31. See, for example, Feliks Gross, *The Seizure of Political Power in a Century of Revolution* (New York: Philosophical Library, 1958), pp. 187–295; Dinko Tomasic, *National Communism and Soviet Strategy* (Washington, D.C.: Public Affairs Press, 1957); Mario Einaudi, Jean-Marie Domenach, and Aldo Garosci, *Communism in Western Europe* (Ithaca: Cornell University Press, 1951); Walter Crosby Eells, *Communism in Education in Asia, Africa and the Far Pacific* (Washington, D.C.: American Council on Education, 1954), Schneider, *Communism in Guatemala*; and Laqueuer, *Communism and Nationalism in the Middle East*.

32. There is one significant qualification to this statement. During these years there was some work done on the "appeals of Communism" to either the masses or middle-level cadres. This was, however, the exception to the rule in a field where leadership strategies received the lion's share of attention. See Adam B. Ulam, *The Unfinished Revolution: An Essay on the Source of Influence of Marxism and Communism* (New York: Random House, 1960); Gabriel Almond, *The Appeals of Communism* (Princeton: Princeton University Press, 1954); Lucien Pye, *Guerrilla Communism in Malaya*; and Richard V. Burks, *The Dynamics of Communism in Eastern Europe* (Princeton: Princeton University Press, 1961).

33. George Taylor, "The Hegemony of the Communists, 1945–1952," *The Annals of the Academy of Political and Social Sciences* 277 (September 1951): 13, 14, 21. See also David N. Rowe, *Modern China: A Brief History* (Princeton: Van Nostrand, 1959); Karl Wittfogel, "The Influence of Leninism-Stalinism on China," *The Annals of the American Academy of Political and Social Sciences* 277 (September 1951): 28, 30–34; Franz Michael, "The Fall of China," *World Politics* 8, 2 (January 1956): 300–306; and R. L. Walker, "How to Misunderstand China," *Yale Review* 40, 3 (March 1951): 437–51.

34. Robert C. North, *Moscow and the Chinese Communists* (Stanford: Stanford University Press, 1953), ch. 1.

35. Benjamin I. Schwartz, *Chinese Communism and the Rise of Mao* (Cambridge: Harvard University Press, 1951), pp. 199, 200–201. See also Schwartz, "Marx and Lenin in China," *Far East Survey* 17, 15 (27 July 1949): 176–78.

36. John K. Fairbank, "Past and Present," *The New Republic* 136, 19 (13 May 1957): 14. See also Fairbank, *The U.S. and China* (Cambridge: Harvard University Press, 1958), ch. 13.

37. John K. Fairbank, "Revolutionary Asia," *Foreign Affairs* 29, 1 (October 1950): 102–104. Note should also be taken of the work of Mary Wright, who also explored the indigenous roots of the Communist movement. See her "Modern China in Transition, 1900–1950," *Annals* 321 (January 1959): 1–5; and "The Chinese Peasant and Communism," *Pacific Affairs* 24, 3 (1951): 256–65.

38. Fairbank, "Revolutionary Asia," pp. 107–108.

39. See, for example, Hsiao Tso-liang, *Power Relations Within the Chinese Communist Movement, 1930–1934* (Seattle: University of Washington Press, 1961); Schwartz, *Chinese Communism*; and North, *Moscow and the Chinese Communists*.

40. Most forcefully stated in Ygael Gluckstein, *Mao's China: Economic and Political Survey* (Boston: Beacon Press, 1957).

41. For example, Theodore Hsi-en Chen, "China: Communism Wins," *Current History* 19, 108 (August 1950): 78–82; Conrad Brandt, Benjamin Schwartz, and John

K. Fairbank, eds., *A Documentary History of Chinese Communism* (Cambridge: Harvard University Press, 1952); Mary Wright, "Modern China in Transition," pp. 3–5; and Tilman Durdin, "The Communist Record," *The Atlantic Monthly* 204, 6 (December 1959): 41.

42. Chalmers Johnson, *Peasant Nationalism and Communist Power: The Emergence of Revolutionary China, 1937–1945* (Stanford: Stanford University Press, 1962).

43. Chalmers Johnson, "Civilian Loyalties and Guerrilla Conflict," *World Politics* 14, 4 (July 1962): 646–61.

44. Johnson, *Peasant Nationalism*, ch. 1.

45. Chalmers Johnson, "Peasant Nationalism Revisited: The Biography of a Book," *The China Quarterly*, no. 72 (December 1977): 766–67.

46. Chalmers Johnson, "The Changing Nature and Locus of Authority in Communist China," in *China: Management of a Revolutionary Society*, ed. John Lindbeck (Seattle: University of Washington Press, 1973), pp. 34–76. In his review of Johnson's book, Benjamin Schwartz was critical of the vagueness with which Communist organization was discussed. *The China Quarterly*, no. 15 (June 1963): 169–70.

47. Johnson, *Peasant Nationalism*, pp. 17–18.

48. Donald G. Gillin, "'Peasant Nationalism' in the History of Chinese Communism," *Journal of Asian Studies* 23, 2 (February 1964): 269, also makes this point.

49. Ibid., pp. 274, 283–85.

50. Most prominently, John E. Rue, *Mao Tse-tung in Opposition 1927–1935* (Stanford: Stanford University Press, 1966); and Shanti Swarup, *A Study of the Chinese Communist Movement* (Oxford: Clarendon Press, 1966).

51. For example, Stuart Schram, "Mao Tse-tung and Liu Shao-ch'i, 1939–1969," *Asian Survey* 12, 4 (April 1972): 274–94; and John Lewis, "Leader, Commissar, and Bureaucrat: The Chinese Political System in the Last Days of the Revolution," in *China in Crisis*, ed. Ho P'ing-ti and Tang Tsou (Chicago: University of Chicago Press, 1968), vol. 1, book 2, pp. 449–81.

52. See, for example, Richard H. Solomon, *Mao's Revolution and the Chinese Political Culture* (Berkeley: University of California Press, 1971); Benjamin I. Schwartz, "China and the West in the 'Thought of Mao Tse-tung,'" in *China in Crisis*, ed. Ho and Tsou, vol. 1, book 1, pp. 365–489; and Peter Seybolt, "The Yenan Revolution in Mass Education," *The China Quarterly*, no. 48 (October-December 1971): 641–69.

53. Johnson himself reports this last criticism in his "Peasant Nationalism Revisited: The Biography of a Book," *The China Quarterly*, no. 72 (December 1977): 784. The quotation is from an article by Richard Pfeffer in *The Nation*, 27 April 1970, p. 506.

54. Chalmers Johnson, "Chinese Communist Leadership and Mass Response," in *China in Crisis*, ed. Ho and Tsou, vol. 1, book 1, pp. 397–437. Johnson later claimed that he still stood by the original argument of *Peasant Nationalism*. Johnson, "Peasant Nationalism Revisited," pp. 766–85.

55. James Sheridan, *China in Disintegration: The Republican Era in Chinese History* (Glencoe: Free Press, 1971), esp. pp. 264–69; and Maurice Meisner, "Yenan Communism and the Rise of the Chinese People's Republic," in *Modern East Asia: Essays in Interpretation*, ed. James Crowley (New York: Harcourt, Brace and World, 1970). The most masterful synthesis can be found in the work of the French historian Lucien Bianco, *The Origins of the Chinese Revolution 1915–1949*, trans. Muriel Bell (Stanford: Stanford University Press, 1971), ch. 6.

56. Mark Selden, *The Yenan Way in Revolutionary China* (Cambridge: Harvard University Press, 1971).

57. See Mark Selden, "People's War and the Transformation of Peasant Society: China and Vietnam," in *America's Asia: Dissenting Essays in Asian-American Relations*, ed. Edward Friedman and Mark Selden (New York: Pantheon Books, 1971), and *The Yenan Way*, p. 277.

58. Ralph Thaxton, "On Peasant Nationalism and National Resistance," *World Politics* 30, 1 (October 1977): 24–57; Tetsuya Kataoka, *Resistance and Revolution in China* (Berkeley: University of California Press, 1974), ch. 4 and 7; and Meisner, "Yenan Communism."

59. Roy M. Hofheinz, Jr. is often credited with laying the greatest stress on the determining role of organization, based on his conclusion in "The Ecology of Chinese Communist Success: Rural Influence Patterns, 1923–45," in *Chinese Communist Politics in Action*, ed. A. Doak Barnett (Seattle: University of Washington Press, 1969), p. 77. However, Hofheinz's later study of the early years of the Communist peasant movement casts doubt on the efficacy of organization or leadership alone as "the yeast of revolutionary growth." *The Broken Wave: The Chinese Communist Peasant Movement, 1922–1928* (Cambridge: Harvard University Press, 1977), p. 286.

60. Ilpyong J. Kim, *The Politics of Chinese Communism: Kiangsi under the Soviets* (Berkeley: University of California Press, 1973), p. 3.

61. Of course, Kataoka's argument does not carry the ideological baggage typical of some Western works published in these years.

62. A very strong case for the importance of organization as a factor contributing to Communist success can be found in Bianco, *Origins of the Chinese Revolution*, ch. 6.

63. For a summary of his argument see Kataoka, *Resistance and Revolution*, introduction and conclusion.

64. Some scholarship on the GMD tends to favor those who minimize the role of the war, suggesting, in contrast to Kataoka, that the power of the GMD was not growing in the prewar period. See Lloyd Eastman, *The Abortive Revolution: China under Nationalist Rule, 1927–1949* (Cambridge: Harvard University Press, 1974); and Hung-mao Tien, *Government and Politics in Kuomintang China, 1927–1937* (Stanford: Stanford University Press, 1972). In a later study, Eastman does underscore the importance of the war in contributing to the Guomindang collapse, while by no means granting it the sole determining role. *Seeds of Destruction: Nationalist China in War and Revolution, 1937–1949* (Stanford: Stanford University Press, 1984), esp. pp. 216–26.

65. Elizabeth J. Perry, *Rebels and Revolutionaries in North China, 1845–1945* (Stanford: Stanford University Press, 1980).

66. Jack A. Goldstone, "Theories of Revolution: The Third Generation," *World Politics* 32, 2 (April 1980): 425–53.

67. Theda Skocpol, *States and Social Revolutions: A Comparative Analysis of France, Russia, and China* (Cambridge: Cambridge University Press, 1979); Jeffrey M. Paige, *Agrarian Revolution: Social Movements and Export Agriculture in the Underdeveloped World* (New York: Free Press, 1975); James C. Scott, *The Moral Economy of the Peasant: Rebellion and Subsistence in Southeast Asia* (New Haven: Yale University Press, 1976); Samuel L. Popkin, *The Rational Peasant: The Political Economy of Rural Society in Vietnam* (Berkeley: University of California Press, 1979).

68. He does not exclude the possibility that political action may occur in rural settings where these notions never had, or no longer hold, currency, but he suggests that for many such, we are no longer discussing "peasant" action at all. Cf: his discussion of the effects of migration, p. 213.

69. Skocpol, *States and Social Revolutions*, p. 171; Scott, "Revolution in the Revolution: Peasants and Commissars," *Theory and Society* 7 (1979): 97–134; Popkin, *Rational Peasant*, p. 259.

70. Skocpol enshrines this question as the title of a review on the subject, "What Makes Peasants Revolutionary?" *Comparative Politics* (April 1982): 351–75.

71. For China, by contrast, the only major attempt to apply these factors in an analytical fashion was a paper by John Wilson Lewis. The paper dealt primarily with peasant rebellions in traditional China but linked the same patterns with the Chinese revolution. Lewis, "Memory, Opportunity, and Strategy," paper for the Research Conference on Communist Revolutions, St. Croix, V.I., January 1972. Lewis argues that the historical memory of repression of rebellion in a locality reduced the propensity to revolt.

72. In Skocpol's words, "Revolutionary situations have developed due to the emergence of politico-military crises of state and class domination. And only because of the possiblities thus created have revolutionary leaderships and rebellious masses contributed to the accomplishment of revolutionary transformation." *States and Social Revolutions*, p. 17. Paige, *Agrarian Revolution*, p. 42; Popkin, *Rational Peasant*, pp. 42–43; Scott, *Moral Economy*, pp. 229–30.

73. Skocpol, "What Makes Peasants Revolutionary?" p. 363. Interestingly, she does not see this as boding ill for peasant interests; rather to the contrary: "Because of this direct mobilization, peasant resources and manpower have ended up participating in the building of new-regime social institutions and state organizations. Peasant participation in this revolutionary pattern is less 'spontaneous' and autonomous than in the first pattern, but the result can be much more favorable to local peasant interests, because during the revolutionary process itself direct links are established between peasants and revolutionary political and military organizations." For Paige's position, see *Agrarian Revolution*, p. 44.

74. Popkin, *Rational Peasant*, p. 259; Scott, *Moral Economy*, pp. 223–25; Paige, *Agrarian Revolution*, pp. 45–49.

75. Scott, *Moral Economy*, p. 236; Popkin, *Rational Peasant*, pp. 43–46, 64, 176–77, 236.

76. In addition to work published or in progress by the authors represented in this volume, we now have the benefit of the definitive study by Yung-fa Chen, *Making Revolution: The Communist Movement in Eastern and Central China, 1937–1945* (Berkeley: University of California Press, 1986).

77. Perry, *Rebels and Revolutionaries*.

78. The classic statement on an exchange analysis of the growth of revolutionary movements can be found in Joel Migdal, *Peasants, Politics, and Revolution: Pressures toward Political and Social Change in the Third World* (Princeton: Princeton University Press, 1974).

79. In line with this perspective on revolution as a political process, see the masterful essay by Rod Aya, "Popular Intervention in Revolutionary Situations," in *Statemaking and Social Movements: Essays in Theory and History*, ed. Susan Harding and Charles Bright (Ann Arbor: University of Michigan Press, 1984), pp. 318–43.

Chapter 2

1. In his essay, "The Jiangxi Period: A Comment on the Western Literature," in Philip C. C. Huang et al., *Chinese Communists and Rural Society* (Berkeley: Center for Chinese Studies, 1978), pp. 85–97, Philip Huang summarizes and critically examines five such studies. They are: John Rue, *Mao Tse-tung in Opposition, 1927–1935* (Stanford: Stanford University Press, 1966); Shanti Swarup, *A Study of the Chinese Communist Movement* (London: Oxford University Press, 1966); Derek Waller, *The Kiangsi Soviet Republic: Mao and the National Congresses of 1931 and 1934* (Berke-

ley: Center for Chinese Studies, 1972); Ilpyong Kim, *The Politics of Chinese Communism: Kiangsi under the Soviets* (Berkeley: University of California Press, 1973); and Trygve Lotveit, *Chinese Communism, 1931–1934: Experience in Civil Government* (Lund, Sweden: Studentlitteratur, 1973). I heartily agree with Huang's assertion that an analysis of power struggles and theoretical arguments will not assist people in understanding a social revolution, and I support his call for more work on the rural context in which revolution occurred. But I would add that such work necessarily includes a serious consideration of the counterrevolutionary forces that were active in the countryside.

2. See Ch'u T'ung-tsu, *Local Government in China under the Ch'ing* (Cambridge: Harvard University Press, 1962), pp. 168–92, for a discussion of the gentry. The composition of this class has been a subject of debate among scholars. Chang Chung-li, *The Chinese Gentry* (Seattle: University of Washington Press, 1955), pp. 3–70; and Ho Ping-ti, *The Ladder of Success in Imperial China* (New York: Columbia University Press, 1962), pp. 26–41.

3. Lloyd E. Eastman, "The Disintegration and Integration of Political Systems in Twentieth-Century China," *Chinese Republican Studies Newsletter* 1, 3 (April 1976): 2–12.

4. *Memoirs of General Hsiung Shih-hui, 1907–Spring 1950*, vol. 1, General Hsiung Shih-hui [Xiong Shihui] Papers, Special Collections Library, Butler Library, Columbia University, p. 52.

5. Ibid.

6. Philip A. Kuhn, "Local Self-Government under the Republic: Problems of Control, Autonomy, and Mobilization," in *Conflict and Control in Late Imperial China*, ed. Frederic Wakeman, Jr., and Carolyn Grant (Berkeley: University of California Press, 1975), p. 293.

7. C. K. Yang, *Chinese Communist Society: The Family and the Village*, vol. 2, *A Chinese Village in Early Communist Transition* (Cambridge: MIT Press, 1959), p. 114. The diversity of the rural elite is illustrated by the six life-histories of Chinese "gentry" families collected by Chow Yung-teh in Fei Hsiao-tung, *China's Gentry: Essays on Rural-Urban Relations* (Chicago: University of Chicago Press, 1953). Also see Chow Yung-teh, *Social Mobility in China: Status Careers among the Gentry in a Chinese Community* (New York: Atherton Press, 1966).

8. Wang Yinxi attributed the growth of the Communist movement in Jiangxi to four fundamental causes. The first two were Communist conversion and coercion of the people. The other two were the bankruptcy of Jiangxi's village economy and exploitation by "local bullies and oppressive gentry." "Wang tingzhang wei qingjiao feigong gao difang guanli ji minzhong shu" (Commissioner Wang's letter to local officials and people regarding the elimination of Communists), *Jiangxi minzheng gongbao* (Jiangxi Civil Affairs Department gazette) (hereafter cited as *JMG*), no. 62 (1 March 1930), *zhuanzai* sec., pp. 1–5. In another piece Wang noted that people blamed the government and "local bullies and oppressive gentry" for the emergence of the Communists. "Wang tingzhang dui Nanchang Xinjian xian zhengfu zhiyuan xunhua" (Commissioner Wang's exhortation to the Nanchang and Xinjian county government workers), *JMG*, no. 67 (16 May 1930), *gongdu* sec., pp. 8–9, and *Jiangxi sheng zhengfu gongbao* (Jiangxi Provincial Government gazette) (hereafter cited as *JSZG*) no. 2 (2 October 1934): 14–15.

9. James Pinckney Harrison, *The Long March to Power: A History of the Chinese Communist Party, 1921–72* (New York: Praeger Publishers, 1972), pp. 154 and 204–12.

10. Xiong Bangyan, "Xiao Jiabi, Guo Mingda fangong di shimo" (The beginning and end of Xiao Jiabi and Guo Mingda's anti-Communism), *Jiangxi wenxian*

(Documents of Jiangxi), no. 4 (2 July 1966): 18–24.

11. "Ningdu Cuiweifeng kang fei xunnan jiyao" (A brief record of the martyrs who resisted the bandits at Cuiweifeng, Ningdu county), GMD Archives, no. 478/7; Dan Shi, "Cuiweifeng kang fei yishi Wei Xuexun xiansheng shilue" (A biographical sketch of Cuiweifeng anti-Communist martyr Wei Xuexun), *Jiangxi wenxian*, no. 26 (2 May 1968): 8–9; and *North China Herald*, 6 February 1934, p. 207.

12. "Ningdu Cuiweifeng kang fei xunnan jiyao."

13. See William Wei, "The KMT in Kiangsi: The Suppression of the Communist Bases, 1930–1934," Ph.D. diss., University of Michigan, 1978, ch. 3, for details on the cooperative societies movement and the New Life movement.

14. Kuhn, "Local Self-Government," p. 294.

15. "Xian zuzhi fa" (County organization law), *Zhongyang zhoubao* (Central weekly), no. 16 (24 September 1928), *zhuanzai* sec., pp. 14–15.

16. Ibid., article 16.

17. Prior to becoming commissioner of civil affairs (October 1929–November 1931), Wang Yinxi served as chief of staff, Third Division. *The China Yearbook* (1932), p. 748.

18. Articles 17 and 18 of the "Xian zuzhi fa." Besides county and branch PSBs, there were also a provincial capital PSB, special city PSBs, and waterway PSBs, which patrolled the Jiangxi waterways. For information of the provincial capital PSB, see Huang Guangtou, "Shinian lai zhi Jiangxi shenghui jing zheng" (Capital police administration in Jiangxi in the last decade), *Ganzheng shinian* (A decade of Jiangxi administration) (Nanchang, 1941).

19. It should be noted that the documents indicate that at least one of these inspectors was accused by a county PSB chief of conspiring with "oppressive gentry" to incriminate him. *JMG*, no. 60 (16 June 1930), *gondu* sec., pp. 49–50. There is no further information on this allegation. The regional inspectors appear to have performed their duties in a professional manner.

20. Wei, "The KMT in Kiangsi," p. 145, table 12, based on documents in *JMG*, nos. 60–70 (1 February–1 July 1930).

21. *JMG*, no. 61 (16 February 1930), *gongdu* sec., pp. 17–18; and no. 62 (1 March 1930), *gongdu* sec., pp. 31–32.

22. "Jiangxi sheng gexian jingcha dui diyiqi jiaoyu jihua biao" (First semester educational plan of Jiangxi province's county police forces), *JMG*, no. 69 (16 June 1930), *zhuanzai* sec., pp. 1–3.

23. *JMG*, no. 68 (1 June 1930), *gongdu* sec., p. 15.

24. This process began in October 1929. "Jiangxi sheng minzheng ting gexian xingzheng tongji" (Jiangxi Civil Affairs Department county administration statistics), *JMG*, no. 60 (1 February 1930), *baogao* sec., p. 6.

25. For a detailed description of the Police Force training program, see the curriculum charts in *JMG*, no. 69 (16 June 1930), *zhuanzai* sec., pp. 1–3.

26. "Jiangxi sheng minzheng ting shijiu nian sanyue fen baogao" (Jiangxi province Civil Affairs Department March 1930 administrative report), *JMG*, no. 60 (16 June 1930), *baogao* sec., p. 8.

27. *JMG*, no. 60 (1 February 1930), *gongdu* sec., p. 4.

28. *JSZG*, no. 1/2 (17 May 1931), p. 92.

29. Hu Guokang, "Gan dong diqu jiaofei huiyi lu" (Recollections of bandit suppression in eastern Jiangxi), *Jiangxi wenxian*, no. 24, part 2 (2 March 1968): 6–9.

30. *JSZG*, no. 32 (20 November 1932): 47–48 and 79–80.

31. Jiang Jieshi zongtong, "Xianzhang shi zhengzhi di jiben liliang" (The county magistrate is the fundamental strength of the administration), in *Jiang Jieshi Zongtong*

quanji (Complete works of President Chiang Kai-shek) (hereafter *JZQ*), 2 vols. (Taibei: Guofang bu yanjiu yuan), pp. 595–601.

32. The following description of the *baowei tuan* is based primarily on the "letter of the law" as it appears in "Xian Baowei tuan fa" (County local militia law), in *Xianzheng ziliao huibian* (Assembled county government data), ed. Liu Zhendong, vol. 2 (n.p.: Zhongyang zhengzhi xuexiao yanjiu bu, 1939), pp. 575–81.

33. "Yansu wanzheng xian zuzhi ji baowei tuan banfa" (Measures for the stern and speedy completion of county organizations and local militia), *JMG*, no. 68 (1 June 1930), *zhuanzai* sec., pp. 1–3. As of June 1930, only twenty-eight counties had finished organizing county governments and the *baowei tuan*. Counties without "bandits" were to complete this work by the end of June. Forty-eight counties with "bandits" were to complete this work by the end of August 1930. Protection was to be provided by the Police Force.

34. Yang Yongtai, in *Guomin zhengfu junshi weiyuanhui weiyuanzhang Nanchang xingying quli jiaofei shengfen zhengzhi gongzuo baogao* (A report by the chairman of the National Government's Military Affairs Council field headquarters at Nanchang on political work in the bandit suppression provinces) (Nanchang, 1934), and *JMG*, no. 60 (1 February 1930), pp. 8–9. Division Commander Luo Lin observed that the county reconstruction committees were controlled by "local bullies and oppressive gentry." *JSZG*, no. 1/2 (16 May 1930), p. 59. A different view was expressed by Xiao Lan, "Feiqu xianzhuang zhi xiezhen" (Sketch of the current situation in the bandit areas), *Jiaochi xuanchuan zhuankan* (A special publication on propaganda for the suppressing of reds), ed. Guomin geming jun lujun diba shi tebie dangbu (Special Party Headquarters of the 8th Division of the National Revolutionary Army) (n.p., 1931), who noted that these committees were controlled by members of the Reorganizationist Clique.

35. Articles 6, 11, and 12 of the "Xian baowei tuan fa."

36. County magistrates were given "rewards and punishments" in accordance with their ability to implement the system. Unfortunately, there are no documents available on who received them or the reasons for their failure to implement the system. "Jiangxi sheng minzheng ting shijiu nian sanyue fen xingzheng baogao," p. 9.

37. Wang Zipu, "Shinian lai zhi Jiangxi minzheng" (A decade of Jiangxi civil affairs), *Ganzheng shinian*, p. 2.

38. Ding Zhongjiang, "Jiangxi wuciweijiao he Xiong Shihui" (The Fifth Encirclement and Suppression Campaign in Jiangxi and Xiong Shihui), *Chun qiu* (Spring and autumn), vol. 20, part 1, no. 5 (May 1974): 1–5. As early as 13 September 1929, Chiang Kai-shek ordered provincial chairmen to impress upon their magistrates the usefulness of the *baojia* as a Communist-suppression institution. *Zhongyang zhoubao*, no. 68 (23 September 1929), *yizhou da shi shuping* sec., p. 7. For regulations governing the *baojia*, see *Jiaofei zhanshi* (A military history of the suppression of the bandits), ed. Guofang bu shizhengju, vol. 6 (Taibei: Zhonghua da dian bianyinhui), app. 6, pp. 1175–83, and app. 8., pp. 1189–97.

39. Hong Yi, "Baiqu gongzuo di jihui zhuyi" (Opportunism of white area work), in *Baiquzhibu gongzuo neirong* (The content of white areas branch bureau work), ed. Zhonggong Gan dongbei sheng wei zuzhi bu (Chinese Communist Northeast Jiangxi Provincial Committee Organization Bureau) (n.p., n.d.), Bureau of Investigation Library, no. 232.5/823.

40. Chen Ching-chih, "The Japanese Adaptation of the *Pao-Chia* System in Taiwan, 1895–1945," *Journal of Asian Studies* 34, 2 (February 1975): 391–416. The Nationalists were well aware of the Japanese use of the *baojia* system and were probably influenced by it.

41. This was probably one of the reasons why Yang Yongtai, secretary-general of Nanchang Headquarters, made the *baojia* an integral part of the Administrative Area

Inspectorate System. Yang Yongtai, *Yang Yongtai xiansheng yanlunji* (Lectures by Yang Yongtai) (n.p.: Ya bi shen shan gongsi, n.d.), p. 50. Tien Hungmao, *Government and Politics in Kuomintang China, 1927–1937* (Stanford: Stanford University Press, 1972), p. 110. For a detailed description of the Adminstrative Area Inspectorate System, see Wei, "The KMT in Kiangsi," pp. 92–101.

42. Tien, *Government and Politics in Kuomintang China*, p. 112.

43. *JSZG*, no. 14 (17 October 1934): 16; no. 15 (22 October 1934): 12–13.

44. *Junshi weiyuanhui weiyuanzhang xingying zhengzhi gongzuo baogao* (Political work report of the field headquarters of the chairman of the Military Affairs Council) (Nanchang, 1935), pp. 17–18.

45. Sometimes this precaution was counterproductive, because a person compromised by a Communist relative or friend might find that the safest course of action was to join the Communists as well.

46. *Junshi weiyuanhui baogao*, pp. 17–18; and Wang, "Shinianlai zhi Jiangxi minzheng," p. 22.

47. *Ganzheng shinian*, ch. 15, p. 16.

48. Kuhn, "Local Self-Government," p. 287.

49. *Jiaofei zhanshi*, vol. 6, app. 8, p. 1191, article 16.

50. Chen Gengya, *Gan Wan Xiang E shicha ji* (Account of a visit to Jiangxi, Anhui, Hunan, and Hubei) (Shanghai: Shenbao yuekan she, 1934), p. 30. Chen was a member of the Rural Land Economic Investigation Group of the Sun Yat-sen Cultural and Educational Institute.

51. The regulations governing the use of a travel permit were stringent. It could be used only in the county in which it was issued. Furthermore, it was restricted to one person and had to be returned to the *baojia* official after it was used. If it was lost, the loss had to be reported to the county magistrate. Ibid., pp. 7–8.

52. Ibid. Peasants were consequently forced to post notices in the streets of their own villages in order to sell their produce.

53. Ibid., p. 26.

54. Ibid.

55. "Jiangxi nongcun jingji" (Jiangxi village economy), *Jiangxi jingji wenti* (Economic problems of Jiangxi), ed. Jiangxi Sheng Zhengfu Jingji Weiyuanhui (Jiangxi Provincial Government Economic Commission) (reprinted Taibei: Xuesheng shuju, 1971), p. 55.

56. Howard L. Boorman, ed., *Biographical Dictionary of Republican China*, vol. 2 (New York: Columbia University Press, 1968), p. 114.

57. *Memoirs of General Hsiung Shih-hui*, 1:32.

58. For a detailed description of the changes in the county *baoweituan* after 1932 see Liao Shiqiao, "Shinian lai zhi Jiangxi baoan" (A decade of peace preservation in Jiangxi), *Ganzheng shinian*, pp. 1–2. Researchers should be cautioned about the different names of the *baowei tuan*; sometimes it is referred to as the *baoan dui*. Yang Yongtai tried to clarify this in his general critique at the Second Peace Preservation Conference held at Nanchang Headquarters on 2 June 1934. *Guomin zhengfu junshi weiyuanhui baogao*. Xiong Shihui took a special interest in the training of the security forces in general and the militia in particular. He wanted them to be as well-trained as military units. In personal discussion with his subordinates and at public lectures, Xiong presented his ideas, which were quite conventional, on the training of soldiers and the attitude officers should have toward them. Hsiung Shih-hui Diary, General Hsiung Shih-hui Papers, Columbia University, 4, 6, 28, and 29 January 1934.

59. Liao Shiqiao, "Shinian lai zhi Jiangxi baoan," p. 1.

60. Ibid. Provincial funds themselves were mostly subsidies provided by the central government. Because Jiangxi was one of the so-called bandit-suppression provinces, it was one of the largest recipients of this largesse. Tien, *Government and*

Politics in Kuomintang China, p. 157. As a close associate of Chiang Kai-shek, Xiong was able personally to intercede on behalf of Jiangxi for government funding. Hsiung Shih-hui Diary, 12 February 1935.

61. *Junshi weiyuanhui baogao*, p. 22.

62. *JSZG*, no. 7 (8 October 1934): 7–8.

63. *Junshi weiyuanhui baogao*, p. 23; and Liao Shiqiao, "Shinian lai zhi Jiangxi baoan," pp. 5–6.

64. For further details on militia skirmishes, see *Jiangxi nianjian*, pp. 457–73, tables 1–12.

65. Wang Zipu, "Shinianlai zhi Jiangxi minzheng," p. 12; *JSZG*, no. 11 (13 October 1934): 16; no. 5 (5 October 1934): 2–3.

66. *China Year Book* (1931), pp. 217 and 178.

67. Liu Mengying, "Jiangxi dianxian jianshe yu jiaofei kang zhan zhi huiyi" (Telecommunications construction in Jiangxi and recollections of the bandit suppression and the war of resistance), *Jiangxi wenxian*, no. 6 (2 September 1966): 21.

68. Tan Bingxun, "Shinian lai Jiangxi gonglu" (A decade of Jiangxi highways), *Ganzheng shinian*, p. 1.

69. Ibid.

70. Liu Mengying, "Jiangxi dianxian jianshe yu jiaofei kang zhan zhi huiyi," p. 22.

71. Liao Shiqiao, "Shinian lai zhi Jiangxi baoan," p. 11.

72. *Memoirs of General Hsiung Shih-hui* 1:43; and T'ang Leang-li, *Suppressing Communist-Banditry in China* (Shanghai: China United Press, 1934), p. 52.

73. *Guomin zhengfu junshi weiyuanhui baogao*, ch. 7, p. 1.

74. *Junshi weiyuanhui baogao*, pp. 87–88.

75. *Guomin zhengfu junshi weiyuanhui baogao*, ch. 3, p. 16.

76. "Annex IV: Report on a Survey of Certain Localities in Kiangsi," *Annexes to the Report to the Council of the League of Nations of Its Technical Delegate on His Mission in China from Date of Appointment until April 1, 1934* (Shanghai: North-China Daily News and Herald, 1934), p. 51.

77. Ibid., p. 30, and *Guomin zhengfu junshi weiyuanhui baoguo*, ch. 5, p. 21.

78. Rui Wei, "Jiangxi gonglu jianshe gaikuang" (The general situation of the construction of Jiangxi highways), *Xiandai shehui* (Contemporary society) 3, 14 (5 September 1934): 30.

79. Ibid.

80. "Jiangxi nongcun jingji," p. 103; Franklin L. Ho, "The Reminiscences of Ho Lien (Franklin L. Ho)" as told to Crystal Lorch, postscript dated July 1966, unpublished ms., Special Collections Library, Butler Library, Columbia University, p. 121; George E. Taylor, "Reconstruction after Revolution: Kiangsi Province and the Chinese Nation," *Pacific Affairs* 8, 3 (September 1935): 309.

81. Rui Wei, "Jiangxi gonglu jianshe gaikuang," p. 30; and *JSZG*, no. 19 (23 October 1934): 12–13. The Nationalist Army also had problems securing sufficient vehicles in the beginning of the fifth campaign. Xue Yue, *Jiaofei jishi* (A record of bandit suppression) (Taibei: Wenxing shudian, 1962), ch. 1, p. 21. Since many of the roads had turns that were too sharp and grades that were too steep, limiting the weight of the vehicles that could travel over them, it was probably safer to travel by foot than by motor transport.

82. Ho, "The Reminiscences of Ho Lien," p. 122.

83. Cao Boyi, *Jiangxi suweiai zhi jianli ji qi bengkui, 1931–1934* (The rise and fall of the Jiangxi Soviet) (Taibei: Guoli zhengzhi daxue Dong Ya yanjiu suo, 1969), p. 598.

84. Liao Shiqiao, "Shinianlai zhi Jiangxi baoan," p. 7. The exact number of blockhouses is difficult to ascertain. Other estimates are much lower than Liao's. Yu

Zhen reported 3,700 blockhouses completed in the entire province by 11 September 1934; Hu Pu-yu reported 2,900 blockhouses built in Jiangxi by 16 January 1934. This figure was confirmed by Xiong Shihui, who noted that there were 2,900 blockhouses built in addition to those on the roads by January 1, 1934. The 2,900 were probably those built on the battlefield and were part of Liao's estimate of 14,000, the difference being those built along the roads and around the villages. Yu Zhen, "Jiangxi jiaofei junshi yu zhengzhi" (The military and political aspects of bandit suppression in Jiangxi), *Xiandai shehui* 3, 14 (11 September 1934): 4; Hu Pu-yu, *A Brief History of the Chinese National Revolutionary Forces*, trans. Wen Hu-xing, 2d ed. (Taibei: Zhong Wu Publishing Co., 1973), p. 96; *Memoirs of General Hsiung Shih-hui*, p. 44.

85. Li Huang, *Jiangxi jiyou* (Travels in Jiangxi) (Taibei: Wenhui chubanshe, 1967), p. 38.

86. Ibid., p. 38.

87. *JSZG*, no. 89 (20 June 1934): 23.

88. For details on the construction of blockhouses see *Jiaofei zhanshi*, vol. 6, app. 6, pp. 1121–42. On pp. 1135–38 there are illustrations of the larger blockhouses.

89. Xue Yue, *Jiaofei jishi*, ch. 1, table 3, n. 3.

90. *Memoirs of General Hsiung Shih-hui* 1:42.

91. *JSZG*, no. 90 (30 June 1934): 38–40; no. 16 (19 October 1934): 7.

92. William W. Whitson and Liu Chi-min, *A Strategy for Counter-Insurgency* (Taibei: n.d.), p. 18. Blockhouses were also built around villages for self-defense. Li, *Jiangxi jiyou*, p. 37. See *Jiaofei zhanshi* 6:1141 for illustrations of the blockhouses used in village defense.

93. Cao Boyi, *Jiangxi suweiai*, p. 601.

94. *Guomin zhengfu junshi weiyuanhui baogao*, ch. 11, p. 3.

95. *Jiaofei zhanshi* 6:1201.

96. Ibid. 6:1200.

97. Ibid.

98. Yu Zhen, "Jiangxi jiaofei junshi yu zhengzhi," pp. 3–11. Hatano Ken'ichi, ed., *Shiryō shūsei Chūgoku kyōsantōshi* (History of the Chinese Communist Party: Collected materials), vol. 3 (Tokyo: Jiji tsushinsa, 1961), p. 23.

99. See *JSZG*, no. 28 (2 November 1934): 18–19, for an example of the justice meted out to a merchant caught blackmarketing oil.

100. Lloyd E. Eastman, *The Abortive Revolution: China under Nationalist Rule, 1927–1937* (Cambridge: Harvard University Press, 1974), pp. 72–73, and *JSZG*, no. 30 (5 November 1934): 3–4.

101. *Guomin zhengfu junshi weiyuanhui baogao*, ch. 11, p. 3.

102. *Jiaofei zhanshi* 6:1202.

103. Ibid., p. 1203.

104. *JSZG*, no. 6 (6 October 1934): 13.

105. *JSZG*, no. 11 (13 October 1934): 14–15.

106. Ibid.

107. *Guomin zhengfu junshi weiyuanhui baogao*, ch. 11, p. 5.

108. *JSZG*, no. 17 (20 October 1934): 4–5.

109. Chalmers Johnson is essentially correct when he asserts that radical agrarian reform would alienate all but the poorest section of the peasantry and thereby defeat the purpose of gaining general rural support in Jiangxi. Johnson, *Peasant Nationalism and Communist Power: The Emergence of Revolutionary China, 1937–1945* (Stanford: Stanford University Press, 1962), p. 19. But his emphasis is misplaced. Communist failure during the soviet period was due less to the lack of support of a significant section of the population than to its timely and active support of the Nationalist blockade-blockhouse strategy.

Chapter 3

1. *Hongse Zhonghua* (Red China), no. 240 (30 October 1934).
2. Apart from some Guomindang accounts of the largely successful mopping-up operations conducted in the first six months after the Long March, this paper is mainly based on a bare handful of more or less contemporary press reports, on interviews with southern guerrilla leaders by sympathetic journalists in the late 1930s, and above all on memoirs from the 1940s and 1950s. There are obvious and well-founded objections to sources of this nature. Autobiographical writings from People's China are almost always politically distorted to some degree, and the evidence they provide is uneven, fragmentary, and often contradictory. Although they sometimes yield interesting and vivid detail, conclusions based on them must be approached with caution.
3. Military History Office, *Military Campaigns in China: 1924–1950* (Taibei: Military History Office, 1966), p. 36.
4. Guofang bu, Shizheng ju, *Jiaofei zhanshi* (Military history of bandit extermination), vol. 3 (Taibei: Guofang bu, Shizheng ju, 1967), p. 437.
5. Agnes Smedley, *The Great Road: The Life and Times of Chu Teh* (New York: Monthly Review Press, 1956), p. 309; and *Jiaofei zhanshi* 3:437–40 and 5:797–800.
6. Ibid.
7. Gan Yue Min E Xiang beilu jiaofeijun disan lujun zong zhihuibu canmouchu, *Wuci weijiao zhanshi* (A military history of the Fifth Encirclement), vol. 1 (Taibei: Zhonghua minguo kaiguo wushi nian wenxian weiyuanhui, 1968), p. 512.
8. Details of road building in this period are in Hunan shengzhi bianzuan weiyuanhui, *Hunan shengzhi* (Hunan provincial gazetteer), vol. 1 (Changsha: Hunan renmin chubanshe, 1959), pp. 640–41.
9. *Hunan shengzhi* 1:648 has an example of a depopulation order.
10. *Jiaofei zhanshi* 5:800.
11. G. E. Taylor, "Reconstruction After Revolution: Kiangsi Province and the Chinese Nation," *Pacific Affairs* 8, 3 (September 1935): 307–308.
12. Ibid., p. 304.
13. See Hung-mao Tien, *Government and Politics in Kuomintang China, 1927–1937* (Stanford: Stanford University Press, 1972), pp. 111–12, for a description of this system.
14. Taylor, "Reconstruction," pp. 309–10.
15. *Jiaofei zhanshi* 3:440.
16. Warren Kuo, *Analytical History of the Chinese Communist Party*, vol. 3 (Taibei: Center for International Relations, 1970), pp. 36–40.
17. *Wuci weijiao zhanshi* 1:510.
18. Helen Snow (Nym Wales), *The Chinese Labor Movement* (New York: Day, 1945), p. 217.
19. The economic crisis did not go unremarked at the time in the Communist press. In Moscow Wang Ming wrote: "The third circumstance leading to the application of new tactical methods by the Red Army is the *necessity of surmounting the material difficulties arising for the Army in the Central Soviet Region.* The incessant military operations stretching over a number of years, the continual aerial and artillery bombardment, the direct pillaging expeditions of white bandit gangs, (and) the severe economic blockade . . . have recently led to a lack of munitions and articles of the first necessity for the Red Army, despite the whole-hearted support and assistance on the part of the civilian population." (*Inprecor*, 8 December 1934, vol. 14, part 62, p. 1659). See also Gong Chu, *Wo yu hongjun* (The Red Army and I) (Hong Kong: Nanfeng chubanshe, 1954), pp. 410–15; *China Weekly Review* for late 1934 and early 1935; and Cai Xiaoqian, "Jiangxi suqu huiyi pianduan" (Memoirs of the Jiangxi

Soviet), *Feiqing yanjiu* (Bandit conditions research) (later renamed *Zhonggong yanjiu* [Chinese Communist research]) 3, 8 (August 1969): 102–107. The second and third parts of this article appeared in *Zhonggong yanjiu* 4, 1 (January 1970), and 2 (February 1970).

20. See, for example, *Xinghuo liaoyuan* (A single spark can light a prairie fire), vol. 4 (Beijing: Renmin wenxue chubanshe, 1961), pp. 198–99.

21. Gong Chu, "Canjia Zhonggong wuzhuang douzheng jishi" (Reminiscences of participating in the Chinese Communists' armed struggles), *Mingbao yuekan*, no. 97 (January 1974): 103; no. 98 (February 1974): 87; Chang Kuo-t'ao, *The Rise of the Chinese Communist Party, 1921–1927* (Lawrence: Kansas University Press, 1970), p. 569; and Kuo, *Analytical History* (1970), 2:620–21.

22. See "Interview with Ch'u Ch'iu-pai [Qu Qiubai]" in Kuo, *Analytical History* 3:60–64; and *Lishi yanjiu* (Historical research), no. 6 (1977): 33.

23. Luo Mengwen, *Douzheng zai Yanggan hongqu yu baiqu* (Struggle in the red areas and white areas of Yanggan) (Beijing: Zuojia chubanshe, 1962), pp. 1–2; and *Lishi yanjiu*, no. 6 (1977): 34.

24. *Hongse Zhonghua*, 20 October 1934, p. 243; and Tso-liang Hsiao, *Power Relations Within the Chinese Communist Movement, 1930–1934*, vol. 1 (Seattle: University of Washington Press, 1961), pp. 300–301.

25. Helen Snow (Nym Wales), *Red Dust* (Stanford: Stanford University Press, 1952), p. 65.

26. See Cai Xiaoqian, "Jiangxi suqu huiyi pianduan," part 2, pp. 120–21, for an account of these campaigns.

27. Estimates of the strength of the rearguard, most of which was distributed over four military districts in southern Jiangxi and western Fujian, range from twenty to forty thousand, with thirty thousand the most commonly given figure. For various estimates of the rearguard's size see Hatano Ken'ichi, *Chūgoku kyōsantō-shi* (History of the Chinese Communist Party) (Tokyo: Jiji tsushin sha, 1961), 4:407–408 and 5:43–44; Gong Chu, *Wo yu hongjun*, pp. 100–101; Ye Husheng, *Jinggangshan di hongqi* (Red flag on Jinggangshan) (Beijing: Gongren chubanshe, 1956), p. 105; *Wuci weijiao zhanshi* 1:507–508; Smedley, *The Great Road*, p. 309; Helen Snow, *The Chinese Labor Movement*, p. 218; and Otto Braun, *Chinesische Aufzeichnungen (1932–1939)* (Chinese Sketches) (Berlin: Dietz Verlag, 1973), p. 109. For information on the leadership of the rearguard as originally constituted see Wang Jianmin, *Zhongguo gongchandang shigao* (Draft history of the Chinese Communist Party), vol. 2 (Taibei: Zheng zhong shu ju, 1965), p. 622; Gong Chu, *Wo yu hongjun*, p. 406; and Kuo, *Analytical History* 3:3.

28. Cai Xiaoqian, "Jiangxi suqu huiyi pianduan," part 3, p. 108.

29. Gong Chu, *Wo yu hongjun*, ch. 17; and Kuo, *Analytical History* 3:54–65. More than one commentator has suggested that Mao used the opportunity of the Long March to rid himself of some of his opponents in the leadership, but more likely the opposite is true. It is well known that Mao's influence in the party's leading bodies was at a low ebb during this period. Chen Yi, Tan Zhenlin, Mao Zetan, He Shuheng, and Ceng Shan, all of whom were left behind in Jiangxi, were recognized Mao supporters. Maoist influence in the rearguard was strengthened by the fact that local cadres, who tended to follow Mao, were more likely to be chosen for rearguard duty than "outsiders." But the appointment of Xiang Ying as the main leader of the rearguard suggests that the then dominant "Internationalists" in the leadership sought to vest overall control of it in one of their own supporters.

30. Braun, *Chinesische Aufzeichnungen*, p. 109; and Edgar Snow, *Scorched Earth*, vol. 1 (London: Victor Gollancz, 1941), p. 125.

31. Braun, *Chinesische Aufzeichnungen*, pp. 109 and 114; and *Wuci weijiao zhanshi* 1:509-14.

32. Gong Chu, *Wo yu hongjun*, pp. 414-15; Nihon kokusai mondai kenkyūjo, Chūgoku-bu kai, *Chūgoku kyōsantō shi shiryō shū* (Collection of materials of the history of the CCP), vol. 7 (Tokyo: Keisō Shobō, 1970-75), p. 411.

33. Smedley, *The Great Road*, p. 309; and Edgar Snow, *Red Star over China* (London: Victor Gollancz, 1968), p. 189.

34. This was completely routed by Guomindang forces.

35. Ye Cao, *Sannian youji zhanzheng* (The three years' guerrilla war) (Hong Kong: Zhengbao chubanshe, 1948?), pp. 24-25.

36. Accounts of this period can be found in volumes of *Xinghuo liaoyuan*; in Jiangxi renmin chubanshe, ed., *Hongse fengbao* (Red storm), 3 vols. (Nanchang: same, 1958); and in other collections of stories and reminiscences.

37. *Hongse fengbao* 2:196-97.

38. For example *Xinghuo liaoyuan* 4:198-99; *Zhongguo gongchandang zai Jiangxi diqu lingdao geming douzheng di lishi ziliao* (Historical materials on the revolutionary struggles led by the Chinese Communist Party in the Jiangxi area) (Nanchang: Jiangxi renmin chubanshe, 1958), pp. 188-89.

39. Ye Cao, *Sannian youji*, p. 14.

40. Gong Chu, *Wo yu hongjun*, p. 448.

41. Ibid., p. 445.

42. Wuhan Night School, *Zhongguo gongchandang zai zhongnan diqu lingdao geming douzheng di lishi ziliao* (Historical materials on the revolutionary struggles led by the Chinese Communist Party in the central area) (n.p.: Zhongnan renmin chubanshe, n.d.), pp. 246-48.

43. *Xinghuo liaoyuan* 4:194 ff.

44. It is hard to believe, however, that military dogma was the main factor, particularly since there is evidence to show that the "Maoist" Chen Yi played a greater part in military decision-making in the early months of the rearguard action than the "Internationalist" Xiang Ying. Gong Chu, *Wo yu hongjun*, pp. 444-45.

45. *Zhongguo gongchandang zai zhongnan diqu*, p. 246; Ye Cao, *Sannian youji*, pp. 15-25; and *Lishi yanjiu*, no. 6 (1977): 37.

46. These conferences were later seen as main turning points in the rearguard struggle and presented as victories for the Maoist line. Their resolutions reportedly bore some resemblance to those taken by the central leadership at Zunyi in January 1935, although the evidence suggests that at that time only the southwestern Fujian leaders knew the details of the Zunyi decisions. Ye Cao, *Sannian youji*, p. 27. But insofar as the conference decisions represented a necessary adjustment to changed local conditions, they may well have independently arrived at conclusions similar to those embodied in Mao's line at Zunyi.

47. *Hunan shengzhi* 1:649-50; *Zhongguo gongchandang zai Jiangxi*, pp. 189-91; *Zhongguo gongchandang zai zhongnan diqu*, pp. 248-49; *Hongqi piaopiao* (The red flag waves), vol. 12 (Beijing: Zhongguo qingnian chubanshe, 1957-58), p. 107; Wang Shoudao, ed., *Zhongguo gongchandang lingdao Hunan renmin yingyong fendou di sanshi nian* (Thirty years of the Hunan people's heroic struggles led by the Chinese Communist Party) (Changsha, 1951), pp. 56-57; *Xinghuo liaoyuan* 4:170-71 and 201-203; *Lishi yanjiu*, no. 6 (1977): 37-39; and Ye Cao, *Sannian youji*, pp. 26-32 and 49.

48. *Lishi yanjiu*, no. 6 (1977), p. 38; and *Xinghuo liaoyuan* 4:171-72.

49. For this paragraph see Mu Qing, *Xiang zhong di hongqi* (Red flag in the countryside) (Zhongnan hongmao shudian chubanshe, 1950), pp. 21-22; *Hongqi piaopiao* 12:106-108; *Zhongguo gongchandang zai zhongnan diqu*, pp. 249-50; *Zhong-*

guo gongchandang zai Jiangxi, pp. 191–93; *Hunan shengzhi* 1:691; Jiangxi sheng funü lianhehui, *Jiangxi funü geming douzheng gushi* (Stories of the revolutionary struggle of Jiangxi women) (Beijing, 1963), pp. 40–43; *Xinghuo liaoyuan* 4:202–209; and Ye Cao, *Sannian youji*, pp. 35–53.

50. *Hongse Zhonghua*, 3 October 1934.

51. *Jiangxi funü*, p. 58; *Hongqi piaopiao* 11:116–17.

52. Ye Cao, *Sannian youji*, pp. 38–40; and *Xinghuo liaoyuan* 4:208.

53. The main account of the three-year struggle in Yanggan is Luo Mengwen, *Douzheng zai Yanggan hongqu yu baiqu*. See also *Xinghuo liaoyuan* 4:325–34; and *Zhongguo gongchandang zai zhongnan diqu*, p. 25.

54. This document has been translated in *Chūgoku kyōsantō shi shiryō shu* 7:411.

55. For example *Jiangxi funü*, p. 63.

56. *Xinghuo liaoyuan* 4:201.

57. Ibid. 4:175 and 200; *Lishi yanjiu*, no. 6 (1977): 42; and *Zhongguo gongchandang zai Jiangxi*, pp. 233–36.

58. For example, *Zhongguo gongchandang zai Jiangxi*, p. 233; and *Hongqi piaopiao* 11:116. In the early period in particular, however, some units persisted with an "ultra-left" land policy (see Ye Cao, *Sannian youji*, p. 88).

59. *Xinghuo liaoyuan* 4:181–82.

60. Ibid. 4:202; and Ye Cao, *Sannian youji*, p. 38.

61. *Hongse fengbao* 3:76; and *Xinghuo liaoyuan* 4:207–208.

62. *Xinghuo liaoyuan* 4:183; Yang Shang-k'uei [Yang Shangkui], *The Red Kiangsi-Kwangtung Border Region* (Beijing: Foreign Languages Press, 1961), pp. 90–93; *Lishi yanjiu*, no. 6 (1977): 43; and *Hongse fengbao* 3:76.

63. *Xinghuo liaoyuan* 4:183 and 350–51.

64. *Hunan dagongbao*, 19 October 1936, reprinted in *Hunan shengzhi* 1:654.

65. Ye Cao, *Sannian youji*, pp. 71–75; and *Lishi yanjiu*, no. 6 (1977): 55.

66. *Zhongguo gongchandang zai Jiangxi*, p. 189. On learning in 1936 of the arrival of the Red Army in Shaanxi, Chen Yi expressed his joy and renewed confidence in verse: "Storm-tossed and homeless,/ We sleep each day in the wild, and constantly change base./ . . . ./Tiny stones can finally fill the sea of blood,/ and we rejoice from afar that our army has crossed the Golden Sand River!" Chen Yi, *Shici xuanji* (Collected Poems) (Beijing: Renmin wenxue chubanshe, 1977), p. 11.

67. *Hongqi piaopiao* 12:114–17; *Zhongguo gongchandang zai Jiangxi*, pp. 193–95; *Jiangxi funü*, p. 43; and Kuo, *Analytical History* 3:353. However, Communists in Hunan towns and cities were active in setting up anti-Japanese mass organizations after the formation of the united front with the Guomindang. *Hunan shengzhi* 1:671–74.

68. *Xinghuo liaoyuan* 4:210–15.

69. For these two paragraphs see *Lishi yanjiu*, no. 6 (1977): 42; *Xinghuo liaoyuan* 4:185–87 and 215–18; Yang Shang-k'uei, *Red Border Region*, p. 116; Chen Yi, *Shici xuanji*, p. 11; and Ye Cao, *Sannian youji*, pp. 64–67. Chen Yi's poem "Guerrilla Fighting in Southern Kiangsi" translated in *Chinese Literature*, no. 7 (1977): 70–72, gives a vivid picture of guerrilla life in this period.

70. Ye Cao, *Sannian youji*, pp. 67–69; and *Hongqi piaopiao* 11:137–38.

71. Yang Shang-k'uei, *Red Border Region*, pp. 131–32; *The Chinese Labor Movement*, p. 218; *Xinghuo liaoyuan* 4:187 and 218–20; *Hongqi piaopiao* 11:136–37; and Ye Cao, *Sannian youji*, p. 79.

72. Yang Shang-k'uei, *Red Border Region*, pp. 145–46; *Xinghuo liaoyuan* 4:188; Edgar Snow, *Scorched Earth* 1:130; *Zhongguo gongchandang zai zhongnan diqu*, p. 258; *Hongqi piaopiao* 11:117; and Asiaticus (pseud.), "Autobiography of General Yeh T'ing," *Amerasia* 5, 1 (March 1941): 28.

73. *Xinghuo liaoyuan* 4:187–88; *Lishi yanjiu*, no. 6 (1977): 58; and Yang Shang-k'uei, *Red Border Region*, pp. 150–51.

74. *Xinghuo liaoyuan* 4:219–26; Ye Cao, *Sannian youji*, pp. 68–79; *Hongqi piao-piao* 11:136–38.

75. *Xinghuo liaoyuan* 4:187–88; Yang Shang-k'uei, *Red Border Region*, pp. 150–51; and Chen Yi, *Shici xuanji*, p. 27. According to the CCP's official account, Chen Duxiu's "right-opportunism" was to blame for the Communists' betrayal and defeat by the Guomindang at the end of the first united front in 1927.

76. In his account of reorganization in the Jiangxi-Guangdong border region Yang Shangkui admits that Communist claims of guerrilla strength in the area were deliberately exaggerated: "The [Guomindang] asked us how many men we actually had, and we gave the figure of more than a thousand because the troop was still being enlarged. They were sly enough to ask us for the roster, giving the reason that pay was allotted accordingly, but actually they just wanted to find out our real strength. After some expansion, we had over six hundred men, who had been reorganized and were beginning gradually to spread out towards the plain." This number was brought up to a thousand with the help of sympathetic peasants who came "just to answer the roll-call." *Red Border Region*, pp. 153–154.

77. On the period of the negotiations and after see *The Chinese Labor Movement*, p. 218; *Xinghuo liaoyuan* 4:188 and 221–27; *Lishi yanjiu*, no. 6 (1977): 59–61; Yang Shang-k'uei, *Red Border Region*, pp. 150 and 158; H. Forman, *Report from Red China* (New York: Holt, 1945), p. 164; Agnes Smedley, *Battle Hymn of China* (New York: Knopf, 1945), p. 178; *Hongqi piaopiao* 11:138–42; and Ye Cao, *Sannian youji*, pp. 81–84.

78. This was no accident, of course, since it was precisely long-term Communist activities in these provinces that had given Chiang Kai-shek the main pretext and opportunity to incorporate them into his fold.

79. Edgar Snow, *Red Star over China*, p. 205.

80. The units that went to make up the New Fourth Army nucleus in late 1937 and 1938 were originally scattered over eight provinces and some forty counties in thirteen or fourteen separate guerrilla areas. *Kang-Ri zhanzheng shiqi di Zhongguo renmin jiefangjun* (The Chinese People's Liberation Army during the War of Resistance against Japan) (Beijing: Renmin chubanshe, 1953), p. 53; and Chen Jun, *Xinsijun manji* (Random notes on the New Fourth Army) (Shanghai: Tongyi chubanshe, 1939), p. 44. Estimates of the total size of the forces ranges from over fifteen thousand to a mere five thousand. Splitting the difference one arrives at the figure of ten thousand, which happens to be the estimate that Chiang Kai-shek has given. Israel Epstein, *The People's War* (London: Victor Gollancz, 1939), pp. 260–61; *New China Information Committee Bulletin* (Chongqing), no. 10 (1939): 14 and 29; *Xinghuo liaoyuan* 6:376; and *The Chinese Labor Movement*, p. 218. For Guomindang estimates see Chiang Kai-shek, *Soviet Russia in China* (Taibei: China Publishing Company, 1969), p. 89; Kuo, *Analytical History* 3:352; and Hsu Long-hsuen and Chang Ming-kai, *History of the Sino-Japanese War (1937-1945)* (Taibei: Chung Wu Publishing Company, 1971), p. 252.

81. Xiang Ying, "Nanfang sannian youji zhanzheng jingyan duiyu dangqian kangzhan di jiaoxun," in Zhu De et al., *Kang-Ri youji zhanzheng lunwenji* (Collection of articles on the anti-Japanese guerrilla war) (n.p., 1938), pp. 149–60.

82. Kuo, *Analytical History* 3:365. The citation was for having "held out in a prolonged heroic guerrilla war and carried out basically and correctly the party line to fulfill the party-assigned missions under extremely difficult circumstances following the evacuation of the main body of the Red Army from the South," and for having

"preserved [guerrilla areas] to this day to serve as major supporting bases for the Chinese people's war against Japan."

83. But they failed completely in their other task of "restoring, consolidating, and developing the Soviet area" (*Hongse Zhonghua*, no. 240, 3 October 1934) and even in linking up the various rearguard units in preparation for such a restoration (Yang Shang-k'uei, *Red Border Region*, p. 2; and *Xinghuo liaoyuan* 4:169).

84. Not all guerrillas fighting in the South ended up at the New Fourth Army assembly points on the Yangze. A small minority stayed behind to staff New Fourth Army rearguard offices. Others—it is hard to say how many, since Communist accounts not surprisingly play down this phenomenon—refused to leave the mountains, and condemned the united front as a surrender and betrayal. Chen Jun, *Xinsijun manji*, p. 46; and Kuo, *Analytical History* 3:353. Some stayed in the South because they feared for the safety of their dependents if the Guomindang and the landlords returned. *Kang-Ri zhanzheng shiqi di Zhongguo renmin jiefangjun*, p. 54. Others refused to leave the south quite simply because after years of hard struggle they preferred to go home rather than to make the arduous trek over distances of up to a thousand kilometers to Central China. See Beierdeng (Jack Belden) et al., *Chengwei shiju zhongxin di xinsijun* (The New Fourth Army, which has become the linchpin of the situation) (Yuandong shudian, 1941), p. 5.

85. Snow, *Scorched Earth* 1:130.

86. Chang Kuo-t'ao, *Rise*, pp. 555–57. Despite Ye Ting's "retirement" from the struggle after 1927, Mao and other Communist leaders were not opposed to his appointment to the leadership of the New Fourth Army. In Ye Ting's own words: "The generalissimo consented and the Communists also agreed" to his proposal that he assume command of the reorganized guerrillas. Asiaticus, "Autobiography of Yeh T'ing," p. 28. Later Xiang Ying's hostility to Ye Ting provoked anger in Yan'an. Ye had accepted Mao's proposals on personnel and had agreed to model the internal organization of the new army on the Eighth Route Army. Chang Kuo-t'ao, *Rise*, p. 555.

87. Mao saw the guerrilla zones in the south as "representing part of the gains of our decade of sanguinary war with the [Guomindang]" and as "our strategic strongholds for the anti-Japanese national revolutionary war in the southern provinces." *Selected Works*, vol. 2 (Beijing: Foreign Languages Press, 1965), pp. 67–68.

88. Mao was certainly not unaware that the forces that had emerged from the southern mountains at the end of the three-year struggle had developed during years of separation from the party under a leadership chosen by his factional opponents.

89. Shilun congkan she, *Shilun congkan, disanji* (Collection of tracts for the times, third volume) (Shanghai: Shilun congkanshe, 1939), p. 62.

90. Beierdeng, *Chengwei shiju zhongxin*, pp. 95–96; and Zhu De, *KangRi youji zhanzheng*, pp. 150–53.

91. Chen Shaoyu, Xiang Ying et al., *Yingyong fendou shiqi nian* (Seventeen years of heroic struggle) (n.p.: Zhenli chubanshe, 1940), pp. 10–28.

92. *China Weekly Review*, 20 August 1938, p. 391.

93. *Xinghuo liaoyuan* 6:397–98.

94. Ye found his position so intolerable that at one point he even attempted to resign his post. Smedley, *Battle Hymn of China*, p. 180. The ultimate "Maoization" of the New Fourth Army was indeed partly effected by the posting of Mao supporters, including Liu Shaoqi, to control its units. *Renmin ribao*, August 22, 1961.

95. Kuo, *Analytical History* 3:365.

96. "Problems of War and Strategy," *Selected Works* 2:228.

97. See, for example, *Xiang Ying jiangjun yanlunji*, pp. 56–57; Beierdeng, *Chengwei shiju zhongxin*, p. 35; and Yuan Guoping, "Xinsijun yinianlai zhengzhi gongzuo di

zongjie ji jinhou renwu'' (A summary of the political work of the past year in the New Fourth Army and its current tasks), *Shilun congkan*.

98. Epstein, *The People's War*, pp. 264–65.

99. Gao was eventually arrested and shot by emissaries from New Fourth Army headquarters in May 1939, after his soldiers had reportedly voted for his death. Smedley, *Battle Hymn of China*, pp. 221–22.

100. Epstein, *People's War*, p. 261; and Ye Cao, *Sannian youji*, p. 87.

101. *The Chinese Labor Movement*, p. 217.

102. Beierdeng, *Chengwei shiju zhongxin*, p. 7; Epstein, *People's War*, p. 264; Snow, *Scorched Earth* 1:133–34; and Balujun dishiba jituanjun zongzhengzhibu xuanchuanbu, *Kangzhan banianlai di balujun yu xinsijun* (The Eighth Route Army and New Fourth Army in the past eight years of resistance war) (n.p., 1945), p. 54.

103. Xiang Ying's conception of guerrilla war may also help to explain the apparent ease, paradoxical at first sight in a veteran leader of one of the bitterest and most unrelenting struggles in the history of Chinese Communism, with which he adopted the more conciliatory positions of Wang Ming after the latter's return to China in late 1937. A central feature of the so-called second Wang Ming line was its comparative neglect of the element of social and political struggle within the united front. Wang was far more prepared than Mao to tone down social and political demands for the sake of cementing the alliance with the Guomindang. During most of the negotiations with the Nationalists Wang Ming was still in Moscow, where Stalin's voice was more easily heard than that of the peasants who formed the party's social base in Northwest China. Not so Mao, who from 1935 onward was daily faced with the urgent need to reconcile the interests of various competing constituencies, including the peasants. Xiang Ying, however, was barely constrained in the same way. To the extent that the southern guerrillas any longer possessed a social base, it was pitifully weak. They had moderated their policies well in advance of similar rightward moves by Communists in the Northwest and participated only in the final stages of the debate on how to integrate resistance, national unity, and class struggle. Thus Xiang Ying had rather more in common with Wang Ming than a past factional link, and it would be facile to reduce his leadership of the early New Fourth Army exclusively to an emanation of the "Wang Ming line."

Chapter 4

1. See Chalmers Johnson, *Peasant Nationalism and Communist Power* (Stanford: Stanford University Press, 1962); Mark Selden, *The Yenan Way in Revolutionary China*, Harvard East Asian Series no. 62 (Cambridge: Harvard University Press, 1971); Tetsuya Kataoka, *Resistance and Revolution in North China* (Berkeley: University of California Press, 1974). The first ascribes the growth of Communist power to peasant hatred of the Japanese, caused by reprisals against the population; the second, though concentrating on an area not subject to Japanese occupation, suggests that social, political, and economic reforms and mass-line leadership methods were the foundations of Communist power. The third stresses the linking of Communist organizations to a tradition of rural self-defense. Only Kataoka significantly explores the limitations on peasant support (see his chapter "The Gun and the Peasants," pp. 276–86), but even for him the limitations were overcome by the use of proper appeals. In his conclusion to that chapter, he suggests that once "tied to a frame of steel," the villages "would have gone wherever the frame would take them."

2. For a useful discussion of the evolution of Japanese pacification strategy, see Lincoln Li, *The Japanese Army in North China, 1937–1941* (Tokyo: Oxford University Press, 1975), pp. 186–213.

3. The entire onus of blame for informing cannot be placed upon the traditional elite. Japanese sources citing specific information from specific informers are rare, and they generally do not comment on the social background of informants. The Chinese Communist sources for the most part make only general allegations about nefarious activities by "evil gentry and local bullies" (*tuhao lieshen*). See, for example, Guan Xiangying, "Lun jianchi Jizhong pingyuan youji zhanzheng" (Maintaining the Central Hebei plains guerrilla warfare), *Balujun junzheng zazhi* 11 (November 1939): 35. Many others undoubtedly provided information, under duress or in return for benefits offered by the Japanese. For a comparative perspective on collaboration by the far from elite elements, see William Hinton, *Fanshen: A Documentary of Revolution in a Chinese Village* (New York: Random House, 1966), pp. 107–27. Peng Zhen was unromantic about the opportunistic tendencies of the *youmin* or lumpen elements in the villages: in his words, lumpen elements tended to the view of "if it gives milk, it's mother." Peng, *Zhonggong "Jin-Cha-Ji bianqu" zhi gezhong zhengce* (n.p.: Tongyi chubanshe, 1942; handcopied), p. 7. Hereafter cited as *Gezhong zhengce*.

4. The policy could, of course, be applied during mop-ups in bases or secure guerrilla areas, but in such cases it had to be applied on a catch-as-catch-can basis and was far less important in both Japanese strategic aims and impact than were the mop-ups themselves.

5. See Kathleen J. Hartford, "Step by Step: Reform, Resistance and Revolution in Jin-Cha-Ji Border Region, 1937–1945," Ph.D. dissertation, Stanford University, 1980, pp. 124–29, 405–15.

6. Ibid., pp. 75–89, for a more detailed description of the early organizing measures.

7. See Liu Bocheng, "Liangnianlai Huabei youji zhanzheng jingyan jiaoxun di chubu zhengli" (Initial consolidation of the lessons and experiences of the past two years' North China guerrilla warfare), *Balujun junzheng zazhi* 10 (October 1939): 25–28; Zhou Shidi, "Jizhong pingyuan youji zhanzheng di jingyan jiaoxun" (Experiences and lessons of Central Hebei plains guerrilla warfare), part 1, *Balujun junzheng zazhi* 2, 5 (May 1940): 32–47; Guan Xiangying, "Lun jianchi Jizhong," p. 34.

8. Li Mengling, "Jizhong junqu di jianlue jieshao" (A brief introduction to the Central Hebei Military District), *Balujun junzheng zazhi* 9 (September 1939): 110; Fan Zixia, "Xingfeng di huiyi" (Recollections of exciting days), in *Hebei geming lieshi shiliao* (Historical materials on Hebei revolutionary martyrs), ed. Hebeisheng minzhengting, vol. 1 (Tianjin: Hebei renmin chubanshe, 1961–62), p. 111.

9. Haldore Hanson, *Humane Endeavour: The Story of the Chinese War* (New York: Farrar and Rinehart, 1939), p. 219.

10. Renmin chubanshe, *Kang-Ri zhanzheng shiqi jiefangqu gaikuang* (Conditions in the liberated areas during the War of Resistance against Japan) (Beijing: Renmin chubanshe, 1953), p. 28; Li Mengling, "Jizhong junqu," pp. 111–12.

11. *Kang-Ri zhanzheng*, p. 28.

12. See, for example, "Jin-Cha-Ji bianqu kang-Ri genjudi shi zenyang chuangzao qilai di" (How the Jin-Cha-Ji Border Region anti-Japanese base area was created), *Balujun junzheng zazhi* 1 (January 1939): 51–63; Li Mengling, "Jizhong junqu," pp. 111–12.

13. Boeicho boei kenkyujo senshishitsu, *Hokushi no chiansen* (Pacification war in North China), vol. 1 (Tokyo: Choun shinbusha, 1968, 1971), pp. 116, 128.

14. Ibid. 1:131–33, 154–59, 173–75; Fang Qiang, "Balujun zai Jizhong di liangnian" (Two years of the Eighth Route Army in Central Hebei), *Balujun junzheng zazhi* 2, 4 (April 1940): 30, 33–34; Zhou Shidi, "Jizhong pingyuan youji zhanzheng," pp. 33–35.

15. Lin Lang, with Wang Tao, "Zai zhandouzhong di Jizhong kangzhan baolei"

(The Central Hebei resistance war bastion in the midst of battle), *Qunzhong* 3, 22 (30 November 1939): 527–28.

16. Yao Yilin, "Yinianlai di Jidong youjizhan" (The past year's guerrilla war in East Hebei), *Balujun junzheng zazhi* 12 (December 1939): 36.

17. Guo Huaruo, "Jin-Cha-Ji bianqu dongji fan 'saodang' di shengli" (The victory of the Jin-Cha-Ji Border Region in the winter counter-sweep), *Balujun junzheng zazhi* 2, 1 (January 1940): 109; Li Mengling, "Jizhong junqu," p. 113; *Hokushi no chiansen* 1:147–52.

18. Lu Zhengcao, "Chuancha zai gouxianzhong di youji zhanzheng" (Guerrilla warfare piercing through the blockade ditch lines), *Qunzhong* 8, 15 (16 September 1943): 415.

19. Lin Lang, "Zai zhandouzhong di Jizhong," p. 527; *Hokushi no chiansen* 1:149–50.

20. Peng Shaohui, "Chuancha Ping-Han tielu di jingyan" (Experiences of piercing through the Ping-Han railroad), *Balujun junzheng zazhi* 10 (October 1939): 38.

21. Zhou Shidi, "Jizhong pingyuan youji zhanzheng," p. 35.

22. Ibid., pp. 40–42; for a detailed report of such a spy from later in the early period, see "Chukyo joho issoku" (Intelligence on the Chinese Communists), *Joho* 34 (15 January 1941): 77–83.

23. Yao Yilin, "Yinianlai Jidong," p. 37.

24. *Hokushi no chiansen* 1:78; Peng Shaohui, "Chuancha Ping-Han," p. 38.

25. *Hokushi no chiansen* 1:149.

26. Ibid. 1:264; see also Yao Yilin, "Yinianlai Jidong," passim.

27. *Kang-Ri zhanzheng*, p. 29; Zhou Shidi, "Jizhong pingyuan youji zhanzheng," pp. 50–51.

28. Zhou Shidi, "Jizhong pingyuan youji zhanzheng," p. 51.

29. Cheng Zihua, "Jizhong pingyuanshang di minbing douzheng" (The militia's struggle on the plain of Central Hebei), *Jiefang ribao*, 7 July 1944.

30. Shu Zihua, "Jin-Cha-Ji junqu budui zuijin zhengzhi gongzuo gaikuang" (Recent political work in the Jin-Cha-Ji Military District units), *Balujun junzheng zazhi* 7 (July 1939): 44–53.

31. Xiao Xiangrong, "Kang-Ri budui baipei di gonggu qilai" (Consolidate the anti-Japanese forces a hundredfold), in Wang Jiaxiang et al., *Zhengzhi gongzuo luncong* (N.p.: Balujun, 1941) 1:157.

32. See *Balujun junzheng zazhi*, 1939–1940.

33. Hartford, "Step by Step," pp. 169–79, 287–99, 319–23.

34. "Kahokusho ichi noson ni okeru Chukyo no tai-noson shisaku" (Chinese Communist village policies in one village of Hebei province), part 2, p. 7. I am grateful to Dr. Yung-fa Ch'en for providing a copy of this invaluable source for me.

35. See Chuyo mekkyo i-inkai chosabu, "Kichuku chubu ni okeru Chukyo no minshu kakutoku kosaku jitsujo chosa hokoku" (Report of the conditions of the Chinese Communists' work of winning over the masses in the central part of Central Hebei), *Rikushi mitsu dai nikki* 40, 142 (1940): part 4, p. 31.

36. I am using the terms "landlord" and "rich peasant" in an economic sense, in accordance with the CCP's definition of rural classes, which changed very little from the soviet period to the final civil war. For a translation of those definitions from the 1933 Land Law of the Soviet Republic, see Chao Kuo-chun, *Agrarian Policy of the Chinese Communist Party, 1921–1959* (Bombay: Asia Publishing House, 1959), pp. 25–26.

Class terminology used by the Communist Party during the Resistance War was often much fuzzier than these terms. "Class" was in fact rarely referred to; "stratum" was the preferred term. Although documents frequently do refer to landlords or rich peasants in those terms, one also frequently encounters the much more ambiguous political class terminology in Resistance War writings. Thus after the introduction of the three-thirds policy, landlords and rich peasants cooperating with the resistance are metamorphosed into "middle elements," while throughout the war those who opposed the resistance or certain border region policies appeared variously as "diehards," "local bullies and evil gentry," etc.

I am indebted to Prof. Lincoln Li for some very perceptive comments relating to the differences between economic and political definitions of the elite in North China. Unfortunately I have not been able to make full use of his insights within the length limits for this essay.

37. See Hartford, "Step by Step," pp. 139–268, passim, for evidence on this point.

38. Peng Zhen, *Gezhong zhengce*, p. 37; "Fuping Shijiagang jianzu jingyan" (Rent reduction experiences in Fuping's Shi family stockade), *Jiefang ribao*, 17 April 1945.

39. The full account of the events that follow can be found in Gen Xiang, "Weiwu buqu di Ming Shuzhen" (Stern and unrelenting Ming Shuzhen), in *Hebei geming lieshi shiliao* 2:68–86.

40. For another example of the "hidden problems" problem, see Zhong Ting, "Jiancha X cun di shibai" (Investigating the failure in X village), *Bianzheng wanglai* (The past and present of the border region government) 1, 8 (December 1941): 19.

41. Liu Lantao, "Beiyuequ dangqian di nongmin tudi zhengce" (Present land policies in Beiyue district), in *Tudi zhengce zhongyao wenjian huiji* (Important documents on land policy), ed. Zhonggong Jin-Cha-Ji zhongyangju xuanchuanbu (n.p., 1946), pp. 56, 61; Peng Zhen, *Gezhong zhengce*, pp. 37–44.

42. *Gezhong zhengce*, p. 37; Gen Xiang, "Weiwu buqu di Ming Shuzhen," pp. 77–78.

43. For examples, see Wang Ruofei, "Jianchi Huabei zhanzhengzhong zhi 'renmin wuzhuang ziweidui'" (The "people's armed self-defense corps" persisting in the war in North China), *Balujun junzheng zazhi* 2, 1 (25 January 1949): 86.

44. Shu Tong, "Jin-Cha-Ji junqu kangzhan sannianlai di zhengzhi gongzuo" (The past three years' political work in resistance war in Jin-Cha-Ji military district), *Jiefang* 120 (1 December 1940): 23.

45. Fan Zixia, "Xingfeng di huiyi," pp. 112–13.

46. Jin-Cha-Ji bianqu xingzheng weiyuanhui, *Liangnianlai bianqu dashiji* (Record of important events in the border region during the last two years) (n.p., n.d.), p. 42. Corroboration on Meng's execution can be found in a GMD intelligence source, Zhang Baoshu, "Zhonggong lingdaoxia di 'Jin-Cha-Ji bianqu' jishi" (A record of the "Jin-Cha-Ji Border Region" under the Chinese Communists' leadership) (n.p., 1940), mimeo, p. 2.

47. *Liangnianlai*, p. 43.

48. Ibid., pp. 88–104.

49. For additional information on Bai's activities in Yingshan county (a BRG-formed county comprising Ying and Shanyin counties, Shanxi) in 1940, see Ding Yuan, "Yingshan gongzuo jinkuang" (Recent circumstances in work in Yingshan county), *Jin-Cha-Ji tongxun* 13 (20 April 1940): 9. Judging by this source, Bai may have been openly working for the Japanese by this point. After Bai's forces had entered the county, several "traitors" (probably meaning armed units led by those people) attacked the Eighth Route Army units stationed in the county, drove out the Border Region's county government, and then began sending "evil gentry, local bullies, and lumpen elements" out as puppet village heads.

50. Here my judgment of the expected effects differs considerably from the inter-

pretations of some other scholars. Samuel B. Griffith suggests that the Hundred Regiments offensive was aimed at provoking Japanese reprisals to help mobilize the peasants: *The Chinese People's Liberation Army*, United States and China in World Affairs Series (New York: McGraw-Hill for the Council on Foreign Relations, 1967), pp. 70–71 and n. 23, p. 335. Chalmers Johnson and Tetsuya Kataoka have both made helpful comments on an earlier draft of this essay, and have taken issue with my reading of the events. Johnson sees the Hundred Regiments as an important learning experience for the CCP in North China and believes that the offensive ultimately served the party's interests because of the greater mobilization that followed the Japanese reaction. Kataoka has argued that Mao used the Hundred Regiments to keep the Japanese in China. (See also Kataoka's essay in this volume.) While I can see some of the reasons why Johnson and Kataoka might interpret the Hundred Regiments in this fashion, I must continue to differ with them. For party leaders in North China at any rate, there is reason to conclude that they expected the Hundred Regiments to provide a major breakthrough in their strategic situation, not by intensifying Japanese repressive measures, but by breaking the growing Japanese stranglehold, and particularly by destroying the Japanese capacity for contingent repression. See, for example, Peng Zhen, "Muqian zhengzhi xingshi" (The present political situation), *Bianzheng daobao* 3, 3/4 (15 January 1941): 11–12.

51. Xue Zizheng, "'Zhian qianghua' yundong toushi" (A perspective on the "pacification-strengthening" movement), *Qunzhong* 8, 1/2 (16 January 1943): 19. The information on population and cultivated area comes from *Hebeisheng gexian gaikuang yijian* (Yearbook of conditions in the counties of Hebei Province) (n.p., 1934), p. 153; Hebeisheng zhengfu mishuchu, ed., *Hebeisheng tongji nianjian* (Yearbook of Hebei province statistics) (n.p., 1931), pp. 3–7, 20–22.

52. Lu Zhengcao, "Chuancha zai gouxianzhong," pp. 415–16.

53. Xue Zizheng, "Zhian qianghua," p. 18; this source also gives a graphic description of the different kinds of road systems built as part of the blockade strategy. See also Lu Zhengcao, "Chuancha zai gouxianzhong," p. 415.

54. Xue Zizheng, "Zhian qianghua," p. 18.

55. Lu Zhengcao, "Chuancha zai gouxianzhong," p. 415.

56. Xue Zizheng, "Zhian qianghua," p. 17.

57. See, for example, Tao Xijin, "Muqian zhanqu youji xiaozu di xiaoneng ji qi lingdao wenti" (The current potential and leadership problems of the guerrilla cells in the war areas), in *Gongfei huoguo shiliao huibian* (Collection of historical materials on Communist bandit national disasters), ed. Guoli zhengzhi daxue guoji guanxi yanjiu zhongxin, vol. 3 (Taibei, 1964–1978), p. 201.

58. "Kahokusho ichi noson," part 2, pp. 5–6, 10.

59. See, for example, Zhong Renfang, "Siyinian di dui wo saodang zhi tedian yu wo fansaodang di jingyan yu jiaoxun" (Special characteristics of the enemy's 1941 sweep against us and the experiences and lessons of our countersweep [campaign]), *Balujun junzheng zazhi* 4, 2 (January 1942): 15.

60. See Jin-Cha-Ji bianqu xingzheng weiyuanhui, ed., *Xianxing faling huiji* (A collection of current laws and ordinances), vol. 1 (n.p., 1945), p. 186.

61. Ibid., pp. 186, 188.

62. "Yuxian hongqianghui panluan jingguo" (The events of the Yu county Red Spears revolt), *Jiefang ribao*, 23 and 24 October 1942.

63. *Xianxing faling huiji* 1:187.

64. Sun Zhiyuan, "Genjudi renmin wuzhuang jianshe wenti" (Problems of base area people's armed forces construction), *Balujun junzheng zazhi* 3, 10 (October 1941): 19–20.

65. E. P. Thompson, *The Making of the English Working Class* (New York: Vintage, 1966), p. 210, n. 1.

66. These sources include, in particular, *Balujun junzheng zazhi*, *Bianzheng daobao* (Border region government leadership), *Bianzheng wanglai* (The past and present of border region government), and materials reprinted in *Gongfei huoguo* shiliao huibian, vol. 3.

67. Hanson, *Humane Endeavour*, p. 191. Hanson also reported that by March 1938, nine puppet magistrates had been killed. Hanson, "The People Behind the Chinese Guerrillas," *Pacific Affairs* 11 (September 1938): 295.

68. "Kahokusho ichi noson," part 2, pp. 9, 12. Similar requirements of higher-level party permission for assassination or execution of traitors obtained elsewhere in the border region as well. See, for example, Liu Fu-hai et al., *Wild-Goose Guerrillas* (Beijing: Foreign Languages Press, 1978), p. 69.

69. "Shin-Satsu-Ki no jokyo" (Conditions in Jin-Cha-Ji), *Joho* 35 (1 February 1941): 36. Charles Loomis provided this translation.

70. Sun Zhiyuan, "Genjudi renmin wuzhuang," p. 13.

71. Even fictionalized accounts may not present a particularly heroic picture of the capacity or tendency of guerrilla groups operating independently to attack the Japanese directly. See, for example, Liu Fu-hai et al., *Wild-Goose Guerrillas*, passim.

72. Ibid., pp. 66–90; see also pp. 46–65. The frame-up was explicitly recommended (as second-best to assassinations) in Jin-Cha-Ji bianqu Jizhong fenqu wuweihui, ed., "Guanyu fangfei sufei di zai zhishi" (Another directive concerning withstanding and eliminating bandits) (n.p., n.d.), mimeo, handcopied.

73. See, for example, Peng Shaohui, "Chuancha Ping-Han," p. 38.

74. For a detailed discussion of the moderate policies, see Hartford, "Step by Step," pp. 183–228.

75. Ibid.; Yao Yilin, "Yinianlai Jidong," p. 38. Moderation had a number of facets not directly related to the socioeconomic reform policies. One of the most prominent was increased control over accusations against traitors. For example, Wang Ruofei, "Huabei youjidui yu minzhong youji zhanzheng fazhan di jingyan," *Balujun junzheng zazhi* 2, 4 (April 1940): 16, cautions against overdoing the confiscation of "traitors" property, lest the Japanese use those disaffected by these measures to "sow discord."

76. *Gongfei huoguo shiliao huibian* 3:408. The caution extended into the final period of the war, for the "new liberated areas" of Jin-Cha-Ji. See Hartford, "Step by Step," pp. 231–40.

77. The Chinese phrase is *jianbi qingye*. It meant carefully planned prior concealment of any grain, animals, or goods of possible use to the Japanese; it later came to include stopping up doors and windows to minimize damage by fire. See Ma Cheng, "Jianbi qingye di diandi jingyan" (A bit of experience in strong bulwarks, clear fields), *Bianzheng wanglai* 1, 8 (10 December 1941): 14–16. The massive group efforts to collect the grain harvest before the arrival of a Japanese mopping-up operation constituted another important method of target-removal.

78. Sun Zhiyuan, "Genjudi renmin wuzhuang," p. 13.

79. "Kichuku chubu," pp. 3, 7, 47–48.

80. See Li Weihan, "Zenyang zhixing dang zuzhishang di jinggan zhengce he yinbi zhengce" (How to implement the better-cadres and concealment policies in party organization), in *Gongfei huoguo shiliao huibian* 3:130–46; Tao Xijin, "Muqian zhanqu youji xiaozu di xiaoneng ji qi lingdao wenti" (The current potential and leadership problems of the guerrilla cells in the war areas), in ibid. 3:198–205; [Wang] Ruofei, "Zhunbei genjudi bian wei youji qudi wuzhuang douzheng" (Preparing for the armed struggle of base areas changing into guerrilla areas), in ibid. 3:205–209; Gao

Feng, "Lun duiyu difang wuzhuang di liangdao wenti" (Concerning problems of leading the local armed forces), in ibid. 3:209–17.

81. Zhou Shidi, "Jizhong pingyuan youji zhanzheng," final part, *Balujun junzheng zazhi* 2, 6 (June 1940): 47.

82. Gao Feng, "Duiyu difang wuzhuang." This source emphasizes the dangers of premature revelation of strength in areas easily entered by the Japanese.

83. "Kahokusho ichi noson," part 1, pp. 41–45.

84. See, for example, Liu Fu-hai et al., *Wild-Goose Guerrillas*, pp. 74–76, 133–34; "Kahokusho ichi noson," part 1, pp. 41–45. Li Fuchun, "Balujun zuozhanqu di qunzhong gongzuo" (Mass work in the areas where the Eighth Route Army is fighting), *Gongchandangren* (The Communist) 2 (1939): 26, called for preparing for infiltration of puppet organs by party members when an area came under Japanese occupation.

85. Wang Ruofei, "Huabei youjidui," p. 20.

86. Sun Zhiyuan, "Genjudi renmin wuzhang," pp. 19–20.

87. See Tao Xijin, "Muqian zhanqu youji xiaozu," p. 204.

88. Cheng Zihua, "Jizhong pingyuanshang di minbing."

89. *Tuji.* I am indebted to Prof. Kenneth Folsom for information on the use of this method during the soviet period. The journal *Bianzheng wanglai* contains a number of accounts on the use of this method. See, for example, vol. 1, no. 8 (10 December 1941): 12–13, 19–20. Repeated references to the method also occur in *Balujun junzheng zazhi.* For an example of use of the method during the early period (especially for tax collection), see "Nianqiniandu zhengshou jiuguo gongliang di zongjie" (A summary of the levy and collection of National Salvation Public Grain in 1938), *Bianzheng daobao* 56 (11 September 1939): 5, 6.

90. The method seems something like the work teams later used by the CCP for trouble-shooting, experimentation, and so forth. But the factor that distinguishes the blitzkrieg work as a special type is its function of moving into a situation and acting so fast and furiously that mass enthusiams are raised to a fever pitch, dismantling the psychological obstacle represented by fear of Japanese (and sometimes elite) repression.

91. Wang Ruofei, "Huabei youjidui," p. 18. On the fears of capitulation by defeatists, see Mao, *Selected Works* 2:55–56; on the effectiveness of the initial victory at Pingxingguan, see ibid., pp. 115–16.

92. Qing Lin, "Shu-Ji wuqu shi zenyang kaibi di?" (How was the fifth district of Shu-Ji county opened up?), *Bianzheng wanglai* 1, 8 (December 1941): 12–13.

93. Tie Yan, "Zhuanqu, xian, qu lianhe jiancha zhengli di XX cun" (XX village, inspected and consolidated by a unified [team from] special district, county, and district [organs]), Shang Wen, "Pinggou yundong zai Xingtang" (The ditch-leveling movement in Xingtang), and Zhong Ting, "Jiancha X cun di shibai," in *Bianzheng wanglai* 1, 8 (December 1941): 17–19, 23–24, and 19–20, respectively.

94. Shu Tong, "Zhuguanzhuyi zai qianfang buduizhong di biaoxian xingshi" (Forms of subjectivism appearing in the front areas' military units), *Balujun junzheng zazhi* 3, 10 (October 1941): 14.

95. Hartford, "Step by Step," pp. 153–68.

96. Meaning that Japan had been sucked into a war of attrition it could not even hope to win without hugely increasing troop commitments, an impossibility once the war had spread into the wider Asian theater.

97. The Japanese had recognized this fact and by 1941 tried tactically to wipe out completely the resistance forces within an area, through the use of repeated and closely spaced sweeps. This necessitated some important tactical changes in the border region's response. See Zhong Renfang, "Siyinian di duiwo saodang," pp. 12–18.

98. The tenuousness was more pronounced in some areas than in others. In this respect, it is important to note that the areas closest to Japanese military presence that were nevertheless resilient against Japanese repression during the first two years of the war were the very areas in which Communist organizers had been most active during the early 1930s. Hartford, "Step by Step," pp. 545–59.

99. I am struck by the contrast between the CCP's (Mao's) gradual expansion strategy during the Jiangsi Soviet years and the expansion strategy formulated for the beginning of the Resistance War. Compare Mao, *Selected Works* 1:64–68, 75–76, 99–102, with 2:93–101. It is possible that rapid expansion in the latter period was devised through learning from earlier mistakes, but I suspect that it was all the more necessary if the party was not going to launch a call for massive redistribution of land.

Chapter 5

1. Hsu Lung-hsuen and Chang Ming-kai, comps., *History of the Sino-Japanese War, 1937–1945* (Taibei: Chung Wu, 1971), p. 469.

2. Zhongyang shujichu, "Zhongyang dui shiju zhishi" (An instruction from the party center on the current situation), 23 December 1939, in *Zhonggongdangshi cankao ziliao*, ed. Zhonggong zhongyang dangxiao dangshi jiaoyanshi, vol. 4 (Beijing: Renmin chubanshe, 1979), pp. 127–28.

3. *Kangri zhanzheng shiqi jiefangqu* (A survey of the liberated areas during the War of Resistance against Japan) (Beijing: Renmin chubanshe, 1953), p. 83.

4. *Qin lieshi Qirong xunguo sazhounian jiniance* (Commemorative volume on the thirtieth anniversary of martyr Qin Qirong's sacrifice for his country) (Taibei: private printing, 1973). This figure is undoubtedly too high.

5. Guo Weicheng, "Kongsu Shen Honglie di zuixing" (Denounce the crimes of Shen Honglie), *Dazhong ribao* 773 (January 1941). This is also a high estimate.

6. Zheng Jun, "Xianle yuanxing di touxiangpai—Bao Zeshan" (Prototype of a capitulationist—Bao Zeshan), *Dazhong ribao* 232 (March 4, 1941).

7. Shandong shifan xueyuan lishixi, "Kangri zhanzheng shiqi Shandong renmin di fandi douzheng" (The Shandong people's anti-imperialist struggle during the War of Resistance against Japan), *Shandong shengzhi ziliao* 1 (1959): 1–36.

8. Frank Dorn, *The Sino-Japanese War, 1937–1945* (New York: Macmillan, 1974), p. 248.

9. Zhongyang shujichu, "Zhongyang dui shiju zhishi."

10. Chen Hualu, "Taihe can'an jishi" (Record of the Taihe massacre), in *Wenshi ziliao xuanji*, ed. Zhongguo renmin zhengzhi xieshanghuiyi Shandongsheng weiyuanhui wenshi ziliao yanjiu weiyuanhui, vol. 6 (May 1979): 104–15. *Kangri zhanzheng shiqi jiefangqu gaikuang*, p. 85.

11. Zhongyang Tongji Diaochaju, Central Bureau of Investigation and Statistics, ed., *Shiba jituanjun ji Xinsijun bufa xingwei ji xianzhu dongtai* (The illegal actions and notable movements of the 18th Group Army and the New Fourth Army) (Chongqing, 1940–1941).

12. Hsu Lung-hsuen, *History of the Sino-Japanese War*, p. 474.

13. Wang Zhaoliang, "Shandong jiefangqu dashi nianbiao" (Chronology of the Shandong liberated area), in *Shandong shizhi ziliao* (Material on Shandong historical records), ed. Shandongsheng difang shizhi bianzuan weiyuanhui, 1, 1 (1982): 87.

14. Zhu Rui, "You shi yizhong 'saodan'" (It's another type of "mop-up"), *Qunzhong* 5 (October 1940): 18–51.

15. Yuan Bo, "Shandong kangzhan xiankuang ji qi qiantu—Xu Xiangqian tongzhi yu Xinhuashe jizhe Yuan Bo tongzhi zhi tanhua" (The present situation and future of the Shandong resistance war—Xu Xiangqian's talk with New China News Agency

journalist Yuan Bo), *Junzheng zazhi* 2, 1 (November 1940): 43–47.

16. Zhongyang diaocha tongjiju (Central Bureau of Investigation and Statistics), ed., *Zhonggong zai Shandong zhi zuzhi yu huodong* (Organization and activities of the Chinese Communist Party in Shandong province) (Chongqing, 1941), pp. 45–46.

17. Mou Zhongheng, "Wo suo jiechu de Shen Honglie" (Shen Honglie as I knew him), *Wenshi ziliao xuanji* 7 (October 1979): 102–14.

18. Guo Weichen, "Kongsu Shen Honglie di zuixing"; Wang Yumin, *Kangzhan banian* (Eight years of resistance war) (Taipei, private printing, 1974), p. 172; Lloyd E. Eastman, "Facets of an Ambivalent Relationship: Smuggling, Puppets, and Atrocities During the War, 1937–1945," in *The Chinese and the Japanese*, ed. Akira Iriye (Princeton: Princeton University Press, 1980), pp. 275–303.

19. Bōeichō bōei kenkyūsho senshishitsu, ed., *Hokushi no Chiansen* (North China pacification war), vol. 1 (Tokyo: Asagumo, 1968), pp. 485–86, 488–90.

20. Luzhong xingzheng gongshu, ed., *Luzhongqu kangri minzhu zhengquan jianshe qinianlai di jiben zongjie ji jinhou jiben renwu* (Basic summary of the last seven years of construction of the Luzhong anti-Japanese democratic regime and our basic tasks for the future) (Central Shandong District, 1945), p. 9.

21. *Kangri zhanzheng shiqi jiefangqu gaikuang*, p. 90.

22. Hu Shifang, "Kang-Ri shidai lunxian di Shandong" (Shandong under occupation during the Resistance War), *Zhangqu* 54 (10 February 1976): 23. This was Wu Huawen.

23. *Hokushi no chiansen* 2:369–70.

24. David M. Paulson, "War and Revolution in North China: The Shandong Base Area, 1937–1945," Ph.D. dissertation, Stanford University, 1982, p. 258.

25. Wang Jichun, "Luo Ronghuan tongzhi zai Shandong geming douzheng jishi" (Record of Comrade Luo Ronghuan's revolutionary struggle in Shandong), *Shandong shifan xuebao* 1 (1980): 8–12.

26. Ibid.

27. Hu Shifang, *Zhangqu* 51 (10 November 1975): 26. This was Yang Yuxun.

28. "Shandong renmin di 'huoshui'—He Siyuan" (A "source of disaster" for the Shandong people—He Siyuan), *Dazhongbao* 1257 (7 October 1945).

29. "He Siyuan toudi ru Ji di qianqian houhou" (The whole story of He Siyuan's capitulation to the enemy and entrance into Jinan), *Dazhongbao* 1273 (26 October 1945).

30. Bo Jian, "Lini Xianliang Zhaoni Baoyuan zai Qingdao Jimocheng yu dikou gongkai heliu" (The open collaboration of Li Xianliang and Zhao Baoyuan with the Enemy Dwarfs at Qingdao and Jimo City), *Dazhongbao* 1133 (9 September 1945). For Li's side of the story, see Li Xianliang, *Kangzhan huiyilu* (Memoirs of the War of Resistance) (Qingdao: Gankun, 1948).

31. Tian Xiangqian, "Wo yu Wu Huawen xiangchu di huiyi" (Memories of my encounters with Wu Huawen), *Wenshi ziliao xuanji* 8 (May 1980): 122–37.

32. Wang Yumin, *Kangzhan banian*, p. 254.

33. Kuwajima Setsuro, *Kahoku senki* (North China war diary) (Tokyo: Tosho, 1978), pp. 208–41.

34. Hsu Lung-hsuen, *History of the Sino-Japanese War*, p. 546.

35. Laurence Tipton, *Chinese Escapade* (London: Macmillan, 1949), p. 202. Even internal intelligence reports on the Guomindang side acknowledged that the Communists were not collaborating with the Japanese. In an October 1944 article entitled "A Report on the Chinese Communists in Shandong and the Decline of Our Forces," He Yingqin's staff office states that "In Shandong we have not yet discovered concrete evidence of collaboration between the Chinese Communists and the enemy." This document can be found in the Nanjing Guomindang Archive, in *Zhongguo xiandai*

zhengzhi shi ziliao huibian (Collection of Materials on China's modern political history) 3, 5, in the volume entitled "Zhonggong lingdao Kang-Ri Balujun Xinsijun zhanji youguan ziliao" (Materials on the accomplishments of the CCP in leading the Eighth Route Army and New Fourth Army in battle against Japan).

36. Ministry of Defense, ed., *Jiaofei zhongyao zhanyi zhi zhuishu yu jiantao* (Description and review of the main Communist extermination battles), vol. 3 (Taipei, 1951), pp. 10–14.

37. Li Zhuru, *Zhandouzhong di Shandong renmin* (The Shandong people in combat) (Shandong Donghai District: Donghai gejiuhui, 5 August 1940).

38. Wang Yumin, *Kangzhan banian*, p. 217, gives the example of Wang's bitter rivalry with Zhao Baoyuan. The information on Wang's unit's performance during Japanese mop-ups came from an interview with Ambassador Arthur Hummel, Jr., in Beijing in August 1982.

39. Hu Shifang, *Zhangqu* 52 (10 December 1973): 61.

40. Guo Weicheng, "Kongsu Shen Honglie di zuixing."

41. Dorn, *The Sino-Japanese War*, pp. 229, 320.

42. Fan Yusui, "Wo ren Guomindang Shandongsheng dangbuzhuren weiyuanhui di huiyi" (Memories of serving on the Guomindang Shandong Provincial Party Executive Committee), *Wenshi ziliao xuanji* 8 (October 1979): 102–14.

43. Wang Zhenqian, Peng Jingwen, and Sun Xueren, "Jiazishan xia zhengqige" (A song of righteousness sung below the Jiazi Mountains), in *Xinghuo* (Spark), vol. 5 (Liaoning: Liaoning People's Press, 1981), p. 98. For more inside details on Communist united front work in the Northeast Army, see Gao Wenhua, "1935 nian qianhou Beifangju di qingkuang" (The Northern Bureau in 1935), pp. 184–88, and Liu Peizhi, "Xi'an shibian qianhou zhengqu Dongbeijun gongzuo di huiyi" (Winning over the Northeast Army at the time of the Xi'an Incident), pp. 189–210, in *Zhonggong dangshi ziliao*, ed. Zhonggong zhongyang dangshi ziliao zhengji weiyuanhui, vol. 1 (Beijing: Xinhua Studies, 1982).

44. Guo Weicheng, "Kongsu Shen Honglie di zuixing."

45. Zhongyang tongji diaochaju, ed., *Zhonggong zai Shandong zhi zuzhi yu huodong*.

46. Wang Zhenqian et al., *Xinghuo*, pp. 70–179.

47. *Hokushi no chiansen* 2:199.

48. Mou Zhongheng, "Wo suo jiechu di Shen Honglie."

49. Hsu Lung-hsuen, *History of the Sino-Japanese War*, p. 475.

50. *Qin lieshi Qirong xunguo sanzhounian jiniance*.

51. *Luzhongqu Kang-Ri minzhu zhengquan jianshe*, p. 4.

52. Zhang Jingwu, "Shandong Balujun zenyang fandui diren di 'saodong'" (How the Shandong Eighth Route Army opposed enemy "mop-ups"), *Junzheng zazhi* 2, 12 (December 1940): 54–61.

53. Evans Fordyce Carlson, *Twin Stars of China* (New York: Dodd, Mead, 1940), pp. 255–56, 259–60.

54. "Shen zhuxi zai Shandong diwuqu zhaokai jiuwang gongzuo taolunhui jiangyanci" (Speech given by Chairman Shen at the opening of the Shandong 5th District salvation discussion meeting), in *Kangzhan jianguo* (Resistance and nation building), ed. Shandong quansheng baoan silingbu zhengzhibu (November 1938), pp. 11–17.

55. Gu Ying, "Guomindang Shandongsheng zhengfu zhixiaxia di shenghuiqu—'Wurenqu' di beican jingshan" (The tragic scene of the "no-man's land"—the special district directly under the jurisdiction of the Guomindang Shandong Provincial Government), *Dazhong ribao* 737 (19 October 1944). Cui Jicheng, "Guomindang Shandongsheng zhengfu zhuxi Shen Honglie" (Shandong Provincial Government Chairman Shen Honglie), *Wenshi ziliao xuanji* 8 (October 1979): 81–101.

56. *Qin lieshi Qirong xunguo sanzhounian jiniance*, p. 19.

57. *Kang-Ri zhanzheng shiqi di Balujun he Xinsijun* (The Eighth Route Army and New Fourth Army in the Anti-Japanese Resistance War period) (1953; reprint, Beijing: Renmin chubanshe, 1980), p. 187. R. G. Tiedemann, "The Persistence of Banditry," *Modern China* 8, 4 (October 1982): 395-434.

58. Gu Ying, "Guomindang Shandongsheng zhengfu zhixiaxia di shenghuiqu 'Wurenqu' di beican jingshang."

59. Tipton, *Chinese Escapade*; Wang Yuming, *Kangzhan banian*; interview with Ambassador Arthur Hummel, Jr., August 1982. Wang helped Hummel escape from internment in a Japanese prison camp at Weixian.

60. Tipton, pp. 158, 147, 175. One regimental commander defied Wang on the tax issue, so Wang had him and his wife buried alive as a lesson to the others.

61. Ibid., pp. 64, 165.

62. Ibid., p. 203. For calumnious propaganda about Wang from the Communist side, see "Wang Yumin budui zai Changping bianqu goujie diren fangong fanrenmin, Changyicheng she banshichu zhuan he diren lianluo" (The Wang Yumin Unit at the Changping Border District colluded with the enemy, opposed communism and the people, and at Changyi Town set up an office to communicate with the enemy), *Dazhongbao* 1186 (21 July 1945). Yang Yongping, "Changping bianqu de zainan shi shui zaocheng di Ji Wang Yumin tongzhixia di renmin shenghuo" (Who created the disaster in the Changping Border District? The people's life under the rule of Wang Yumin), *Dazhongbao* 1187 (23 July 1945).

Chapter 6

1. Mao Tse-tung, "China's Two Possible Destinies," *Selected Works of Mao Tse-tung*, vol. 3 (Beijing: Foreign Languages Press, 1967), p. 202.

2. Mao, "The Situation and Our Policy After the Victory in the War of Resistance against Japan," *Selected Works* 4:11-22.

3. Suzanne Pepper, *Civil War in China: The Political Struggle, 1945-1949* (Berkeley and Los Angeles: University of California Press, 1978), pp. 3-195.

4. An unpublished paper by Edwin A. Winckler, "Military Outcomes in the Chinese Civil War," provides an extremely stimulating schema for tackling this problem.

5. "Report on an Investigation of the Peasant Movement in Hunan," *Selected Works* 1:23-56.

6. See Angus McDonald's perceptive comments on the role of cities in revolution in *The Urban Origins of Rural Revolution: Elites and the Masses in Hunan Province, China, 1911-1927* (Berkeley and Los Angeles: University of California Press, 1978), p. 319.

7. *Dongbei ribao*, 16 February 1947, p. 2. Hereafter cited as *DBRB*.

8. Ramon Myers, "Socioeconomic Change in Villages of Manchuria During the Ch'ing and Republican Periods: Some Preliminary Findings," *Modern Asian Studies* 10, 4 (1976): 591-620.

9. Cited in Joel S. Migdal, *Peasants, Politics, and Revolution: Pressures Toward Political and Social Change in the Third World* (Princeton: Princeton University Press, 1974), p. 74.

10. *DBRB*, 15 November 1947, p. 2, for a report on tenant rich peasants, for example.

11. G. William Skinner suggests that at certain times Chinese peasant communities were well integrated into the larger society and economy (open) and at other times deliberately cut themselves off from the outside world (closed). See his "Chinese

Peasants and the Closed Community: An Open and Shut Case,'' *Comparative Studies in Society and History* 13, 3 (July 1971): 270–81.

12. Ibid., for the general thesis.

13. McDonald notes a similar phenomenon among local elites in the 1920s during the establishment of peasant associations in Hunan. *The Urban Origins of Rural Revolution*, p. 272.

14. Report by Changbai County Party Committee in *DBRB*, 21 August 1947, p. 2.

15. Migdal, *Peasants, Politics, and Revolution*, p. 233.

16. *DBRB*, 6 January 1947, p. 1.

17. In the fury of the land reform campaign, party propaganda undoubtedly exaggerated the extent of this phenomenon in order to heighten cadre vigilance, but there is no reason to doubt it was widespread.

18. *DBRB*, 9 March 1947, p. 1.

19. See, for example, the report from Suibin county in *DBRB*, 30 January 1947, p. 2.

20. *DBRB*, 8 March 1947, p. 2.

21. Migdal, *Peasants, Politics, and Revolution*, p. 41, notes that "The key to the power of lords on every level lay in their degree of monopoly over essential rural resources and the external forces they could call in to protect that monopoly."

22. Chong-sik Lee, *Counterinsurgency in Manchuria: The Japanese Experience* (Santa Monica, Ca.: Rand Corporation, 1967).

23. Willian Whitson, *The Chinese High Command* (New York: Praeger, 1973), pp. 306–308.

24. Although Manchuria was endowed with the best developed rail network, the Communists did not make use of it until the latter stages of the campaigns in the Northeast. Rather, by incapacitating the railroads in the early period of the war, they denied their use to the Nationalists, who had no alternative system to fall back upon.

25. *DBRB*, 21 May 1947, p. 1.

26. NEAC had been established in the summer of 1946 by the Communists as a regional administration for Manchuria. It was effectively under the control of the CCP's Northeast Bureau of which Lin Feng was a member.

27. *DBRB*, 27 August 1947, pp. 1–2.

28. *DBRB*, 26 October 1947, p. 1.

29. Ibid.

30. *DBRB*, 27 October 1947, p. 1.

31. Wang I-shou, "Chinese Migration and Population Change in Manchuria, 1900–1941," Ph.D. diss., University of Minnesota, 1971.

32. *DBRB*, 8 May 1947, p. 2.

33. Chandler Davidson, "On the 'Culture of Shiftlessness,'" *Dissent* (Fall 1976).

34. *DBRB*, 9 March 1947, p. 2.

35. *DBRB*, 11 November 1947, p. 2, for Hejiang province.

36. Ibid.

37. Pepper, *Civil War in China*, pp. 173–74.

38. For some comments on traditional labor exchange and cooperation see Ramon Myers, "Cooperation in Traditional Agriculture and Its Implications for Team Farming in the People's Republic of China," in *China's Modern Economy in Historical Perspective*, ed. Dwight Perkins (Stanford: Stanford University Press, 1975), pp. 261–77.

39. *DBRB*, 20 March 1947, p. 2, for traditional labor exchange in Mulan county. See also Samuel L. Popkin, *The Rational Peasant* (Berkeley and Los Angeles: University of California Press, 1979), p. 97.

40. Statistical data for the period are very sparse. The *Dongbei ribao* for the second

half of 1948 might contain such data, but the issues for these months are not available outside of China, and they may not even be available there.

41. Pepper, *Civil War in China*, pp. 201–204.

42. *DBRB*, 13 June 1947, p. 2.

43. *DBRB*, 5 July 1947, p. 2.

44. *DBRB*, 1 February 1947, p. 1.

45. *DBRB*, 4 April 1947, p. 2. Desertion was a major problem among the peasants impressed during the warlord conflicts. Hsi-sheng Ch'i, *Warlord Politics in China, 1916–1928* (Stanford: Stanford University Press, 1976).

46. *DBRB*, 3 January 1947, p. 3.

47. *DBRB*, 4 April 1947, p. 2; and June 13, 1947, p. 2.

48. *DBRB*, 13 July 1947, p. 1.

49. Peter Schran, *Guerrilla Economy: The Development of the Shensi-Kansu-Ninghsia Border Region, 1937–1945* (Albany: SUNY Press, 1976).

50. Nanniwan was the district near Yan'an famous for its economically self-sufficient troops.

51. The Soviets provided substantial quantities of arms and ammunition to the Communists in 1945–46 from Japanese stocks and traded machinery, transport equipment, petroleum products, and so forth to the Communists in northern Manchuria in exchange for grain, soybeans, and other agricultural commodities.

52. Gavan McCormack, *Chang Tso-lin in Northeast China* (Stanford: Stanford University Press, 1977); Ronald Suleski, "Manchuria under Chang Tso-lin," Ph.D. diss., University of Michigan, 1974; Chong Sik Lee, *Counterinsurgency*.

53. The *Dongbei ribao* of the civil war period is filled with stories of patriotic contributions from the rural and urban laborers as well as exhortations to make additional sacrifices to support the war effort. Furthermore, taxes were levied on a wide range of daily commodities as well as luxury items, an indication too that the war burden was borne by the masses to a considerable extent.

54. I have found the following to be among the more stimulating recent works on peasant politics: James Scott, *The Moral Economy of the Peasant* (New Haven: Yale University Press, 1976); Migdal, *Peasants, Politics, and Revolution*; Popkin, *The Rational Peasant*; and Jeffrey Race, "Toward an Exchange Theory of Revolution," in *Peasant Rebellion and Communist Revolution in Asia*, ed. John W. Lewis (Stanford: Stanford University Press, 1975), pp. 169–204.

55. Migdal, *Peasants, Politics, and Revolution*, pp. 232–33.

56. Ibid., p. 211; Popkin, *The Rational Peasant*, p. 262.

57. Race, "Exchange Theory of Revolution," passim.

58. Popkin, *The Rational Peasant*, p. 24.

59. Race, "Exchange Theory of Revolution," pp. 183–85; Popkin, *The Rational Peasant*, p. 262.

60. Migdal, *Peasants, Politics, and Revolution*, pp. 263–64.

INDEX